T0330857

Gender, Asset Accumulation and Just Cities

With more than half the world's population now living in urban areas, urbanisation is undoubtedly one of the most important phenomena of the twenty-first century. However, despite increasing recognition of the critical relationship between economic and social development in cities, gender issues are often overlooked in understanding the complexities of current urbanisation processes. This book seeks to rectify this neglect.

Gender, Asset Accumulation and Just Cities explores the contribution that a focus on the gendered nature of asset accumulation brings to the goal of achieving just, more equitable cities. To date neither the academic debates nor the formulated policy and practice on just cities has included a focus on gender-based inequalities, discriminations, or opportunities. From a gender perspective, a separate discourse exists, closely associated with gender justice, particularly in relation to urban rights and democracy. Neither, however, has addressed the implications with women's accumulation of assets and associated empowerment for transformational pathways to just cities.

In this book, contributors specifically focus on gender and just cities from a wide range of gendered perspectives that include households, housing, land, gender-based violence, transport, climate, and disasters.

Caroline O.N. Moser is Emeritus Professor at the University of Manchester, UK, and Advisor to the Ford Foundation New York Just Cities Initiative, USA.

Gender, Asset Accumulation and Just Cities

Pathways to transformation

Edited by Caroline O.N. Moser

LONDON AND NEW YORK

First published 2016
by Routledge
2 Park Square, Milton Park, Abingdon, Oxon OX14 4RN

and by Routledge
711 Third Avenue, New York, NY 10017

Routledge is an imprint of the Taylor & Francis Group, an informa business

© 2016 selection and editorial matter, Caroline O.N. Moser; individual chapters, the contributors

British Library Cataloguing in Publication Data
A catalogue record for this book is available from the British Library

Library of Congress Cataloging in Publication Data
A catalog record for this book has been requested

ISBN: 978-1-138-02401-4 (hbk)
ISBN: 978-1-138-19353-6 (pbk)
ISBN: 978-1-315-77611-8 (ebk)

Typeset in Times New Roman
by Wearset Ltd, Boldon, Tyne and Wear

Contents

Figures

Tables

Contributors

Sarah Bradshaw, Senior Lecturer, Middlesex University London, UK.

Sylvia Chant, Professor, Department of Geography, London School of Economics and Political Science, UK.

Beth Chitekwe-Biti, Slum Dwellers International (SDI), Harare, Zimbabwe.

Caren Levy, Vice-Dean, Development Planning Unit, University College London (UCL), UK.

Brian Linneker, Freelance Researcher.

Cathy McIlwaine, Professor, Department of Geography, Queen Mary University of London, UK.

Paula Meth, Senior Lecturer, Department of Town and Regional Planning, University of Sheffield, UK.

Diana Mitlin, Professor of Global Urbanism, University of Manchester, UK.

Caroline O.N. Moser, Emeritus Professor, University of Manchester, UK.

Carole Rakodi, Emeritus Professor, University of Birmingham, UK.

Sally Roever, Women in Informal Employment: Globalizing and Organizing (WIEGO).

Alfredo Stein, Lecturer in Urban Development Planning, University of Manchester, UK.

Acknowledgements

The genesis of this book is an outcome of my association with the Ford Foundation's Asset Building and Community Development Program, first with vice president Pablo Farias, and more recently with Don Chen, senior programme officer. As part of their 'just cities' initiative, Don suggested I organise a networking event on gender, asset building, and just cities at the World Urban Forum 7 (WUF7), Medellin, in Colombia, April 2014. This challenge to specifically address 'gender and assets' made me realise that in my asset work to date, I had tended to 'add women and stir'; I had never really analytically conceptualised assets from a gender perspective.

Grounded in the WUF7 theme of urban equality, and the importance of 'building' just cities, the Medellin forum provided the opportunity for a briefing paper incorporating gender into the debate on assets and just cities, as well as a panel event. Partners from the global south shared experiences from Brazil, Bangladesh, and Zimbabwe with northern researchers analysing urban drivers such as transport and violence. The excellent background papers, written by participants such as Cathy McIlwaine, Caren Levy, and Beth Chitekwe-Biti, together with their interest in taking this debate to further stages, was an important catalyst in the decision to further explore these issues through an edited book.

The methodology behind this edited book is similar to that of an earlier volume focusing on assets, titled *Reducing Global Poverty: The Case for Asset Accumulation* (Brookings Institution, 2007), in which an introductory chapter set the stage for a workshop debate that informed contributors as they addressed specific issues around this theme in an edited volume. In this way, the co-production of this book has been a collective endeavour. In July 2014, seven of the contributors met in London to discuss the overall asset framework, to debate conceptualisations of empowerment and transformation, to exchange ideas about interpretation of just cities, and above all to reach a consensus about the nexus linking the three. The outcome of this important and fascinating discussion, continued by email with the five other contributors unable to join us in London, was an agreement on the overall theoretical focus and the contents of this book. I would like to express my gratitude to all my book collaborators for embracing this methodology as a way of cohesively contributing to the critical debate relating to gendered asset accumulation and transformation to just cities.

This initiative has benefited from the Ford Foundation's generous financial support to the WUF7 event in Medellin. I would also like to thank the following: first and foremost, Pablo Farias and Don Chen for their continuing support and commitment to my work on asset accumulation; the University of Manchester for the production of briefing papers (and USB sticks!) for the WUF7 event; Cathy McIlwaine, who hosted our London workshop at Queen Mary's University of London; each contributor, who as part of the methodology kindly reviewed another's chapter, with special thanks to Alfredo Stein and Cathy McIlwaine who did more than their share; and Monica Hicks, who provided meticulous copy-editing without which the book would not have reached completion. Finally, my thanks to Peter Sollis for his unflagging good humour.

1 Introduction

Towards a nexus linking gender, assets, and transformational pathways to just cities

Caroline O.N. Moser

The twenty-first century is undoubtedly an urban age. However, despite increasing recognition of the critical relationship between Global South cities and their countries' economic and social development, and a proliferation of international programmes to support their greater 'sustainability' and 'resilience', important gaps remain in understanding the complexities of current urbanisation processes. One limitation relates to gender; while the gendered nature of urban poverty has been widely debated, both theoretically and empirically,[1] the gendered nature of urban asset ownership, and the accumulation of asset portfolios, has received far less attention (Moser 2008; 2009). This book seeks to rectify this neglect, and in so doing to explore the contribution that a focus on the gendered nature of asset accumulation brings to the goal of achieving just, more equitable cities.

From an asset perspective the relationship between gender and just cities has two sides, or faces. On the one hand are gender-related constraints to achieving just cities, through persistent gender-based inequalities, disparities, and exclusions in access to financial, physical, productive, human and social capital. Affecting these are structural 'driving forces' such as economic globalisation, demographic transition, and associated urban spatial agglomeration, as well as political change, climate change and disasters, and violence and insecurity. Related intermediary factors, or barriers, include cultural norms affecting gendered divisions of labour and female mobility, which have implications not only for earnings but also for rights to participate in urban public life. On the other hand, through their agency in the choice of solutions and interventions to accumulate or to adapt assets, women seek to empower themselves, with impacts both on poverty reduction and on increased equality. Accumulated assets may not only empower women, but also may successfully challenge power relations in a transformative manner, thereby contributing to just, and more inclusive, cities.

The framework of gendered asset pathways to empowerment and transformation, elaborated and illustrated diagrammatically later, in Figure 1.1, informs this introduction as well as guiding all the subsequent chapters in this book. By way of introducing the framework, this chapter starts with a brief summary of the context, which defines the book's relevance, before introducing three background issues that comprise conceptual debates as well as operational concerns.

First, it describes the asset accumulation framework; second, it identifies the nexus linking gender, assets, and just cities; and third, it reviews academic feminist debates on the conceptualisation of 'transformation'. In sum, these three issues provide the background for the introduction of a framework of gendered asset pathways to empowerment and transformation that contribute to achieving more equal, just cities. Finally, the chapter briefly introduces relevant perspectives and debates on a range of gendered asset pathways explored in detail in the chapters that follow.

Two contextual issues are of particular relevance at the outset. First is the development of a conceptual framework and associated operational programme addressing a wide range of asset-related issues in cities of the Global South, which I have developed, together with colleagues, over the past decade. Initially this focused on asset accumulation and associated intergenerational poverty reduction (see Moser 1998; 2007; 2009); subsequently its focus extended to asset erosion as a consequence of urban violence and conflict (see Moser and McIlwaine 2004; 2006), and most recently has addressed issues relating to community-based asset adaptation to climate change (see Moser and Satterthwaite 2010; Moser and Stein 2011; Stein and Moser 2014). While gender issues have been 'mainstreamed' throughout this work, to date, with one exception (see Moser and Felton 2010) it has not focused specifically on the gendered accumulation, erosion, or adaptation of assets.

A second contextual issue concerns the increased focus on urbanisation processes in the Global South and the politico-economic tension between the potential for economic growth and progress, associated with improved standards of living, jobs, and housing, and the concrete reality in which the majority of the population still contend with substandard housing, poor infrastructure, unsafe and unsanitary conditions, and significant social isolation, all of which constrain their access to economic opportunities. Associated with this is a body of research and practice on the conceptualisation of 'just cities'. Lefebvre (1991), for instance, articulates this in terms of 'rights' to the city, as the inclusion of all city users within its space. Fainstein (2011) in turn associates the 'building' of just cities with equity, democracy, diversity, and intersectionality. In their Just City Initiative, the Ford Foundation identify a need to build truly just cities, shaped by fairness, opportunity and a commitment to shared prosperity. The programme states that 'the struggles of urban transformation – from the need for basic services to the rising demands of a growing middle class – will test countries' capacities to foster prosperity, social justice, sustainability and resilience'.[2] Thus it argues that the challenge of making urban growth more socially inclusive, in terms of both processes and outcomes, needs to be achieved within the fields that are driving metropolitan growth and change – urban planning, housing, and transportation infrastructure.

To date neither the academic debates nor the formulated policy and practice on 'just cities' has included a focus on gender-based inequalities, discriminations, or opportunities. From a gender perspective, a separate discourse exists, closely associated with gender justice, particularly in relation to urban rights and democracy (Molyneux and Razavi 2002; UN-HABITAT 2013). Neither, however, has addressed the implications for women's accumulation of assets and associated empowerment for just cities. In this book, therefore, contributors specifically focus on gender and 'just cities' from a wide range of gendered perspectives that include households, housing, land, gender-based violence, transport, climate and disasters.

Conceptual background: the asset accumulation framework

This section provides the conceptual background for further exploring gendered asset pathways to empowerment and transformation. It briefly introduces the main components of the asset accumulation framework, one of a number of approaches first developed in relation to the diagnosis of poverty, as well as urban poverty reduction interventions, in terms of the following three questions.

What is an asset? Is it an instrumental or transformative concept?

An asset is generally defined as a 'stock of financial, human, natural or social resources that can be acquired, developed, improved and transferred across generations. It generates flows or consumptions as well as additional stock' (Ford Foundation 2004). The extensive debate about the 'technification' and 'decontextualisation' of poverty provides a useful background for a parallel debate as to whether an asset is an instrumental or transformative concept. As Harriss (2007) argues, the 'depoliticisation' of poverty reduces poverty to the characteristics of individuals or households, abstracted from class and other power relations. It fails to recognise poverty as 'multi-dimensional' deprivation, rather than just a lack of income, that includes a lack of capabilities, assets, entitlements and rights. In reality, poverty is a social relation, not an absolute condition. Poverty is not a thing to be 'attacked' but rather the outcome of specific social relations that require investigation and transformation (Green 2006).[3]

In a similar manner, assets are not simply resources that people use to build livelihoods. As Bebbington (1999) argues, *assets give people the capability to be and to act*. Thus the acquisition of assets is not a passive act but one that *creates agency* and is linked to the *empowerment of individuals and communities* (Sen 1997). The concept of asset accumulation draws on theoretical and policy-focused literature on asset-based development approaches (Sherraden 1991; Carter and Barrett 2006), but emphasises the importance of context and political economy both associated with the distribution of economic resources and political power. Assets exist, not in isolation but embedded within social processes, structures, and power relationships, all of which mediate access to them and the accumulation of their value.

Assets can be tangible and intangible, and individual or collective, depending on the asset type. The most widely recognised assets are natural, physical, social, financial, and human capital (see Box 1.1). The identification of these assets related to the fact that they could be econometrically measured in an asset matrix (see Moser and Felton 2009; Moser 2009). However, a far broader range of non-tangible, often symbolic assets exists, influenced, among others, by the work of Bourdieu (1986; 1990; see also McIlwaine 2012). These include aspirational

---

Box 1.1 Definitions of widely recognised tangible and intangible capital assets

Physical capital: the stock of plant, equipment, infrastructure, and other productive resources. This includes housing and consumer durables owned by individuals and households, as well as infrastructure and other collective assets.

Financial capital: the financial resources accumulated by people through wages, income-generating activities, and savings credit. This includes transfer income from rent or remittances.

Human capital: investments in education, health, and the nutrition of individuals. Labour is linked to investments in human capital; health status determines people's capacity to work; and skills and education determine the returns from their labour.

Social capital: an intangible asset, defined as the rules, norms, obligations, reciprocity, and trust embedded in social relations, social structures, and societies' institutional arrangements. It is embedded within informal institutions within communities, and within households, as well as in formal institutions in the marketplace, the political system, and civil society.

Natural capital: the stock of environmentally provided assets such as soil, atmosphere, forests, minerals, water, and wetlands. In rural communities land is a critical productive asset for the poor; in urban areas land for shelter is also a critical productive asset.

Source: adapted from Moser (2009)

(Appadurai 2004), psychological (Alsop *et al.* 2006), civic (Ginieniewicz and Castiglione 2011), and political assets, most commonly associated with human rights (Ferguson *et al.* 2007).

What is an asset accumulation framework?

In debates about asset-based approaches, 'asset building' and 'asset accumulation' are overlapping, often conflated terms. However, in both the academic and policy-focused literature, 'asset building' is more closely associated with a US debate about increasing the state's institutional support to assist the poor build assets (Boshara and Sherraden 2004), while asset accumulation is more commonly associated with the Global South context, where the state's role is more limited and the process of acquiring and consolidating assets is not only lengthy but also primarily achieved 'bottom-up' by individuals, households, and local communities themselves (Moser 2007, 2; 2008).

An asset accumulation framework can be identified in terms of two related tools or instruments. First is an asset index, an analytical and diagnostic tool for understanding poverty dynamics and mobility. It quantitatively or qualitatively measures the accumulation, adaptation, or erosion of different assets over time and clarifies the interrelationship between different assets within an asset port-folio. Second is an asset accumulation policy, an associated operational instru-ment that focuses on creating opportunities for low-income people to accumulate and sustain complex asset portfolios. Asset accumulation policy is not a set of top-down interventions. Although it may include interventions that concentrate on strengthening individual assets, it is essentially a framework that provides an enabling environment with clear rules, norms, regulations, and support structures to allow households and communities to identify and take advantage of oppor-tunities to accumulate assets and overcome inequalities and barriers to justice.

To facilitate asset accumulation as later shown diagrammatically in Figure 1.1, it is necessary to recognise three interrelated processes.[4] First are the *driving forces* in the wider structural context that have direct and indirect impacts on accumulation, adaptation, or erosion of assets at household and intra-household level. These include the urban economic context, the city planning processes, environmental factors (particularly in relation to climate-change related chang-ing weather conditions) and security (associated with levels of conflict and viol-ence). Such driving forces demonstrate that the reduction in inequality or increased social justice associated with asset accumulation is not a technocratic, instrumental process, but a structural one. Driving forces vary according to context; equally, they are not static, but change over time.

Second are the *intermediary factors* relating to institutions and actors at city and local level that can help or hinder asset accumulation. These include public, private, and civil society organisations, all of which are critical in providing an 'enabling environment' for the accumulation of assets; while the state can estab-lish normative and legal frameworks that can either block initiatives or provide incentives, private sector entities, including micro-finance institutions, support opportunities and facilitate access to promote asset accumulation. Since the pro-cesses of accumulating assets involve complex political contestation, national and local level non-governmental organisations (NGOs) and membership-based organisations (MBOs), are critical in collective action, the creation of com-munity social capital, and as brokers to negotiate social power relations associ-ated with transformative processes.

Third are the *outcomes* of asset accumulation strategies that show how assets are not static, and in the changing global political, socio-economic and environ-mental situation there are constant processes of revalorisation, transformation, and renegotiation. The accumulation of one asset often results in the accumula-tion of others, while insecurity in one can also affect other assets. At an opera-tional level, therefore, an asset accumulation policy framework recognises prioritisation, sequencing, trade-offs, and negotiation potential, as well as com-bining a range of context-specific strategy options.

Are there stages or 'generations' of asset strategy implementation?

Assets are not simultaneously accumulated, and therefore it is also important to distinguish different stages or 'generations' of asset accumulation strategies

(Table 1.1). First-generation strategy is by far the most widespread, and aims to access assets that focus on the provision of 'basic needs' including water, roads, electricity, housing plots, better health care and education and micro-finance.

Essential for getting out of poverty and inequality is this primary emphasis on human, physical, and financial capital. However, once assets are provided, planners and policy makers assume that individual well-being improves and 'development' occurs. Yet the conditions for accessing assets do not necessarily bring the expected development outcomes. Second-generation asset accumulation strategies, therefore, are intended to ensure their further consolidation and prevent erosion – including the intergenerational transfer of assets. Such strategies go beyond the provision of practical basic services to embrace a range of strategic empowerment concerns relating to citizen rights and security, governance and the accountability of institutions. Third-generation asset accumulation strategies identify interventions that can maximise the linkages between different types of inter-dependent assets, thereby ensuring empowerment and transformation. The underlying pathway in this three-stage framework, therefore, is relevant for the following framework that focuses specifically on gender and assets.

The nexus linking gender, assets, and just cities

To explore the relationship between gender, assets, and just cities requires an examination of the nexus linking the three. This builds on previous nexuses developed to identify the key dimensions of gender equality, as well as gender empowerment. For instance, the 2012 World Development Report on Gender Equality and Development identifies a nexus linking *endowments* (education, health, and physical assets), the use of these endowments to take up *economic opportunities* and generate income, and the application of these endowments to take actions, or *agency*, affecting individual and household well-being (World Bank, 2012, 4). Turning to the nexus that grounds this book, it is important to

Table 1.1 Aims and programmes of different asset generation strategies

	First generation	*Second generation*	*Third generation*
Aims	Accessing an asset portfolio within the context of driving forces	Strategic empowerment through consolidating assets and preventing erosion	Maximising linkages between interdependent assets to ensure empowerment and transformation
Type of programme	Provision of land, housing, basic services and infrastructure, and microfinance	Citizen rights and security, good governance and accountability, including intergenerational transfer of assets	Securing long-term financial and institutional sustainability of agencies, economic growth, permanent employment, and income

Source: adapted from Moser (2009).

start by recognising that the relationships are not straightforward. First, the extent to which the accumulation of assets empowers women depends on whether such assets have intrinsic rather than instrumental values; second, while individual women may be empowered, this does not necessarily have transformative results in terms of changing gendered power relations. This, in turn, has implications for achieving equitable and more just cities, if it is assumed that such transformations are essential. These issues are further explored below, with the first section focusing on gendered asset accumulation and empowerment, and the following section on pathways to transformation.

Gender, asset accumulation, and empowerment

Just as the relationship between assets, agency, and empowerment is informed by the differentiation between instrumental and intrinsic values, described above, so too is the relationship between gender, assets, and empowerment. Indeed, the gender and development literature abounds with descriptions of its instrumentalism (see Moser 2014). Feminists such as Cornwall *et al.* (2008) have argued that the political project of gender and development has been reduced to a technical fix, while Mukhopadhyay (2004, 95) has commented that gender 'becomes something that is ahistorical, apolitical and decontextualised'. International institutions have also sought to recognise this dualism; for instance, the World Bank's World Development Report 2012 identified that the millennium development goals (MDGs) recognise the intrinsic and instrumental value of gender equality – with gender equality and women's empowerment serving as development objectives in their own right as well as serving as critical channels for achieving other MDGs (World Bank 2012, 4). However, despite this distinction, the overarching emphasis on the instrumental, technocratic incorporation of gender issues into the MDGs has been widely critiqued (Kabeer 2005).

In the 1980s, developing gender planning as a framework to assist women achieve equality with men in development, I distinguished between (instrumental) practical gender needs as the needs women identify in their socially accepted roles in society, and the transformative potential of (intrinsic) strategic gender needs as those that women identify in their subordinate position to men in their society (Moser 1993; Moser 2014). In the past 30 decades, gender debates have advanced theoretically and practically in challenging the continuing complexities of gender inequalities. Of particular relevance in exploring the relationship between gender and assets is Kabeer's gender empowerment framework (1999; 2005; 2008), with its interrelated dimensions of agency, resources, and achievements. This helps identify the circumstances and conditions under which women are empowered, defined by Kabeer as 'the processes by which those who have been denied the ability to make choices acquire such ability' (2008, 18).

Building on Kabeer's work, it is important to identify a framework that specifically distinguishes how the gendered nature of asset accumulation empowers women – which in turn can lead to transformations in gender relations. This depends first on *agency* (either individual or collective), which represents the decision-making processes by which choices are made and put into effect, including the ability to impose one's will on others through the legitimate use of authority. Agency gives women the capability to have increased control and command over tangible and intangible *assets*, and as such are the means through which agency is exercised.[5] Finally, *accumulated assets* are the concrete outcomes or achievements of agency that may or may not empower women. Such accumulated assets affect women's sense of agency, providing the bases for future exercise of 'transformative agency' (Kabeer 2008, 25).

Feminist discourses on pathways to transformation

The pathway leading from individual and/or collective empowerment to transformation again is not necessarily direct. As mentioned above, women's individual agency may be empowered through their accumulation of assets, but this does not necessarily lead to transformative results in terms of changing gender power relations. Since transformation is such a key concept in this framework, it is necessary to digress slightly to better understand how the term transformation has been defined and used, whether as a process or an outcome.

Starting with definitions, a recent review[6] of the key word 'transformation' and associated terms, used in the context of gender relations and gender mainstreaming, shows that the term has been integrated extensively into feminist discourse. At the same time, there is no single accepted definition, as is the case with the term 'gender mainstreaming'. The following six key usages of the term 'transformation' can be identified: social transformation; transformation of women; transformation of gender/gender relations; transformative/transformational agenda/project; institutional transformation (development agencies/ political structures); transformative change/transformative. Often terms lack precise definition or elaboration, varying in syntax from verbs to nouns to adjectives; indeed in some cases, as shown below, all three usages often appear in the same sentence. Following the Oxford University Press dictionary definition of transformation as 'a marked change in form, nature, or appearance', feminists' usages convey the explicit or implicit idea of change, although what is to change or be changed, how change occurs, and who effects change varies greatly.[7]

The 1995 Fourth World Conference on Women in Beijing 1995, both before and after the event was undoubtedly a major springboard for launching and popularising its usage. Although the word does not appear in the Beijing Declaration, or Platform for Action (PfA), the event itself was seen as the culmination of a major transformation in global policy for gender equality and women's empowerment, with Subrahmanian referring to 'the enormous agenda of transformation and change that was identified [in Beijing 1995]' (2007, 112). Thus the PfA was based on the premise that improvement in the status of women could only be achieved by transforming gender relations. However, what occurred subsequently was an erosion in its translation into practice. As Eyben (2013, 18) states: 'The 1995 Beijing Women's Conference developed a vision of global social transformation; the transformational promise of Beijing failed to bring about a policy shift in favour of women's empowerment.'

Despite the lack of clear definition, the term 'transformation' has been widely recognised by both Southern and Northern feminists as an inherently political act, and closely associated with changing social or gendered power relations. As a political act it questions the status quo and in so doing alters the underlying power dynamics that perpetuate gender inequality. However, to engage with gender as an issue of power and injustice requires strong organisational support and willingness (Hillenbrand, 2010, 424).

The 'how' and 'who' that transforms gender power relations is closely inter-related and is neither easy nor straightforward. As Parpart (2014, 392) comments, 'there is no one-shot solution to gender transformation, nor are solutions readily apparent'. While transformation takes place through social institutions, it is often difficult to identify the specific intervention that helps to transform such gender relations (Hunt and Kasynathan 2001, 49). Equally, the positioning of institutional actors can influence their identification as to how transformation occurs. Thus UN WOMEN (2013, 2–3) emphasises that change is structural and 'top down': 'For gender relations to be transformed, the structures that underpin them have to change; [when] the structural causes of gender-based discrimination are left unchanged ... transformation in gender relations is not achieved.'

In contrast, for Sweetman, working within the NGO Oxfam, the elements of social economic and political transformation are more of a 'bottom up' process that only occur in response to collective group demands. (2013, 223). Finally, there are those who identify transformation as both 'top down' and 'bottom up', simultaneously transforming the lives of women while also transforming bureaucracies, so that they become a tool in transforming the lives of women (O'Neil and Eyben 2013, 89).

While changes at the level of individual consciousness and capacity are essential in processes of transformation, collective struggles of the oppressed for 'representation, redistribution and recognition' (Fraser 2000) have generally proved far more effective in challenging the structure of oppression than individual acts. Often it is the capacity of women to organise around their needs, interests, and rights that is most likely to result in public recognition of their rights as workers, as women, and as citizens (Kabeer 2008, 27).

There is no consensus as to whether transformation is a process or an outcome, a means or an end in itself. Goetz and Sandler (2007, 161) argue that while it should be the outcome of successful mainstreaming, 'Gender mainstreaming is a "pathetic illusion of transformation;" [this] militates against continuing with gender mainstreaming as the principle or only strategy for transformation'. Sandler and Rao (2012), in contrast, identify transformation as a process, with change effected in three ways: first is symbiotic transformation which occurs when it extends and deepens the empowerment of previously marginalised individuals or groups while helping elites solve practical problems; second is interstitial transformation, where empowerment is built cumulatively in niches and margins of society without posing a threat to elites – which could enlarge the transformative scope in the whole of society; third is ruptural transformation that denotes change that entails the destruction of existing institutions and the building of new ones rapidly. Interestingly, Eyben and Turquet build on the second process identified above, drawing on Bourdieu's concept of 'transformative change' to show how this, 'occurs through the actions of a minority among those in privileged and powerful positions, whose identity places them in a relative position of subjection vis-à-vis their peers' (Eyben and Turquet 2013, 194).

Gendered asset accumulation: pathways to reducing poverty, increased empowerment, and transformation?

This brief summary of the various meanings and eclectic usage of the term 'transformation' provides a useful background to a discussion of gendered asset accumulation pathways to transformation. Here, an important distinction can be made between pathways that address immediate inequalities (practical needs) and those that are used to initiate longer-term processes of change in power structures (strategic interests). This clarifies the fact that while the strategic exercise of agency can erode inequalities, it does not necessarily completely destabilise the wider structural inequalities. Thus the extent to which gendered asset accumulation contributes to the goal of achieving just, equitable cities depends on both empowerment and transformation, with the latter both a process and an outcome. The following questions then may be useful to identify stages in this process:

- Does gendered asset accumulation reduce gendered poverty?
- Does gendered asset accumulation also lead to greater gender equality and women's empowerment?
- How far is this transformative in terms of changing unequal power relations in cities leading to more equal just cities?
- How far does this also, or simultaneously, transform gender power relations?

Figure 1.1 provides a diagrammatic representation of the pathways through which gendered asset accumulation has the potential to lead to empowerment, as well as the further transformation required to bring about the goal of achieving just, more equitable cities. The first column lists a range of driving, or structural, forces that influence asset accumulation, including broader economic trends linked to globalisation, as well as urbanisation and city-level planning and policies that can influence the capacity of women to accumulate assets.

Intermediary factors in cities, shown in the second column of Figure 1.1, can provide important opportunities for the accumulation of a range of assets, while the gendered outcomes, as discussed above, range from poverty reduction, equality, and empowerment, through to the gendered transformations that achieve just and equitable cities.

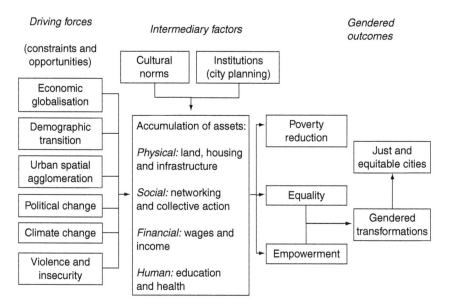

Figure 1.1 Gender asset accumulation pathways to empowerment and transformation.

Constructing the nexus: the evidence base on gendered asset accumulation, empowerment and transformation for just cities

The chapters in this collection provide the evidence base that cumulatively describes, analyses, and critiques the contribution that gendered asset accumulation or adaptation brings to the goal of achieving just and more equitable cities. Each chapter in its own way demonstrates that these are neither straightforward nor direct processes, but rather are fraught with constraints and obstacles associated with external drivers as well as embedded class and gender power relations. This final section of the introduction, therefore, briefly highlights some of the main messages that underlie chapters focusing on different aspects of gendered asset accumulation and empowerment. It also outlines how women negotiate drivers and intermediary factors, make choices and identify opportunities not only to empower themselves but also to effect transformative changes that facilitate if not guarantee the achievement of greater gender and social justice in cities.

Gendered assets that are important for creating just cities

As discussed earlier in this chapter, assets can be tangible and intangible, and individual or collective, with the most commonly cited assets relating to natural, physical, social, financial, and human capital (see Box 1.1). The identification of this core asset portfolio, which I describe in Chapter 3, relates to the fact that it could be econometrically measured in a longitudinal study of asset accumulation in Guayaquil, Ecuador. However, as is well recognised, a far broader range of assets exist, particularly those that are non-tangible, often symbolic assets. Thus, authors identify assets relevant to the focus of their particular chapters. Most radical is Sylvia Chant's assertion in Chapter 2, that female household headship should be considered a 'portable' asset with a role to play in making cities of the future more gender-equitable. She argues that female-headed households may be construed as offering 'enabling spaces' for a wider range of rights for women and girls than is possible within some male-headed households. Female headship may also assist in raising consciousness of gendered inequities and provide a basis for (re)-negotiating gender roles and relations. At the same time, the experience of managing livelihoods affords a sense of achievement and 'empowerment' to women themselves and to other members of their domestic units.

Given the current book's focus on cities and the importance of the links between equitable, accessible urban spaces and just cities, a number of authors identify different aspects of urban space as an intangible asset. For instance, Sally Roever in Chapter 8, in discussing informal workers' livelihoods, classifies public space worksites – as well as stock – as essential assets, particularly for street sellers. Sarah Bradshaw and Brian Linneker, focusing in Chapter 10 on gendered assets and disasters, identify environmental assets as including urban blue and green space and their ecosystem services. At the same time, assets are not static, as illustrated in the case of disasters, as well as climate change, described in Chapter 11 by Alfredo Stein and me; not only does the accumulation of one asset often result in the accumulation of others, insecurity in one can also affect other assets.

Consequently, while some chapters initially focus on a specific asset, they soon find it important to identify the way in which linkages between different assets are essential for accumulation processes. In some cases these are checklists of the range of assets, such as the case of an extensive range of tangible and intangible gendered assets associated with vulnerability and disaster risk, mentioned in Chapter 10. In other cases, asset linkages are further explored, such as Caren Levy's examination of gender equality in transportation in Chapter 8. She identifies the importance of transport in addressing the spatial distances between urban activities, facilitating the linkages between social capital at home and work-related productive capital assets in order to access asset-generating activities. Another example of linkages comes from Chapter 3, where I describe the relationship between different capital assets in Marta's household in Indio Guayas, Guayaquil, in which household social capital around reproductive care contributed to productive work associated with financial capital. Along with her work as community president, Marta masterminded a complex cooking and childcare system, cooking two meals daily, eaten by 15 people, while releasing four female kin from cooking, washing, and childcare.

Finally, there is a systematic examination of assets in terms of the different generations or stages of asset-accumulation strategies, as outlined in the first section of this introduction (see Table 1.1). Thus, for instance, in Chapter 9 Cathy McIlwaine uses this framework for the analysis of the relationship between gender-based violence (GBV) and assets, examining how wider structural phenomena intersect with a series of risks specific to urban living, that precipitate the likelihood of experiencing GBV in cities. Both of these are closely interrelated with the erosion of women's asset portfolios, or failure to even accumulate assets, identified in relation to first-, second-, and third-generation assets.

Individual agency and empowerment

One central theme in the book relates to the ways women seek to empower themselves through their individual agency in the choice of interventions to accumulate or to adapt assets – with associated impacts on both poverty reduction and increased equality. Access to, and accumulation of, a wide range of different assets is fundamental to facilitating such individual agency and empowerment. At the same time it is important to acknowledge that the physical/productive asset of housing is widely recognised as the most critical individual asset prioritised by women. It is regularly asserted that ownership or joint entitlement empowers women, providing them with bargaining power, protecting them from domestic violence, and increasing their security (Chant, Chapter 2 in this volume). But is this always the case? Given the importance of agency related to housing, this section focuses on this specific asset and includes the three chapters that examine the relationship between housing and empowerment from different perspectives.

First, in Chapter 5, Carole Rakodi reviews gendered inequalities in access to land and housing. Her chapter, drawing primarily on evidence from southern Africa, paints a bleak picture of the insuperable constraints women in urban areas experience in accessing both land and secure tenure rights. With the availability of housing determined by the market, policies, law, and practice, access to and control over it is unequally distributed between and within households, with women household heads worst affected. This is further reinforced by discrimination against women in culturally determined inheritance laws. Despite a few recent examples of gender-sensitive titling programmes, in general women's access to and control over housing assets cannot be enhanced unless existing housing delivery channels provide adequate supplies of affordable and well-located serviced plots and houses. However, she argues that to date most southern cities are neither capable of providing adequate low-cost housing nor are they gender sensitive in their policies.

In contrast to this overview, two subsequent chapters provide examples of the complexities of housing initiatives that seek to empower women, through both 'top down' and 'bottom up' interventions. First, in Chapter 6 Paula Meth analyses the gendered contradictions in South Africa's 'top down' state mass-housing programme that since 1994 has provided over three million formal houses to low-income residents, with both positive and negative outcomes for women. The programme's qualification criteria have increased women's access to housing, with more than 50 per cent of houses allocated to female beneficiaries. Thus for women, house acquisition represents the accumulation of a key gendered asset with economic, social, and material value. While specific social outcomes include improvements in safety and security, gains in privacy, reductions in domestic tension and violence, and re-defined empowered identities, at the same time a number of downsides undermine the accumulated asset. These relate to house construction quality, location, and cost. Above all, however, are the impacts on social processes such as tensions over competing claims to housing as an asset, and the associated increase in different forms of violence (usually from male relatives) that directly undermine gendered asset accumulation.

A second gendered housing example, in this case 'bottom up', is the extensive Slum Dweller International (SDI) federation-led initiative across southern African and Asian cities. In Chapter 7, Beth Chitekwe-Biti and Diana Mitlin reflectively critique the evolution of SDI strategies in terms of the limitations of first attempts to secure gender justice, particularly in relation to 'getting to scale'. The well-known SDI process starts with women collectively strengthening their financial assets by saving in small groups. Over time, financial, human, knowledge, and social capital are all acquired through SDI organising, with groups successful in acquiring tenure security, land and housing, and infrastructure improvements. While SDI networks first prioritised greenfield development, as well as housing financed by both savings and donors, success brought new challenges, including accumulation that favoured existing power relations rather than radical transformative processes. Greenfield developments, while individually empowering, were not collectively transformative, and reinforced anti-poor development patterns that disadvantaged lowest-income households, many of whom were headed by women. Consequently the emphasis has shifted to building collective capabilities to negotiate with local authorities and other institutions to upgrade existing low-income settlements, both formal and informal, as illustrated in the case of Zimbabwe. Rather than a small number of households receiving a large asset such as a house, a much larger number of households are reached with an incremental model of upgrading.

From empowerment to transformation: the critical role of community social capital

As Chiketwe-Biti and Mitlin state in their chapter: 'SDI was set up to "unite and empower the urban poor to articulate their own aspirations for change and develop their capacity, from the local to the global, to become critical women-led actors in the transformation of their cities".'

Essential to the complex political contestation needed to negotiate social power relations associated with transformative processes is community social capital linked to collective action. Along with the example of SDI, described above, in many chapters of the book the evidence is overwhelming that this is the dominant asset to achieve such transformative change. This includes detailed examples such as my chapter on Guayaquil, as well as in sector analyses such as Caren Levy's analysis of the constraints associated with 'routes to the just city'.

In Chapter 4, for instance, Sally Roever examines the extent to which informal workers' organisations can themselves be understood as collective assets with transformational capacity, challenging power relations based on class rather than gender. She describes how formally constituted MBOs, such as waste pickers' cooperatives in Bogotá, Colombia, contribute not only to the accumulation of financial and human capital assets at the individual level, but also to physical and social capital formed as members of a collective cooperative. A key dimension of the cooperative's transformative strategy is to combine capacity building with tactics for challenging underlying perceptions of waste pickers, emphasising their environmental role in developing their professional identity. Another transformation strategy relates to the sense of agency that recyclers achieve through the organisation's ability to mediate between workers and the city authorities, creating leverage through marches, demonstrations, protests, and legal strategies that place pressure on authorities, particularly in relation to multinational waste companies and politicians' threats to eliminate informal recycling.

Transformation as a process: longitudinal and intergenerational perspectives

It is important to understand that community social capital is not the panacea for transformative processes, since along with positive examples there are also contexts where there is limited capacity to accumulate social capital. Such would appear to be the case in severe- and extreme-weather related situations, whether dramatic disasters as discussed by Sarah Bradshaw and Brian Linneker in Chapter 10, or the invidious slow weather changes associated with climate change, which Alfredo Stein and I describe in the case of Cartagena in Chapter 11. In both cases weather change erodes individual, household, and small business assets, with a 'lack of political clout' to collectively address local-level social, legal, and physical infrastructure vulnerability. At the same time, in moving from a static analysis of the erosion of assets to the subsequent reconstruction or rebuilding of assets that occur after such severe weather events, this may include processes of revalorisation and renegotiation in which transformative processes may occur. As is the case with conflict, disasters can potentially be 'transformative' in nature, opening up new gendered spaces and opportunities. Of critical importance are the local planning institutions and their associated legal frameworks, and, as described in the case of Cartagena in Chapter 11, the implementation of participatory planning processes in which women have an inclusive role in collective decision-making. A final example illustrating the symbiotic relationship between the erosion and accumulation of assets is provided by the relationship between GBV and assets. In Chapter 9, for instance, Cathy McIlwaine provides evidence to show that while the lack of assets can precipitate GBV, equally the gradual consolidation of assets over time also can potentially reduce GBV.

Ultimately, pathways both to empowerment and to transformation to just cities may often occur, not only step by step, as identified in the case of SDI in Chapter 7, but also as part of longitudinal intergenerational processes. Two examples in this book provide empirical examples to illustrate intergenerational changes in gendered power relations, as well as the complex cultural norm and constraints that so often still limit their effective transformation. In Chapter 2 on female household headship as an asset, Sylvia Chant discusses the important intergenerational attitudinal changes young men in female-headed households experience that testify to the social and psychological asset-building fomented through female household headship. Sons in female-headed households tend to take on more reproductive tasks than those in male-headed units, often forced by circumstance, with a culture of undertaking responsibility for the collective physical and emotional well-being of the family unit at a young age in many cases persisting into adulthood, among both male and female household members.

In Chapter 3, I examine the intergenerational accumulation of gendered asset in households in Guayaquil, with trend data comparing household headship as well as individual assets within households. Education represents the most dramatic intergenerational change; the second generation has more human capital than the first, with daughters better educated than sons. Parental preference in investing more in the education of their daughters than sons, suggests changing perceptions, linked to changing gender relations about potential job market returns, with women more likely to use this educational benefit. However, despite educational successes, 'cultural norms' continue to be important intergenerational intermediary factors constraining women's agency. Even though third-generation granddaughters are more educated than the previous two, and with knowledge of contraception, they are still expected to stay at home until married and to go from the control of a father to that of a husband. They are not expected to live on their own, since this implies promiscuity, and still have the same pressures as their mothers to marry as soon as possible. However granddaughters are resisting, wanting to complete education, with their most important priority a good job rather than a good relationship with a man, highlighting the importance of the relationship between women's agency around education and their individual empowerment. In both of these examples processes of individual empowerment underpin wider processes of transformation as we move towards more just cities.

Concluding comment

The chapters in this book point to the fact that while the accumulation of assets may empower women, this process does not always successfully challenge power relations in a transformative manner, thereby contributing to just and more inclusive cities. Equally those transformative actions that do change power relations in cities do not necessarily transform gender power relations. While in many contexts, as described above, women play critically important leadership roles in accumulating the community social capital essential to drive negotiations, contestation, and collaboration to effect transformations with local authorities and other powerful institutions, most frequently these are not 'women's organisations', but more likely are community or member-based organisations. Therefore the role that women play in achieving transformative change in cities may itself in turn be more of a priority than transformations in gender power relations. This means that pathways that transform cities into more equitable, just spaces simultaneously are also critical catalysts to create transformations in gender relations, with the outcome of more equal gender relations. Ultimately, transformative cities and transformative gender relations are interrelated processes that mutually reinforce each other. As the world becomes increasingly urbanised, such interrelated process will undoubtedly become of critical significance.

Notes

1 For a comprehensive review of the debates, see Chant (2010).
2 See www.fordfoundation.org/issues/metropolitan-opportunity/just-cities.
3 See Moser (2009, 18–25) for a detailed elaboration of this issue.
4 This is adapted from Moser's asset accumulation framework (2009); useful insights come from WIEGO's IEMS narrative framework (WIEGO, 2012).
5 This framework follows Sen (1997) and Bebbington's (1999) identification of assets, which Kabeer refers to more generally as resources (2008, 20).
6 Yara Evans undertook this review as a commissioned background document for this chapter.
7 Indeed the frequent mentioned 'transformative change' may be considered somewhat of an oxymoron.

References

Alsop, R., Bertelsen, M.F., and Holland, J. (2006) *Empowerment in Practice: From Analysis to Implementation.* Washington, DC: World Bank.
Appadurai, A. (2004) 'The Capacity to Aspire: Culture and the Terms of Recognition', in Rao, V. and Walton, M. (eds), *Culture and Public Action.* Stanford, CA: Stanford University Press, pp. 59–85.
Bebbington, A. (1999) 'Capitals and Capabilities: A Framework for Analysing Peasant Viability, Rural Livelihoods and Poverty'. *World Development* 27 (12): 2021–44.
Boshara, R. and Sherraden, M. (2004) *Status of Asset Building Worldwide*, Washington, DC: New America Foundation.
Bourdieu, P. (1986) 'The Forms of Capital', in Richardson, J. (ed.) *Handbook of Theory and Research in the Sociology of Education*, pp. 241–58. Westport, CT: Greenwood Press.
Bourdieu, P. (1990) *The Logic of Practice.* Stanford, CA: Stanford University Press.
Carter, M.R. and Barrett, C.B. (2006) 'The Economics of Poverty Traps and Persistent Poverty: An Asset-Based Approach'. *Journal of Development Studies* 42 (2): 178–99.
Chant, S. (ed.) (2010) *The International Handbook of Gender and Poverty*, Cheltenham: Edward Elgar.
Cornwall, A., Harrison, E., and Whitehead, A. (2008) *Gender Myths and Feminist Fables*, Malden, MA: Blackwell Publishing Ltd.

Eyben, R. (2013) 'Gender Mainstreaming, Organizational Change, and the Politics of Influencing', in Eyben, R. and Turquet, L. (eds) *Feminists in Development Organizations*, pp. 15–36, Rugby: Practical Action Publishing Ltd.

Eyben, R. and Turquet, L. (2013) 'Introduction: Feminist Bureaucrats. Inside–Outside Perspectives', in Eyben, R. and Turquet, L. (eds) *Feminists in Development Organizations*, pp. 1–14, Rugby: Practical Action Publishing Ltd.

Fainstein, S. (2011) *The Just City*, Ithaca, NY: Cornell University Press.

Ferguson, C., Moser, C., and Norton, A. (2007) 'Claiming Rights: Citizenship and the Politics of Asset Distribution', in Moser, C. (ed.), *Reducing Global Poverty: The Case for Asset Accumulation*. Washington, DC: Brookings Institution Press.

Ford Foundation. (2004) *Building Assets to Reduce Poverty and Injustice*. New York: Ford Foundation.

Fraser, N. (2000) 'Rethinking Recognition'. *New Left Review*, May–June, 107–20.

Ginieniewicz, J. and Castiglione, C. (2011) 'State Response to Transnational Asset Accumulation: The Case of Argentina'. *Bulletin of Latin American Research*, 30: 133–47.

Goetz, A. and Sandler, J. (2007) 'Swapping Gender: From Cross-cutting Obscurity to Sectoral Security?', in Cornwall, A., Harrison, E., and Whitehead, A. (eds) *Feminisms: Contradictions, Contestations and Challenges*, pp. 161–76, London: Zed Books.

Green, M. (2006) 'Representing Poverty and Attacking Representations: Perspectives on Poverty from Social Anthropology'. *Journal of Development Studies* 42 (7): 1108–29.

Harriss, John (2007) 'Why Understanding Social Relations Matters More for Policy in Chronic Poverty than Measurement'. *Q Squared Working Paper* 34 (April). Center for International Studies, University of Toronto.

Hillenbrand, E. (2010) 'Transforming Gender in Homestead Food Production'. *Gender and Development* 18 (3): 411–25.

Hunt, J. and Kasynathan, N. (2001) 'Pathways to Empowerment? Reflections on Microfinance and Transformation in Gender Relations in South Asia'. *Gender and Development* 9 (1): 42–52.

Kabeer, N. (1999) 'Resources, Agency, Achievements: Reflections on the Measurement of Women's Empowerment', *Development and Change* 30: 435–64.

Kabeer, N. (2005) 'Gender Equality and Women's Empowerment: A Critical Analysis of the Third Millennium Development Goal', *Gender and Development* 13 (1): 13–24.

Kabeer, N. (2008) 'Paid Work, Women's Empowerment and Gender Justice: Critical Pathways of Social Change'. *Pathways Working Paper 3*, Institute of Development Studies, University of Sussex, Brighton.

Lefebvre, H. (1991) *The Production of Space*, Malden, MA: Blackwell Publishers.

McIlwaine, C. (2012) 'Constructing Transnational Social Spaces Among Latin American Migrants in Europe: Perspectives from the UK'. *Cambridge Journal of Regions, Economy and Society* 5: 289–303.

Molyneux, M. and S. Razavi (eds) (2002) *Gender Justice, Development and Rights*, Oxford: Oxford University Press.

Moser, C (1993) *Gender Planning and Development: Theory, Practice and Training*, London: Routledge.

Moser, C. (1998) 'The Asset Vulnerability Framework: Reassessing Urban Poverty Reduction Strategies'. *World Development* 26 (1): 1–19.

Moser, C. (ed.) (2007) *Reducing Global Poverty: The Case for Asset Accumulation*, Washington, DC: Brookings Institution Press.

Moser, C. (2008) 'Assets and Livelihoods: A Framework for Asset-Based Social Policy', in Moser, C. and Dani, A. (eds), *Assets, Livelihoods and Social Policy*, Washington, DC: World Bank, pp. 43–84.

Moser, C. (2009) *Ordinary Families: Extraordinary Lives: Assets and Poverty Reduction in Guayaquil, 1978–2004*, Washington, DC: Brookings Press.

Moser, C. (2014) 'Gender Planning and Development: Revisiting, Deconstructing and Reflecting'. *DPU 60 Working Paper Series: Reflections No 165/60*, Development Planning Unit, UCL.

Moser, C. and Felton, A. (2009) 'The Construction of an Asset Index: Measuring Asset Accumulation in Ecuador', in Addison, A., Hulme, D., and Kanbur, R. (eds), *Poverty Dynamics: A Cross-Disciplinary Perspective*, Oxford: Oxford University Press, pp. 102–127.

Moser, C. and Felton, A. (2010) 'The Gendered Nature of Asset Accumulation in Urban Contexts: Longitudinal Evidence from Guayaquil, Ecuador', in Beall, J., Guha-Khasnobis, B., and Kanbur, R. (eds), *Urbanisation and Development: Multidiscipline Perspectives*, Oxford: Oxford University Press, pp. 183–202.

Moser, C. and McIlwaine, C. (2004) *Encounters with Violence in Latin America*, London: Routledge.

Moser, C. and McIlwaine, C. (2006) 'Latin American Urban Violence as a Development Concern: Towards a Framework for Violence Reduction'. *World Development*, 34 (1): 89–112.

Moser, C. and Satterthwaite, D. (2010) 'Towards Pro-Poor Adaptation to Climate Change in the Urban Centres of Low and Middle-Income Countries', in Mearns, R. and Norton, A. (eds), *Social Dimensions of Climate Change: Equity and Vulnerability in a Warming World*, Washington, DC: World Bank, pp. 231–58.

Moser, C. and Stein, A. (2011) 'A Methodological Guideline for Implementing Urban Participatory Climate Change Adaptation Appraisals'. *Environment and Urbanization* 22 (2): 463–86.

Mukhopadhyay, M. (2004) 'Mainstreaming Gender or "Streaming" Gender Away: Feminists Marooned in the Development Business'. *IDS Bulletin* 35 (4): 95–103.

O'Neil, P. and Eyben, R. (2013) 'It's Fundamentally Political: Renovating the Master's House', in Eyben, R. and Turquet, L. (eds), *Feminists in Development Organizations*, pp. 85–100, Rugby: Practical Action Publishing Ltd.

Parpart, J. (2014) 'Exploring the Transformative Potential of Gender Mainstreaming in International Development Institutions'. *Journal of International Development* 26: 382–95.

Sandler, J. and Rao, A. (2012) 'The Elephant in the Room and the Dragons at the Gate: Strategising for Gender Equality in the 21st Century'. *Gender and Development* 20 (3): 547–62.

Sen, A. (1997) 'Editorial: Human Capital and Human Capability'. *World Development* 25, 12: 1959–61.

Sherraden, M. (1991) *Assets and the Poor: A New American Welfare Policy*, Armonk, NY: ME Sharpe.

Stein, A. and Moser, C. (2014) 'Asset Planning for Climate Change Adaptation: Lessons from Cartagena, Colombia'. *Environment and Urbanization* 26. doi:10.1177/0956247813519046.

Subrahmanian, R. (2007) 'Making Sense of Gender in Shifting Institutional Contexts: Some Reflections on Gender Mainstreaming', in Cornwall, A., Harrison, E. and Whitehead, A. (eds), *Feminisms in Development: Contradictions, Contestations and Challenges*, London: Zed Books, pp. 112–21

Sweetman, C. (2013) 'Introduction: Feminist Solidarity and Collective Action'. *Gender and Development*, 21 (2): 217–29.

UN-HABITAT (2013) *State of Women in Cities 2012–13*, Nairobi, Kenya: UN-HABITAT.

UN WOMEN (2013) *A Transformative Stand-alone Goal on Achieving Gender Equality, Women's Rights and Women's Empowerment: Imperatives and Key Components*, New York: UNWOMEN.

WIEGO (2012) IEMS Narrative Framework for Data Analysis, mimeo.

World Bank (2012) *Gender Equality and Development*, Washington, DC: World Bank.

2 Female household headship as an asset?

Interrogating the intersections of urbanisation, gender, and domestic transformations

Sylvia Chant

Introduction

The focus of this chapter is female household headship, which appears to be increasing in the context of ongoing urbanisation in the Global South, and has frequently been the subject of quite heated debate about what this means for women and well-being. Despite a general consensus that urbanisation is conducive to greater gender equality, and that cities are 'good for women', this does not necessarily encompass female-headed households, whose growth in numbers and proportions in the past few decades has commonly been linked to a 'feminisation of poverty'. While polarised generalisations of female household heads as 'victims' or 'heroines' have met with justifiable criticism (Varley 2013), this chapter interrogates whether, and to what extent, female household headship might be considered as an 'asset' with a role to play in making cities of the future more gender-equitable.

As the nominal 'poorest of the poor', women who head households purportedly fare worse than they would in male-headed households, and end up entrapping themselves and those who reside with them in situations of cumulative privation. Young dependent household members are thought to be particularly exposed to an 'inter-generational transmission of disadvantage', which does little to unsettle pervasive stereotypes of female-headed households as income-deprived, vulnerable and inferior to a patriarchal 'norm'. Yet when a more holistic and multidimensional view of poverty (and well-being) is taken into account, not to mention the immense heterogeneity of female-headed households, it is apparent that these units do not suffer unilaterally or universally from pecuniary disadvantage and other privations (Chant 1997; Klasen *et al.* 2014). Indeed, in some instances female-headed households might be construed as 'enabling spaces' which offer scope for the assertion of a wider range of rights for women and girls than is possible within some male-headed households. In turn, female headship may also assist in raising consciousness of various inequities which typically face women in both the domestic and extra-domestic domain. Indeed, not only does it appear that female-headed households provide a basis for (re)-negotiating gender roles and relations, at least within the home, but also the experience of managing livelihoods under female headship seems to afford a sense of achievement and 'empowerment' to women themselves and to other members of their domestic units. The latter arguably contributes to building psychological and emotional, as well as practical, resilience. Given rising levels of female headship in several parts of the Global South and especially in cities, could these various corollaries help to sow seeds for gendered social change from the 'bottom-up', especially on an inter-generational basis? In other words, might dynamics operating at the 'micro-level' of the domestic unit extend their cumulative influence into the more macro-level context of the urban environment? Although much of my discussion of the possible impacts of a mounting 'critical mass' of female-headed households in cities is speculative, I draw on evidence to support my ideas from first-hand ethnographic material collected over several years with low-income urban women in Mexico, Costa Rica, the Philippines, and Gambia (see Chant 1997, 2007).

The chapter begins with a brief synopsis of the diversity of pathways into female household headship, the different forms that female-headed households take, and how blanket associations between female household headship and the 'feminisation of poverty' are conceivably misguided. The discussion proceeds to explore the relationships between female household headship and key assets, such as property and social capital, before turning to the question of how female headship itself might be viewed as an asset. Here I suggest that being part of a female-headed household, in the short or long term, can act as a conduit for shifts in personal and domestic dynamics with potential to undermine patriarchal structures, advance women's interests, and strengthen demands to create more gender-equitable 'just cities'.

Female household headship, urbanisation, and domestic transformations

In several parts of the Global South, as well as in the Global North, household and family trajectories have displayed rather similar tendencies since the late twentieth century. These include declining marriage rates, falling fertility (along with a higher percentage of out-of-wedlock births), shrinking household size, mounting levels of divorce and separation, and what Buzar *et al.* (2005, 414) have summarised as a 'wider palette of family and domestic situations'. This expanding suite of domestic configurations is often referred to as the 'second demographic transition', and is conceivably most pronounced in respect of diversity in household forms and intimate networks in post-industrial advanced economies (Buzar *et al.* 2005). However, middle- and low-income countries too have seen a rising share of lone-person units, 'blended family' households (which come about through remarriage or the establishment of homes with second or subsequent partners combining children from different unions), and households headed by women (see Chant and McIlwaine 2009, chapter 9; also Budlender and Lund 2011, 926–7 on South Africa; Kinyanjui 2014, 8 on Kenya).

Households are usually defined as female-headed when the principal female adult member is unpartnered or lives in the absence of another senior male. Despite the fact that patriarchal bias in self- or proxy-reporting can distort figures, data from the United Nations Demographic Yearbook based on 109 countries between 1995 and 2003 suggest that one-fifth of households worldwide are headed by women. The highest proportions are in the Global North, and although the lowest recorded incidence of female headship is in Asia and Oceania (13.4 per cent), in other developing regions, notably Latin America and the Caribbean, and Africa, levels are nearly one-quarter (at 23.9 per cent and 23.8 per cent, respectively) (Varley 2014, 399, table 7.3.1). Interestingly, these latter regions correspond with the most and least urbanised parts of the developing world, although this does not detract from the fact that there seem to be strong links between urbanisation and female household headship generated through a confluence of direct and indirect forces.

One of the most direct influences is demographic. That 'cities are increasingly becoming feminised in demographic terms' (Kinyanjui 2014, 13), appears to be a marked corollary of rising levels of urban female household headship (Chant 2013; Tacoli and Chant 2014). Put simply, a skew towards women in the urban population makes female household headship more likely.

Latin America possesses the most consistently feminised urban sex ratios in the Global South, partly due to the cumulative legacy of female-selective rural–urban migration. Here, female household headship is often significantly greater in towns than in the countryside (see Chant and McIlwaine, forthcoming, chapter 1 on Costa Rica; Sardenburg 2010, 91 on Brazil), with a rural–urban 'transfer' of female-headed households adding impetus to this process (Bradshaw 1995; Chant 1998).

In regions where rural–urban migration has traditionally been male-selective, such as Africa and South Asia, female headship has historically been more pronounced in rural areas. However, the fact that not all women 'left behind' can rely on spousal support, and that some women who are widowed or divorced not only face a dearth of local livelihood opportunities, but land and property dispossession and/or social opprobrium (see Huisman 2005), seems to be giving rise to greater female rural–urban movement. Indeed, in a number of African and Asian countries, where gender disparities in migrant selectivity have started to diminish only recently, female-headed households are now more common in urban than in rural areas, if only by a relatively small margin in some instances (see Tacoli and Chant 2014, 592, table 48.2).

Demographic factors alone are accordingly not the only reason for the growing presence of female-headed households in towns and cities. Indeed, between the late 1980s and end of the first decade of the twenty-first century, female-headed households increased as a proportion of urban households in all countries in Latin America, despite variations in levels of urbanisation and the relative balance of women in urban populations (see Chant 2013, table 1). Vital additional (and frequently related) factors in the growing preponderance of urban female-headed households include greater access by women to employment and independent earnings in cities, higher levels of female land and property owner-ship, and diminished entanglement in, and control by, patriarchal kinship systems (see Chant and McIlwaine, forthcoming, chapter 1). In turn, and picking up on some of the suggestions I made at the outset of this chapter, it behoves speculation as to whether a growing constituency of female-headed households in urban areas is important in its own right: once a critical mass of women begin to fend for themselves (and in many instances their dependants too), does this play a role in inculcating or strengthening the perception that women in cities do not need to be reliant on men to survive? On top of this, does the relative anonymity and social fluidity of urban environments afford more scope for women, especially those who decide to leave oppressive conjugal relationships and establish households on their own, to escape surveillance from former part-ners and their families, or their own kin? (see Chant with Craske 2003, 235–6)? Exploring some of the pathways into, and patterns of, female headship arguably sheds a little light on the possibility that urban environments may be somewhat freer of restrictive social conventions associated with patriarchal family norms in rural settings, and thus be more conducive to women assuming domestic leadership.

Pathways into female household headship in cities

Pathways into female household headship in cities include migration (especially, although not always, where this is female-selective), non-marriage, separation, divorce, and widowhood (see Chant 1997), and in some contexts, polygamy, as observed in the context of majority Muslim countries such as Gambia (Chant 2007) and Bangladesh (Habib 2010). While all such routes apply to rural areas, non-marriage, divorce, and separation tend to be more prevalent in cities. This is even the case in patriarchally conservative countries such as Bangladesh, where Tanzima Zohra Habib's (2010) study of Rajshahi City found that only 32.9 per cent of female heads who were not presently married were widows, and the rest divorced, separated, or 'abandoned' (Habib 2010, 177, table 1).

This is not to deny that generalisations remain elusive when in some urban contexts widowhood prevails, as in Mekelle, Ethiopia, for instance, where a small-scale ethnographic study conducted by Weldegiorgis and Jayamohan (2013, 36) revealed that 58 per cent of female heads reached this state via wid-owhood, 38 per cent through separation or divorce, and a mere 4 per cent (one case in this sample) because of a professed 'desire to be independent'. Indeed, as Ann Varley (2013, 131) notes more generally, in a context of population ageing, and in which women are generally younger than their husbands, widowhood is 'above all a female experience, and one that will become increasingly common in the urban areas of less wealthy countries' (see also Lenoël 2014, chapter 4).

Patterns of female household headship in cities

As might be expected from the plethora of processes leading to female headship, women-headed households are as diverse in their characteristics as a group, as in their formation. As summarised in previous work (Chant 2007, 108):

> Differentiation occurs through routes into the status (whether by choice or involuntarily, and/or through non-marriage, separation, divorce, widow-hood, migration), by rural or urban residence, by race, by composition, by stage in the life course (including age and relative dependency of offspring), and by access to resources from beyond the household unit (from absent fathers, kinship networks, state assistance and the like).

Age is a big factor in this equation, and despite a persistently stereotypical assumption that young (unmarried) lone mothers represent a major constituency among female heads, in actuality these are more likely to form 'embedded' female-headed 'sub-families' within larger extended households, often headed by their own parents or other consanguineous kin (see Chant 1997 on the Philip-pines; Moser 2010 on Ecuador). As such, female headship is typically more applicable to women in their middle or later years. In Bangladesh, for example, Habib's (2010) survey found that 72 per cent of female heads were aged between 30 and 49, with part of the reason being societal resistance to independence among younger women (Habib 2010, 176). Although Habib's designation of female heads was based on whether women were the main breadwinners in their households and this might clearly exert a bias against women aged 49 or more, given older women's lower likelihood of being economically active, it is instruc-tive to consider Ann Varley's (2014, 400) point, drawn on the more conventional classification of female heads as women lacking co-resident male partners, that in many regions of the Global South, the highest proportion of woman-headed households lies in the 60-plus age group. In Latin America and the Caribbean, for example, aggregated data for seven countries suggest that 37 per cent of heads of household over 60 are female, and that women heads aged 60-plus con-stitute over one-third (39.8 per cent) of all female heads in the region, compared with an 18.1 per cent share of male heads in the 60-plus category (Varley 2014, 401, table 7.3.2).

Older age and widowhood are frequently used as proxies for one another, but while they are often linked, it is advisable to remember that age gaps between spouses can be considerable in some contexts, especially in polygamous unions, such that it is difficult to generalise (Chant 1997). This said, Varley (2013, 132) highlights that old or young, widows are prone to poverty given that they are commonly discriminated against in terms of labour market access and inherit-ance laws and practices.

Certainly, there is little doubt that the seniority of female household heads in some contexts may be inimical to personal and household well-being. In Egypt, for example, Bibars (2001, 67) relates that many female heads are poor because they are 'old, illiterate and unable to work'. However, in many cases it is younger female household heads, especially those with dependent children, who may be poorer, as in Costa Rica and Chile (see Chant 2003, 19). Part of the reason for an inability to draw systematic disparities in the poverty experiences of younger and older women is that in some contexts, social protection might play a role in qualifying the risks attached to female headship at later stages of the life-course (see Dubihlela and Dubihlela 2014, 165 for South Africa). On top of this, older women may be in a privileged position in respect of receiving income from older children in work who remain in the household, or who are not co-resident but remit money (Chant 2003, 19).

Thus, female-headed households do not just consist of lone women, or mothers and dependent children, but are very frequently extended in nature. In many instances household extension is a deliberate strategy adopted by female heads to maximise the utility of paid and unpaid labour (see Bradshaw 1995, 2002 on Honduras and Nicaragua; Chant 1997 on Mexico, Costa Rica, and the Philippines; Wartenburg 1999 on Colombia). Even if households themselves are not extended, access to social assistance and embeddedness in kin networks can also be crucial platforms for viability. In the Dominican Republic, for instance, Helen Safa (2002, 13) identifies how female heads of household have historically maintained strong relationships with consanguineous kin.

Female household headship and the 'feminisation of poverty'

The common stereotype that female-headed households are 'poorest of the poor', and that their rising share of the household population is responsible for poverty's increasingly 'female face', forms one of three apparently intuitive pillars of the 'feminisation of poverty' thesis. The remaining two – related – precepts are that women are poorer than men and that the incidence of poverty among women is increasing relative to men over time (Chant 2007). Yet each of these elements in the feminisation of poverty is open to question on conceptual and/or empirical grounds. The assertion that women are poorer than men, for example, is static, and therefore anomalous within a construct whose very nomenclature implies dynamism.

It is also questionable that the incidence of poverty among women is increasing relative to men. Notwithstanding the lack of specified time parameters, a dearth of sex-disaggregated panel data in developing regions makes it very difficult to establish whether gender gaps in poverty are widening over the medium to long term. And even where such data are available, no obvious trajectory emerges in the direction of mounting economic privation among women. For example, Medeiros and Costa's (2006) analysis of sex-disaggregated statistics on income poverty compiled by the Economic Commission for Latin America and the Caribbean (ECLAC) for eight countries between the early 1990s and early 2000s drew the conclusion that there was 'no solid evidence of a process of feminisation of poverty' (Medeiros and Costa 2006, 13). This interpretation was based not only on the per capita income figures for women and men in general and according to male- and female-household headship, but also took into account the incidence, severity, and intensity of poverty.[1]

Although Medeiros and Costa's analysis provides one of the few really rigorous studies of quantitative panel data, and there is ample further evidence from qualitative research to suggest that female household headship is not systematically associated with a 'feminisation of poverty' (see Chant 2007, chapter 3), this is not to deny that some female-headed households in some contexts, including urban ones, are at disproportionate risk of economic privation (see Habib 2010 on Bangladesh; Lenoël 2014 on Morocco; Rogan 2013 on South Africa).

Moreover, it is also important to consider, as noted by Klasen *et al.* (2014, 4), that female-headed households might be more *vulnerable to falling into poverty* because their asset bases in respect of land, credit markets, labour markets, insurance schemes, and social capital are less robust and diverse than in households headed by men.

Female-headed households and assets

The potential vulnerability of female-headed households to poverty is pertinent in the context of quite widespread observations about their low rates of acquisition of material assets such as land and property. This is discussed, inter alia, by Caroline O.N. Moser (2010) on Guayaquil, Ecuador, and by Deere *et al.* (2012, 525) for Latin America more generally. In the latter case, women may be comparatively favoured in land and shelter acquisition than elsewhere in the world, but in only two out of eleven countries in the region studied by these authors – Nicaragua and Panama – has gender parity been achieved in home ownership.

By the same token, Nestor Gandelman (2009) concludes that while women have less probability than men of home ownership in Chile, Honduras, and Nicaragua, female heads of household fare better, even if owning property in the first place may serve as an important element in women's decisions to assume headship. In turn, the prospect of being able to access property *as* a female household head may also play a part in the equation, with Alejandra Ramm (2014) pointing out that for Chile the expansion of social protection and targeting of vulnerable groups in the wake of post-1990 democratisation has led to unmarried women being far more likely to receive a state-housing subsidy than men, especially compared with the authoritarian regime of the 1970s and 1980s. Although post-1990 developments in Chile were premised on the assumption that female household heads were likely to be poorer and more vulnerable than their male counterparts, the upshot has been to benefit single women to the extent that more women now apply for housing subsidies and are regarded as household heads, even if they actually have a male partner in tow. Thus, rather than being a sign of growing vulnerability, Ramm (2014, 13) talks about a 'strategic' and 'empowering' use of lone motherhood being significant in explaining a virtual doubling in the share of Chilean households headed by women between 1990 (20 per cent) and 2011 (nearly 40 per cent), even if female-headed households are almost 50 per cent among the poorest quintile. In this instance, it must be recognised that state-denominated 'vulnerability', while inevitably problematic on a number of counts in respect of what it implies for citizenship, rights, and claim-making, can in some instances work to the favour of 'marginalised' groups such as female-headed households (see Skrabut 2014 on Peru; Zeiderman 2013 on Colombia).

Whatever the processes involved, compared to their rural counterparts urban women are commonly regarded as better-placed in respect of access to land and housing, partly because they have greater opportunities to earn income in their own right, and partly because a greater proportion of property is allocated through the market (or state) rather than through gender-discriminatory custom-ary inheritance practices (UNFPA 2007, 19). In turn, home ownership can sub-stantially strengthen women's asset base – and ipso facto – their 'fall-back' position, not only because of the potential exchange value of land and housing, but also because this affords possibilities for part-sale or rental, as well as for productive use, and as a resource which they can also pass on to children (see Moser 1998, 2010; Rakodi 2014). In my fieldwork in Costa Rica, these were major considerations for women keen to exit unhappy or dysfunctional relation-ships, as in the case of Sonia, living in a low-income settlement in the town of Santa Cruz in the north-west of the country.

Sonia, in 2005, was 44 years old and lived with her three children, aged between 16 and 24. Each child had a different father, and Sonia had only con-ceded to moving in with the youngest's father, a bus driver, because this offered the prospect of securing '*un hogar para mis hijos*' (a home for my children). After a three-month 'honeymoon' period, however, the relationship soured on account of her spouse's drinking and violence, which for at least a decade subse-quently made Sonia feel fearful of leaving him. Nonetheless, on the basis of her own earnings and those of her eldest son, Sonia eventually managed to scrape enough income to buy the plot next door in her own name (in secret), as a form of personal insurance. Once she and her spouse had not had sexual relations for a year, Sonia then divided their living arrangements. If she ever settles down with her current *novio* (boyfriend) – a married man of 52 – she says she will need him to provide her with another house in order that she can leave her exist-ing property to her children, as well as retreat there in the event of a future split (see Chant 2007, 306–8).

Another issue beyond women's acquisition of property per se, whether during a partnership or as a female household head, is that once alone they may put more effort into improving shelter quality, as I observed in research on housing consolidation in three low-income settlements in Querétaro, Mexico in the early 1980s. Here, a disproportionate number of female-headed households had managed to enhance not only the comfort of their dwellings, but also their market value. This was not necessarily because they were financially better-off than male-headed households, but compared with a number of the latter in which the appearance and amenity of 'home' signified relatively little to men who spent the vast bulk of their time at work and/or 'on the street', female heads had prioritised housing investment over other forms of expenditure (Chant 1997, 227–8).

However, not all female heads may be able to access the owner-occupancy market, with many discriminated against even in respect of rental tenure. This is documented, inter alia, by Penny Vera-Sanso (2006) for southern Indian cities where rental accommodation may be hard to secure in the face of aspersions about the sexual propriety of women without male 'guardians'. In the slums of Ahmedabad, in north-western India, Bipasha Baruah (2007, 4) notes that although women-headed households are more likely to rent than to own, land-lords' concerns about their economic security can act as an additional barrier to access. In this way, Klasen *et al.*'s (2014) observation with regard to the precari-ous asset base of female-headed households has greater traction.

Aside from gender discrimination in land and housing, as well as in labour and credit markets, except through micro-finance schemes which offer few pro-spects for lifting women out of poverty and may even deepen indebtedness (Fed-erici 2014), another element in Klasen *et al.*'s (2014) argument which is potentially pertinent to vulnerability to poverty among female heads is their putative lack of 'social capital'.

Social networks are often anticipated to be more limited for female-headed households because women may be cut-off from their partners' kin (and some-times their own), or because they do not have the time to cultivate ties with others, or because they lack inclination to engage in relationships where they may not be able to reciprocate on an equal basis (see Chant 2003, 10–11). Cer-tainly, my research in Mexico, Costa Rica, and the Philippines showed that the social networks of urban female-headed households may be constrained through a combination of factors, including how they are viewed by others, and self-imposed barriers to social mixing which come about not just due to lack of time, but also because they wish to play down their relative freedoms as a means of garnering moral 'legitimacy'.

This said, when moving beyond poverty as an income- and material asset-bound construct to accommodate a more multidimensional conceptualisation, in which issues of power, voice, subjectivity, and agency come to the fore, not only does the 'feminisation of poverty' seem to be a rather tenuous proposition, but it is arguably possible to regard female household headship as an asset in its own right.

Female household headship as an asset

In thinking about the potential for female household headship to act as a positive influence in women's lives which may increase their resilience, as well as open avenues for transformations in gender, it is helpful to consider the concept of 'portable' assets, as discussed in the context of northern Uganda by Bird *et al.* (2010). In an environment vulnerable to the destruction or loss of material or physical assets, as well as the disruption of social networks, the authors emphasise the value of 'portable' assets such as education, which individuals or households can carry with them and use as a platform for rebuilding lives and livelihoods. In this chapter I suggest that the experience of being a head of household, or growing up in a household headed by a woman, can provide something akin to a portable asset in respect of its psychological legacy.

Given the common links between poverty and social pathology, female household headship may not appear to give women or the members of their households any kind of personal, material, or psycho-social advantage, with such households perceived to be more vulnerable and 'at risk' (Chant 1997; Skrabut 2014). Indeed, in the context of widespread patriarchy, women without co-resident spouses or partners are frequently regarded as anomalous and unfortunate, if not 'deviant'. This also extends to their offspring, especially sons who, deprived of a primary male 'role model', are thought to be prone to disaffected behaviour. However, I would argue that experience of female household headship can potentially build capacities, especially in societies which are discriminatory or hostile to this group.

Indeed, some women 'choose' female headship, and this itself can be a pivot for change. In many respects women show strength and agency by stepping out of 'bad marriages', or by deciding to form a household on their own or with children. In a similar vein, resisting a subsequent marriage or co-residential union, which appears to be more common than not, can also be very empowering in its own right (Chant 2003, 27). This is not to deny that in some cases women eschew new relationships on account of the sensibilities of their children, who may become jealous or resentful if their mothers take-up with new partners, or through fear that the latter may abuse step-daughters (Chant 1997, 221).

Nor is this to gloss over the fact that female household headship can be a struggle, especially in the early stages, where women not only have to juggle the demands of fending for themselves and other household members (especially young dependent children), but also to cope with the emotional fall-out of separation, divorce, or bereavement. This was clear in the case of Socorro, a middle-aged woman in Querétaro, Mexico, who had spent most of her adult life as a female household head, despite having three partnerships from which she had nine children. Socorro reported that she had always felt that her situation was precarious, and as the household's only enduring (and usually sole) economic provider, worried constantly about getting ill or having an accident, while feeling drained by multiple demands upon her time (Chant 1997, 203).

For many women embarking on household headship, finding property is a major challenge, especially if they don't have their own house already (see earlier), and another is work. For poor female heads, especially those with young children, gender discrimination in the labour market, coupled with lack of affordable childcare, poses major problems. Sometimes this forces women into running their own informal businesses in or near the home, leaving children in the care of friends or neighbours, enlisting the help of under-age children to boost finances, or extending their households. Socorro, introduced above, for example, invited her elderly father to stay with her in order to have someone around to mind the children while she went out to her cleaning job, even though her father also needed care, and represented another mouth to feed.

Another major challenge, especially for unmarried female heads, or victims of broken marriages, is having to cope with negative attitudes from others.

In contexts in which out-of-wedlock birth is deemed a matter of disgrace, as in the Philippines, for example, young women are frequently discriminated against or turned out by their own families; even if this does not happen, they may take it upon themselves to move away to spare 'family honour' (Chant 1997, 181–2). In turn, even if women migrate to towns or cities where they are unknown, in the communities in which they set-up residence, neighbours often regard them with a 'combination of fear, disrespect and/or disdain' (Chant 1997, 198). In Mexico and Costa Rica, too, female heads often report that they are the butt of gossip and surveillance by other women. In the wake of speculation as to their morals, and concerns on the part of married women that lone women pose a threat to the fidelity of their own husbands, the behaviour of female household heads is also often demonstrably conservative – for example, taking the form of 'keeping themselves to themselves', avoiding flamboyant dressing, or going to great lengths to keep relations with other men discreet, to a minimum, or even eschewing male contact altogether (Chant 1997, 198–9).

This is often difficult when female heads are frequently subject to the unwelcome advances from men who not only seek to exploit their perceived 'loneliness' and vulnerability, but also their conjectured financial viability. As reported by Lidia, a 30-year-old lone mother of one, living in Cañas, Costa Rica, who had declined dates with several men since her husband deserted her seven years previously: 'Men know that single mothers have to work, so they not only come after you for sex, but also for your money!' Indeed, many women with histories of unsuccessful unions do not wish to repeat the dose, especially after a second (or subsequent) experience in which they felt they had been abused financially, sexually, and emotionally. Eida (52 years) from Santa Cruz, Costa Rica, whose husband left her at the age of 46, and who headed an eight-member household, was vehement about not cohabiting with anyone else in the future. Observing that young men in the interests of having an easier life often seek out the company of older women, she affirmed: 'I prefer to clean houses than to sell myself to young men' (Chant 2007, 321).

From struggle to survival and 'success': asset-building in female-headed households

In facing up to an immense array of economic, social, and emotional challenges, it is important to recognise that this may require extreme ingenuity and strength, and personal effort in problem-solving, especially where there is little support from state and society. This conveys a sense of accomplishment, as well as positive framings of coping, self-esteem and self-efficacy on the part of female heads, not to mention others around them. In the town of Santa Cruz, Costa Rica, for example, a 67-year-old married woman, Juanita, affirmed that 'even when women are alone, they still manage to survive'.

While such views on female headship run counter to prevailing wisdoms that this is necessarily poverty-inducing, a further paradox is presented by the fact that in actuality many women pragmatically and psychologically find living without partners a positive alternative. Female headship seems to offer women, inter alia, more power and independence, greater occupational choice, more control over household finances, enhanced mobility and freedom, less exploitation, less insecurity, and greater peace and well-being. For example, Nuvia, a 49-year-old female head working as a cleaner in Villareal, Costa Rica, declared that since splitting with a violent, alcoholic spouse:

> Of course I am happier now, because now I know that I can buy rice and beans, and eat in peace. While when I was with him … if he left at six o'clock in the morning to work, he didn't come back until six o'clock the following morning, drunk and causing me trouble, and me there perhaps without food. Whatever I have had to suffer, I don't wish that on any other woman.
>
> (Chant 2007, 320)

Floribet, a 49-year-old female head from Santa Cruz, Costa Rica, who has had eight children by four different fathers, admitted to having suffered as a lone mother, although she also felt that long lapses between partners had given her a better opportunity to provide for her offspring. This was because she could do any job she wanted without having to undergo protracted and conflictive negotiations. In her various efforts to raise her children Floribet had worked as a waitress, a cleaning lady, and claims at times to have come close to prostitution. Now she has only two children at home and on top of making a modest living selling *arroz con leche* (rice with milk) and *tejidos* (knitwear), receives money from her eldest son and daughter who now have their own families. Although she is far from well-off, she welcomes the security attached to being the manager of household income. Managing to give her children a reasonable start in life has also given her a sense of pride, added to which she now feels able to put men behind her altogether. Floribet joined a small Costa Rican Evangelical church in 2003, and having become a full-fledged *hija de Dios* (child of God), declares that 'the only husband for me from now on will be Jesus Christ!' (see Chant 2007, 320–1).

The sense of triumphalism and pride when women look back on their pasts, as evidenced in Floribet's case, reinforces the fact that few female household heads seem to regret extricating themselves from unhappy or conflictive relationships, or having the opportunity to manage their own affairs.

Despite all the difficulties 44-year-old Costa Rican female household head Sonia had encountered during three effectively dysfunctional relationships, she has a strong sense of self-esteem which has come from raising her children with little help from men. Declaring: '*Yo puedo sola … soy la madre y el padre*' ('I can go it alone … I am the mother and the father'), she said she has proved herself to be capable without a man, and that she doesn't need to ask anyone for assistance. In turn, Sonia does not think that households headed by women are worse-off. For Sonia, the idea that women are the *sexo débil* (weak sex) is a *mentira* (lie). 'A woman doesn't need a man. She has capacity' (Chant 2007, 306–8).

Dolores, a middle-aged female head in Puerto Vallarta, Mexico, also maintained that she had always seen herself as the 'man and woman in this house' (Chant 1997, 203). She called herself a 'heroine' for having raised her family more or less single-handedly, first as the wife of a man 30 years her senior who played a very small role in household management or income provision, and subsequently as a widow. Dolores was immensely proud that she had seen all her children through a good education and into jobs.

While positive personal post-hoc reminiscences and rationalisations of female headship may clearly be construed as justifications for having somehow 'failed' to live-up to normative ideals of marriage and motherhood, there is also quite robust evidence that female headship takes women and their household members into an 'empowering' terrain of new responsibilities and leadership, new activities and aspirations, and changes in gender norms among younger generations.

For example, in order to help her get over the break-up with her youngest son's father in 2001, Sonia, from Costa Rica, took advantage of free state-provided adult education, an opportunity to which she would have been otherwise denied. She is just entering the fifth and final year of her high school diploma (*bachillerato*), and although this requires a commitment of three hours each evening, and she does not get home until after 9 p.m., Sonia has managed to secure reputable grades, and is hoping eventually to enrol part-time on a university degree course and to become a teacher. This is a far cry from the types of job which Sonia has done since age 11, when she was sent by her parents to work as a live-in servant in the capital, San José.

Despite provisos about the precariousness of social networks (see earlier), female household headship may also not necessarily weaken 'social capital', including with affinal kin. For example, in some instances the desire of former in-laws to maintain contact with their grandchildren can keep relationships with female heads close and supportive. This applied to Layla in Cañas, Costa Rica, who after she split with her first husband, on account of his drug-dealing and violence, was given the opportunity to camp on her parents-in-law's patio as a temporary stopgap.

Not only can female household heads salvage relationships with their in-laws, but they can also be presented with the possibility of forging relationships of solidarity with other women. For example, female household heads often counsel as well as console one another, which detracts from their sense of isolation as well as providing an immense source of psychological and emotional, as well as practical, support (see Chant 1997, 206–7). This is apparent in the Philippines, where prospective female household headship can be encouraged through exchanges between women who are either household heads already or with partnered women in similar situations. One such case is Girlie, a market trader in Boracay, who, in the process of advising a girlfriend whose husband is openly having an affair and only comes back to his wife when he needs to eat or to get a change of clothes, has helped her see serious fissures in her own marriage, from which she is now planning to escape (Chant 1997, 207).

On the matter of inter-generational transformations, the experiences of young men in female-headed households may also bring about important attitudinal changes that testify to the social and psychological asset-building fomented through female household headship. One major factor is that sons in female-headed households tend to take on more reproductive tasks than those in male-headed units. Often this is forced by circumstance, especially given constraints on the time of female heads, who in some cases instil in all their children the idea that everyone has to pitch in or no-one will 'get by' (Chant 1997, 204–6). The number, ages, and sex of children can influence the distribution of caring and domestic chores, and boys often do the heavier tasks which might have normally fallen to their fathers, or take on part-time jobs to help fund their own schooling or contribute to household income. Nonetheless, a culture of undertaking responsibility for the collective physical and emotional well-being of the family unit at a young age seems in many cases to persist into adulthood, among both male and female household members.

María Cruz, in Querétaro, Mexico, for example, now in her forties, had raised two young sons and a daughter after terminating her relationship with their 'violent and irresponsible father'. Aside from sharing the domestic work with their sister, both of María's sons (aged six and eight years at the time of the split) soon started topping up their mother's earnings from her part-time breakfast business by running errands for neighbours, clearing stones and other debris from people's land plots, and charging for delivering water from one of the community's few and intermittently slow-flowing standpipes. Although by the age of 22 María's elder son had a partner and a three-year-old daughter with whom he lived nearby on his parents-in-law's compound, his visits to María were frequent, and he aimed in due course to build on María's plot so that he could continue to help his mother (Chant 1997, 241).

That these are not just claims made by female heads themselves is also evidenced in the case of Tereso (46 years old) who had grown up in a household with a violent and financially irresponsible father who eventually abandoned his spouse and children altogether. Vowing never to repeat this history with his own wife, Paula, and having played more than his fair share of domestic and caring work, Tereso has now enjoyed a 26-year relationship with a woman who describes him as an 'exceptional husband'. Tereso has also constantly impressed upon their own four sons that they need to be financially secure before taking on the commitment of looking after a family (Chant 1997, 242).

Aside from gender-sensitivity among sons, other inter-generational spin-offs of female household headship extend to daughters, with many female household heads, especially lone mothers, being concerned to equip their daughters with the best possible chance of 'defending themselves' in later life. Indeed, in female-headed households, levels of education among offspring typically reveal not only smaller gender gaps, but in some cases higher levels of attainment among girls than boys (Chant 1997, 222–3).

From the household to the city: female headship as a public as well as a personal and portable asset?

As female household headship begins to form part of the lived experience of larger proportions of urban populations, absolutely and relatively, across the Global South, it is possible that greater consciousness of the many gender inequalities which inhibit the viability of urban livelihoods will arise. At the same time, I would argue that women who have to 'go it alone' prove themselves capable, albeit by dint of considerable self-sacrifice, to overcome major structural hurdles, and that this will gather momentum and lead to a more informed and persuasive basis for change. As articulated by Buzar *et al.* (2005, 424): 'In their entirety, the demographic, cultural and economic outcomes of household-level dynamics constitute a powerful force for urban transformation.' On a similar note, Kinyanjui (2014, 86) stresses on the basis of her research on informal women entrepreneurs in Nairobi, Kenya, that:

> In the eyes of women in economic informality, change in the city begins at the household level. It is where knowledge is created and nurtured and the power balance is generated. By women being actively involved in economic informality, they are able to become active citizens in households and eventually in the city.

The impact on people beyond those directly affected by female household headship should also be recognised. Alice Evans (2014) identifies how the encroachment of women into formerly masculinised jobs in the town of Kitwe in the Zambian Copperbelt is exerting a strong and sustainable influence on gendered attitudes and behaviours. In the case of female household headship, appreciation among others of the success of many female heads of household and their members could also contribute to growing awareness and tolerance of female-headed households as a more 'normal', viable, and indeed respected form of domestic organisation.

Concluding comments

In this chapter I have outlined the potential to identify female household headship to be an asset in the process of building more gender-equitable cities. Whether female household headship is necessarily a personal or public 'asset' is qualified by the rather mixed contexts in which they are situated, and how these are mediated by their individual circumstances. As noted by Habib (2010, 184) for Rajshahi City, Bangladesh: 'Female headship may bring women some escape from male subordination within the household, but it also brings a range of disadvantages.' However, it could also be argued that these self-same disadvantages raise consciousness of inequalities faced not only by unpartnered women, but women in general. Urban women without husbands or partners have a putatively greater need to fight personal corners in the wider space of the city, on behalf of themselves, and ipso facto, women as a group, and frequently have a greater margin of freedom to do so.

Female household headship can open up new lines of solidarity among women, even on a small scale, and if widened and strengthened could represent a positive force for change. In the context of Nairobi, for example, Kinyanjui (2014, 8) points out that many women entrepreneurs, who often head their own households and hail from different social classes 'are feminising the city by sharing spaces, identifying livelihood opportunities and organising collective action'. She further notes that 'The tenets of unity, solidarity, togetherness and comradeship serves as strategies for rescuing women from material deprivation and exclusion from spaces of action (p. 106).

As a growing constituency in urban contexts of the Global South, there is scope for female-headed households to add impetus to demands for cities to become less male-privileged places, especially in respect of matters such as housing, affordable childcare, and jobs.

As summarised by Buzar *et al.* (2005, 429):

> The household ... operates as a vibrant nexus for wider developments in the economic, cultural, demographic and spatial realm. The urban agency of the household is embodied in the myriad connections between the socio-economic changes brought about by the sum of these interactions, on the one hand, and the wider transformations of the built environment, on the other. Therefore, a greater analytical emphasis on the hitherto 'quiet' demography of urban transformation can open the path for ... energising urban geography with the multiple social transformations projecting from this scale.

The 'time poverty' of female heads of households and their members may clearly stand in the way of catalysing the dedicated group-based political mobilisation which might be necessary for an 'urban revolution' in the immediate future. However, it is tempting to think that the 'quiet demography of urban transformation' may produce a groundswell for sustainable change towards more gender-sensitive cities, building on the proven practical and personal assets developed in the context of female household headship.

Acknowledgements

Thanks are due to Cathy McIlwaine and Caroline O.N. Moser for their valuable comments on earlier versions of this chapter, as well as to the many women interviewed in Costa Rica, Gambia, Mexico and the Philippines, whose observations and opinions over the years have constituted vital inputs to my knowledge and thinking.

Note

1 The incidence of poverty measures the proportion of the poor in a given population and is the most commonly used indicator when assessing poverty differentials between women and men, or between female- and male-headed households. The intensity of (income) poverty is measured by the aggregated difference between the observed income of poor populations and the poverty line, while the severity of poverty refers to 'some combination of the incidence and intensity of poverty and inequality among the poor' (Medeiros and Costa 2006, 20n).

References

Baruah, Bipasha (2007) 'Gendered Realities: Exploring Property Ownership and Tenancy Agreements in Urban India', *World Development*, 35:12, 2096–109.

Bibars, Iman (2001) *Victims and Heroines: Women, Welfare and the Egyptian State* (London: Zed).

Bird, Kate, Higgins, Kate, and McKay, Andy (2010) 'Conflict, Education and the Intergenerational Transmission of Poverty in Northern Uganda', *Journal of International Development*, 22, 1183–96.

Bradshaw, Sarah (1995) 'Female-headed Households in Honduras: Perspectives on Rural–Urban Differences', *Third World Planning Review*, 17:2, 117–31.

Bradshaw, Sarah (2002) *Gendered Poverty and Power Relations: Looking Inside Communities and Households* (Managua: Puntos de Encuentro).

Budlender, Debbie and Lund, Francie (2011) 'South Africa: A Legacy of Family Disruption', *Development and Change*, 42:45, 925–46.

Buzar, Stefan, Ogden, Philip E., and Hall, Ray (2005) 'Households Matter: The Quiet Demography of Urban Transformation', *Progress in Human Geography*, 29:4, 413–36.

Chant, Sylvia (1997) *Women-headed Households: Diversity and Dynamics in the Developing World* (Houndmills: Macmillan).

Chant, Sylvia (1998) 'Households, Gender and Rural–Urban Migration: Reflections on Linkages and Considerations for Policy', *Environment and Urbanization*, 10:1, 5–21.

Chant, Sylvia (2003) *Female Household Headship and the Feminisation of Poverty: Facts, Fictions and Forward Strategies*. London School of Economics, Gender Institute, New Working Paper Series, Issue 9.

Chant, Sylvia (2007) *Gender, Generation and Poverty: Exploring the 'Feminisation of Poverty' in Africa, Asia and Latin America* (Cheltenham: Edward Elgar).

Chant, Sylvia (2013) 'Cities Through a "Gender Lens": A Golden "Urban Age" for Women in the Global South?', *Environment and Urbanization*, 25:1, 9–29.

Chant, Sylvia with Craske, Nikki (2003) *Gender in Latin America* (London: Latin America Bureau).

Chant, Sylvia and McIlwaine, Cathy (2009) *Geographies of Development in the 21st Century* (Cheltenham: Edward Elgar).

Chant, Sylvia and McIlwaine, Cathy (forthcoming) *Cities, Slums and Gender in the Global South: Towards a Feminised Urban Future* (London: Routledge).

Deere, Carmen Diana, Alvarado, Gina E., and Twyman, Jennifer (2012) 'Gender Inequality in Asset Ownership in Latin America: Female Owners Vs Household Heads', *Development and Change*, 43:2, 505–30.

Dubihlela, Job and Dubihlela, Dorah (2014) 'Social Grants Impact on Poverty Among the Female-headed Households in South Africa: A Case Analysis', *Mediterranean Journal of Social Sciences*, 5:8, 160–7.

Evans, Alice (2014) 'Gender Sensitisation in the Zambian Copperbelt', *Geoforum*, 59, 12–20.

Federici, Silvia (2014) 'From Commoning to Debt: Financialisation, Microcredit, and the Changing Architecture of Capital Accumulation', *The South Atlantic Quarterly*, 113:2, 231–44.

Gandelman, Nestor (2009) 'Female-headed Households and Homeownership in Latin America', *Housing Studies*, 24:4, 525–49.

Habib, Tanzima Zohra (2010) 'Socio-Psychological Status of Female Heads of Households in Rajshahi City, Bangladesh', *Antrocom Online Journal of Anthropology*, 6:2, 173–86.

Huisman, Henk (2005) 'Contextualising Chronic Exclusion: Female-headed Households in Semi-Arid Zimbabwe', *Tijdschrift voor Economische en Sociale Geografie*, 96:3, 253–63.

Kinyanjui, Mary Njeri (2014) *Women and the Informal Economy in Urban Africa: From the Margins to the Centre* (Uppsala/London: NordiskAfrikainstutet/Zed Books).

Klasen, Stephan, Lechtenfeld, Tobias, and Povel, Felix (2014) 'A Feminization of Vulnerability? Female Headship, Poverty, and Vulnerability in Thailand and Vietnam', *World Development* (accessed online, http://dx.doi.org/10.1016/j.worlddev.2013.11.003).

Lenoël, Audrey (2014) 'Burden or Empowerment? The Impact of Migration and Remittances on Women Left Behind in Morocco'. Unpublished PhD dissertation, Faculty of Social Sciences and Law, University of Bristol.

Medeiros, Marcelo and Costa, Joana (2006) *Poverty Among Women in Latin America: Feminisation or Over-representation?* Working Paper No. 20, International Poverty Centre, Brasilia. www.ipc-undp.org/pub/IPCWorkingPaper20.pdf.

Moser, Caroline O.N. (1998) 'The Asset Vulnerability Framework: Reassessing Urban Poverty Reduction Strategies', *World Development*, 26:1, 1–19.

Moser, Caroline O.N. (2010) 'Moving Beyond Gender and Poverty to Asset Accumulation: Evidence from Low-income Households in Guayaquil, Ecuador', in Sylvia Chant (ed.), *The International Handbook of Gender and Poverty: Concepts, Research, Policy* (Cheltenham: Edward Elgar), 391–8.

Rakodi, Carole (2014) *Expanding Women's Access to Land and Housing in Urban Areas* (Washington, DC: World Bank Group).

Ramm, Alejandra (2014) 'Housing Subsidies and Unmarried Mothers in Post-dictatorial Chile'. Paper presented at Society of Latin American Studies, 50th Annual Conference, Birkbeck, University of London, 3–4 April.

Rogan, Michael (2013) 'Alternative Definitions of Headship and the "Feminisation" of Income Poverty in Post-Apartheid South Africa', *Journal of Development Studies*, 49:1, 1344–57.

Safa, Helen (2002) 'Questioning Globalisation: Gender and Export Processing in the Dominican Republic', *Journal of Developing Societies*, 18:2–3, 11–31.

Sardenburg, Cecilia (2010) 'Family, Household and Women's Empowerment in Bahia, Brazil, Through the Generations: Continuities or Change?', *IDS Bulletin*, 41:2, 88–96.

Skrabut, Kristin (2014) 'Multi-house Homes: Aspiration, Abandonment and Contingent Time in Urban Peru'. Paper delivered at Cities, Space and Development Seminar Series, London School of Economics, 18 November.

Tacoli, Cecilia and Chant, Sylvia (2014) 'Migration, Urbanisation and Changing Gender Relations in the South', in Susan Parnell and Sophie Oldfield (eds), *The Routledge Handbook on Cities of the Global South* (London: Routledge), 586–96.

United Nations Fund for Population Activities (UNFPA) (2007) *State of the World's Population 2007: Unleashing the Potential of Urban Growth* (New York: UNFPA).

Varley, Ann (2013) 'Feminist Perspectives on Urban Poverty: De-essentialising Difference', in Linda Peake and Martina Rieker (eds), *Rethinking Feminist Interventions into the Urban* (London: Routledge), 125–41.

Varley, Ann (2014) 'Gender, Families and Households', in Vandana Desai and Robert Potter (eds), *The Companion to Development Studies*, 3rd edition (London: Routledge), 397–402.

Vera-Sanso, Penny (2006) 'Conformity and Contestation: Social Heterogeneity in South Indian Settlements', in Geert de Neve and Henrike Donner (eds), *The Meaning of the Local: Politics of Place in Urban India* (London: Routledge/Cavendish), 182–205.

Wartenburg, Lucy (1999) 'Vulnerabilidad y Jefatura en los Hogares Urbanos Colombianos', in Mercedes González de la Rocha (ed.), *Divergencias del Modelo Tradicional: Hogares de Jefatura Femenina en América Latina* (México DF: Centro de Investigaciones y Estudios Superiores en Antropología Social/Plaza y Valdés Editores), 77–96.

Weldegiorgis, Tsehaye and Jayamohan, J.K. (2013) 'Livelihoods and Coping Strategies: Looking Beyond Poverty – A Study of Female Headed Households in Urban Ethiopia', *Asia Pacific Journal of Social Sciences*, 5:1, 31–51.

Zeiderman, Austin (2013) 'Living Dangerously: Biopolitics and Urban Citizenship in Bogotá, Colombia', *American Ethnologist*, 40:1, 71–87.

3 Longitudinal and intergenerational perspectives on gendered asset accumulation in Indio Guayas, Guayaquil, Ecuador

Caroline O.N. Moser

Introduction

The demographic, political, and economic drivers of urbanisation and the growth of cities in the Global South have exacerbated challenges of poverty, inequality, and exclusion. Closely associated with this, gender and development research and debates have focused on the gendered nature of urban poverty. Key milestones along the way have included the gendered urban impacts of neoliberal reforms in which 'male bias' in macroeconomic structural adjustment and subsequent economic globalisation processes has forced women to increase their labour both within the market and within the household (Elson 1991; Moser 1993), with associated precarious employment and work conditions (Pearson 2003). Closely linked has been the well-known stereotype, first elaborated back in the 1970s by Buvinic and Youssef (1978), that female-headed households are poorer than those headed by men. Since the 1990s, UNICEF, the World Bank, and various bilateral agencies have popularised this as the 'feminisation of poverty' (Jackson 1998). Given widespread evidence of the diversity among female-headed households, and the fact that the 'feminisation of poverty' tends to victimise women, it remains a contentious debate – useful for donor support but not necessarily empirically accurate (Chant 2008).

The quantitative evidence on both gendered urban labour markets and household headship as contributors to poverty has been primarily based on income or consumption measurements. During the past decade, as the limitations of such poverty measurements as static and one-dimensional have been generally recognised, if not specifically in relation to gender, a range of new approaches has been introduced.[1] These have included sustainable livelihoods (DFID 2000), social protection, identified as one of the three 'pillars' of the World Bank's Development Report on Poverty (World Bank 2000), and more recently, asset-based approaches and their associated asset-accumulation strategies (Bebbington 1999; Carter and Barrett 2006; Moser 2007).[2]

Yet, to date the gendered nature of asset ownership and accumulation has received far less attention, as already recognised in the introduction to this book. Why is there so little research on this? It is generally explained in terms of the lack of adequate data, as well as an appropriate methodology. For instance, surveys of the ownership of land, housing, livestock, and other productive assets tend to collect data at the household rather than the individual level. At the same time, is it important? In one of the few studies that specifically focuses on the gender dimensions of asset ownership, Deere *et al.* (2007) argue that the limited existing information focusing primarily on rural land ownership shows that women are far less likely than men to own or control assets, and also may not benefit from assets held by men in the same household, putting them at a greater risk of poverty and economic vulnerability. This is particularly the case with individual asset ownership of rural land (Agarwal 1994). In itself, this conclusion points to the importance of deconstructing the relationship between the gendered accumulation of assets within households and the extent to which it is associated with the empowerment of women.

Three issues stand out as of particular relevance to discuss in this chapter. First, is to provide empirically based evidence on gender and asset accumulation in cities, as against the nature of gender and poverty. This is intended to show that just as household poverty data may not directly reflect the welfare of individuals (Sen 1990), so too household asset data may not reflect individual ownership within it. Second, since existing studies tend to focus either on a single asset, such as education or housing (see Rakodi, Chapter 5; Chiketwe-Biti and Mitlin, Chapter 7; and Meth, Chapter 6), or to describe a temporally bound static 'snap shot' at a point in time, this chapter seeks to provide a longitudinal perspective on gendered similarities and differences in accumulating asset portfolios over time. Although men and women use income in different ways with associated well-being impacts (Haddad *et al.* 1997), they may not accumulate the same assets at the same rate. Through their agency in making choices around interventions to accumulate assets, women may realise achievements that empower them. Does the accumulation of assets not only empower individual women, but also contribute to their successfully challenging power relations in a transformative manner, thereby contributing to just, more inclusive cities?

The third issue is to 'push the envelope', by exploring the intergenerational transfer of assets, to both sons and daughters still living with or near their parents as well as those who have migrated to other urban contexts. While it is generally assumed that each generation benefits from the assets of the previous one, in reality is this so, with daughters consequently more empowered than mothers? Of particular significance in urban contexts is the transfer of intergenerational gendered property rights and collective social capital and the extent to which daughters, like their mothers, challenge power relations in a transformative manner.

To address urban gendered asset accumulation both longitudinally and across generations, the concept of household headship, long invisibilised, is important because of its relevance in terms of changing gender roles and relations around headship. While Chant focuses on female headship as an asset in its own right (see Chapter 2), this chapter first provides comparative longitudinal data on patterns of male and female headship.[3] It also identifies trends in the ownership of capital assets, differentiating between male- and female-headed households. Second, moving beyond headship, intra-household data provide a gendered breakdown around specific capital assets at the individual level. Again, a longitudinal perspective contributes to identifying intergenerational asset ownership comparisons.

The research methodology

The dearth of data on the gendered nature of capital assets is unsurprising, given the complexity of undertaking this type of research. In examining the gendered nature of asset accumulation over a 26-year period between 1978 and 2004, in Indio Guayas, a low-income community on the periphery of the city of Guayaquil, Ecuador my methodology combines longitudinal quantitative and qualitative household and intra-household data. It uses de la Rocha's (1994) distinction between expanding, consolidating, and contracting households to capture the way in which household life course changes occur alongside broader economic and political driving forces that underpin the dynamics of urbanisation.

The research was based on anthropological participant observation fieldwork living in the community combined with a longitudinal sociological survey – a panel data set of 51 households that had been visited and interviewed with the same questionnaires in 1978, 1992, and 2004.[4] In 2004, half the panel data second-generation participants still lived on the family plot, while the rest were in other areas of Guayaquil, other cities in Ecuador, or abroad. A survey was undertaken with 46 adult sons and daughters who had left the family plot but were still living in Guayaquil in 2005, while a further small survey was conducted with sons and daughters who had migrated to Barcelona, Spain (and extended to include partners and other migrants from Indio Guayas).[5]

The data analysis included the invention of 'narrative econometrics': a cross-disciplinary 'qual–quant' methodology that combines the econometric measurement of changes in asset accumulation derived from the panel data surveys, with in-depth narratives (Sollis and Moser 1991; Kanbur 2002). The qualitative anthropological evidence comes from three decades of observations, diaries, and interviews, and above all the shared experience of daily life in extremely basic conditions that made it possible to better understand complex, causal social relations. The quantitative measurement of different assets, and their accumulation or erosion, required the construction of an asset index, drawing on earlier research on asset vulnerability (Moser 1996; 1997; 1998) (see also Carter and May 2001; Filmer and Pritchett 2001). The asset index identifies four types of capital as physical, social, financial, and human capital,[6] and their associated asset index categories, each of which contains a number of index components. The empirical data set ultimately identified which assets could be quantitatively measured with composite asset indexes associated with each capital asset (see Table 3.1).[7]

Table 3.1 Asset types by index categories and components

Capital type	Asset index categories	Index components
Physical	Housing	Materials for: roofs, walls, and floors Lighting source Type of toilet
	Consumer durables	Television (none, black and white, colour, or both) Radio, washing machine, bike, motorcycle VCR, DVD player, record player, computer
Financial-productive	Employment security	State employee Private sector permanent worker Self-employed Contract or temporary worker
	Productive durables	Refrigerator, car, sewing machine
	Transfer-rental income	Remittances Rental income
Human	Education	Level of education: illiterate; some primary school; completed primary school; secondary school or technical degree; some tertiary education
Social	Household	Jointly headed household Other households on plot 'Hidden' female-headed households
	Community	Whether someone on the plot: attends church; plays in sports groups; participates in community groups

Source: Moser and Felton 2007a; 2007b.

Household headship and asset accumulation in Indio Guayas 1978–2004

Gendered opportunities and constraints in asset accumulation are contextualised within the urban space in which the community of Indio Guayas is located. This has changed over 30 years from a physically insecure marginalised squatter settlement on mangrove swamp to a recognised suburb of the city, but one in which drug-related violence and crime increasingly threaten personal safety. This positioning within the processes of urbanisation reveals the extent to which external drivers as against internal life course issues are determinants of levels of asset accumulation. Guayaquil represents the changing urban environment of a city that has experienced rapid spatial expansion and settlement consolidation associated with three macro-economic and associated political changes over three decades. These include the 1975 to 1985 oil boom and democratisation process, the 1985 to 1995 collapse of the oil economy and associated structural adjustment policies, and the 1995 to 2005 globalisation and dollarisation crisis. Associated with each were changes in the labour market and a highly unstable local governance structure.

In Guayaquil, as in other rapidly urbanising Latin American cities, land ownership historically varied according to the terrain (see Gilbert and Ward 1978). In the early 1970s in Cisne Dos, where Indio Guayas was located, 'professional squatters' opened up municipality-owned swampland for low-income, 'self-help' housing by clearing the mangroves and nominally 'selling' off individual 10×30 m plots. Indio Guayas was settled through plot-by-plot squatting, by a population desperate to take advantage of the opportunity to acquire a 'free' physical asset, with all of the 1978 panel data household plot owners. When these first 'homeowners' arrived in the waterlogged swamp, the area lacked dry land and had bamboo catwalks for roads, and no basic services such as electricity, running water, or plumbing, nor social services such as health or education. Zoila, a newly arrived woman with four children, described such perilous conditions as follows:

> To live on the catwalks without light, without water, without anything was excessively terrible. Often there would not even be a drop of water to drink. If one wanted to eat one would have to bring the tank of water from over there, and they charged so much for bringing it here in canoe.

The incentive for moving into Indio Guayas for this young, fairly homogeneous population, many just starting families, therefore, was to own a home of their own. While men and women averaged 30 years of age, children averaged seven years. The average household size was six members and the average number of working members per household was 1.6 members.

Changing headship patterns and associated household structures

In 1978 almost all households were male-headed nuclear families; of the 51 households in the panel data set only five were headed by women, of whom two were widows and the other three had never been in a stable relationship (see Table 3.2). During the following decade Guayaquil's growth was fundamentally affected by economic crises, while at the same time the city experienced incremental improvement and infrastructure upgrading, achieved through extensive

Table 3.2 Household headship in Indio Guayas, 1978–2004

Headship type	Year					
	1978		1992		2004	
	No.	%	No.	%	No.	%
Male-headed	46	90	38	75	33	65
Female-headed	5	10	13	25	18	35
Total	51	100	51	100	51	100

Source: Moser 2009.

political mobilisation linked to election votes (see below). The 1992 data show that this was the consolidation period in household life courses where most households were less likely to grow in numbers, but for existing members to strengthen their household social capital (Gonzalo de la Rocha, 1994). However, differences in household composition had begun to slowly occur, with one-quarter now headed by women, due to death, desertion, or separation of their husband or partner. At this time female-headed households were smaller and had a lower dependency ratio than those headed by men. At the same time there were fewer workers within households.

The final period between 1992 and 2004 again was one of national economic turmoil, with political instability increasing and the financial crisis prompting increased out-migration to 3 per cent of the country's population by 2003, resulting in an increase in remittance flows. Guayaquil by 2004 was the country's largest city and most important port, as well as being identified as a 'modern' city with the regeneration of the riverside and central city public space (Villavicencio, 2003). By this time, Indio Guayas was a stable settlement with physical and social infrastructure and no longer on the periphery, but integrated into the city as one of the working class suburbs.

Also by 2004, the number of female heads had grown to one-third of all households and were likely to contain 'hidden' female-headed sub-units. These were unmarried female relatives raising their children within the household to share resources and responsibilities with others. This was also the period in which de la Rocha's 'contraction' stage in the family life course occurred, when the children of the original settlers had reached adulthood and started families of their own, either in the same community or elsewhere. Yet, more than half still lived on the family plot, either as 'hidden' household heads or independently 'nesting' (see below).

Headship and poverty

In 1978 most households lived below the Ecuadorian urban poverty line.[8] As Marta, the community leader, explained to me in 1978.

> Most people have come here because they are in the same state as me. Salaries are so low they don't cover food, let alone rent. We are all poor; you cannot describe it any other way. Anyone who has money would not come here; only those who are poor and really in need.

Were female-headed households poorer in terms of income than male-headed households? In 1978 the small number of female-headed households makes conclusions about headship difficult. In 1992 the vast majority of households were still below the poverty line regardless of headship, reflecting the severe external economic contextual drivers associated with the economic structural adjustment crisis and associated rising unemployment and increased inflation. Female-headed households were slightly less likely to fall below the line than male-headed households, but those that were poor tended to be very poor. Although widows headed a few households, as mentioned above, in 1992 this was mainly because of separation or divorce, reflecting a common second stage in longitudinal adult male serial monogamy patterns. Frequently, young men formed their first relationship with an older, more mature woman with whom they had their first children. By middle-age, however, such men abandoned these women for younger wives. The 1992 trend continued, and by 2004, despite having lower dependency ratios, male-headed households were more likely to fall below the poverty line. While fewer than one-third of the male-headed households were not poor, more than half the female-headed households had successfully moved out of income poverty.

Headship and assets

While income poverty data are important, understanding household accumulation of assets complements this by identifying numerous complexities. It shows how some households were more income-mobile than others, how some households successfully pulled themselves out of poverty when others failed, and which types of assets were particularly important for poverty reduction. Above all, it shows that the accumulation of assets might ultimately be more important for household well-being than pure income measures.

Table 3.3 shows the amounts of different types of asset acquired by the households, with similarities and differences in the asset ownerships of male- and female-headed households. Most had significantly negative scores in 1978 (a positive or negative score does not mean anything in itself – it is simply relative to the average for the entire data set). Between 1992 and 2004 most households had positive acquisition of every asset type except for community social capital, which declined. In turn, Figure 3.1 graphically demonstrates overall differences in the longitudinal processes of asset accumulation. Male-headed households accumulated faster than female-headed households, even though male-headed

Table 3.3 Asset accumulation by headship in Indio Guayas, 1992–2004 (standard deviations above average)

Headship type	Capital assets					
	Housing	Consumer durables	Human capital	Financial capital	Community social capital	Household social capital
1992						
Male-headed	1.226	0.856	1.124	0.923	1.317	1.132
Female-headed	1.086	0.737	0.906	1.062	0.751	0.082
2004						
Male-headed	1.346	1.590	1.146	1.573	0.877	1.373
Female-headed	1.379	1.784	1.089	1.567	0.681	0.797

Source: Moser and Felton 2010.

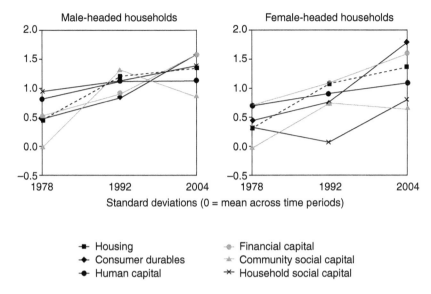

Figure 3.1 Asset accumulation over time in male- and female-headed households.

households had less household social capital. In the long run, female-headed households were less likely to be income-poor than male-headed households, but on balance still had slightly fewer assets. While asset accumulation was individually measured, in reality accumulation of one asset was frequently linked to the accumulation of another, as shown by the anthropological narratives below.

The data show that the accumulation of housing was an important first-generation asset (see Chapter 1) for both household types, increasing over time particularly for those headed by women. Yet hidden behind these figures are intra-household arrangements that over time also expanded the numbers of members living on the plot. This includes first the phenomenon of 'invisible' household heads where mainly single young mothers continue to live in their parents' home, and second, 'nesting', an important support system in which family members, usually children, who could not afford to buy their own plots or independently construct their own homes built structures on their parents' plot either separately or attached to the parental house structure – on the second floor or at the side. This was an intermediate strategy between household extension, where assistance was provided on a daily basis, and the formation of totally independent households. Nesting benefited children's accumulation of human and financial assets. It also provided advantages for host households in the form of time efficiencies through sharing reproductive tasks as well as assisting sons and daughters to care for elderly parents living independently.

Between 1992 and 2004 the impact of the external driver of globalisation patterns was reflected in a city flooded with cheap electrical and technological goods. Consumer durables rose as households sought to acquire so-called 'symbols of modernity'. Interestingly, in 2004 female-headed households had higher levels of consumer durables than male-headed households. With higher income levels and larger household size, especially more adult income-earning children that had remained in the extended family, there was greater demand for consumer goods, especially televisions and mobile phones, from second-generation children.

Unpacking another first-generation asset, financial capital, helps understand why female-headed households were more likely to be above the poverty line in 1992. Although more women than men were unemployed in every year surveyed, female-headed households had more people employed in well-paid private industry or government jobs. Men were more likely to be self-employed or working with temporary job status. However, male-headed households did as well or better on the other aspects of financial capital, including taking in lodgers and remittance income sent from families abroad (see Table 3.3). Although high dependency ratios were often associated with poverty, in female-headed households a high level of dependants also meant that households often adopted complex intra-household divisions of labour that released some adult females into the labour market while others undertook the cooking, childcare, and other household chores. Here again the interrelationship between different capital assets is important. Marta's household illustrated how household social capital around reproductive care can contribute to productive work. In 1992 she masterminded a complex cooking and childcare system along with her work as community president, cooking two meals daily, eaten by 15 people, thus releasing a daughter, two sisters, and a sister-in-law all living nearby from cooking and washing. In addition, she balanced cooking with childcare of one sister's two sons, as well as a granddaughter.

The fact that female-headed households had lower levels of household social capital was in large part because male-headed households, with an adult couple or partners, counted positively as one of the index components. This obviously is weighted against women-headed households that by definition were in almost all cases headed by a single individual, and can be considered a limitation of the index. At the same time, the fact that male-headed households had higher levels of community social capital reflected a number of different issues; in 1992 female participation in two components of community social capital, particularly community organisations, was much higher among the spouses of male-headed households than women household heads, who frequently were so overstretched managing both productive and reproductive tasks that they had no time for community managing work (Moser 1993). As described below, women's participation in community mobilisation and negotiation with political parties, and then international agencies, was critical for the acquisition of essential physical and social infrastructure. By 2004, when most of this infrastructure had been acquired and external agencies had withdrawn, participation in both activities had declined to levels lower than those of 1992. Higher levels for male-headed households in 2004 reflected male participation in street-level football leagues, the outcome of an upgraded paved street. While the econometric data suggest that the two kinds of social capital as measured in the index were less critical to alleviating income poverty than other kinds of assets, this points to the limitations of the asset index and the need to complement it with anthropological narratives of both community and intra-household social capital to clearly identify further complexities in the interpretation of the data.

Intergenerational asset accumulation and changing gender relations

While headship is an important starting point for identifying the gendered nature of asset accumulation over time, assets are aggregated at the level of the household. A second data analysis relates to asset ownership *within* the household, and the gendered breakdown of specific capital assets at the individual level. This provides a more comprehensive picture of the gendering of assets both between mothers and fathers, as well as across generations, between them and their children. To what extent is the accumulation of an asset associated with individual empowerment? While some of the comparative asset data are quantitative, and measured econometrically, in other cases the qualitative data from individual households complements the picture, particularly the narratives of the women members of five families who lived in the same street over 30 years – Marta the local community leader, and her close neighbours Alicia, Lydia, Carmen, and Mercedes (Moser 2009).

Education and intergenerational constraints on women's agency

The positive effects of educational human capital on women's agency in relation to individual empowerment has been widely documented, with changing cognitive ability identified as essential to women's capability to question and act on the condition of their lives. This can affect their power relations within and outside the household, and their capacity to deal with violent husbands, thus suffering less gender-based violence (Sen 1999; Kabeer 2005; McIlwaine, Chapter 9 in this volume). In Indio Guayas, educational human capital demonstrated a second-generation asset strategy, representing the most dramatic intergenerational change in asset accumulation when disaggregated by gender. Within generations, fathers were better educated with more human capital than mothers, with an average of seven years of primary education, as against five years of primary education for mothers. Across generations, the second generation had more human capital than the first, but with daughters better educated, with seven years of secondary, than sons, with five years of secondary. The fact that parents consistently invested more in the education of their daughters, with larger numbers in private schooling, than was the case with their sons, suggests changing perceptions, linked to changing gender relations about potential returns, with women more likely to use this educational benefit in a changing job market. For the third generation, education had not improved in the newer peripheral areas, where many second-generation parents lived, by 2004, with around the same proportion, one-third, sending their children to private school.

To achieve such extraordinary educational outcomes, households made considerable sacrifices. Not only did they consciously use family planning to limit family size, but they also invested substantial resources to get the best education possible, with education being the single largest category of service expenditures. For instance, Marta always had higher aspirations for her daughters:

> For my daughters I want something better. I want them to go to school, to go to university, to be something in this life. Because of this I only have two girls; when one has many it is impossible to give them education, but when one only has few one can manage.

Both daughters completed high school and went on to university, while their mother, who only completed primary school as a child, atypically gained a night school secondary education when aged 40. While the younger daughter completed her degree in industrial psychology, her subsequent employment as school secretary at the local secondary school provided a stable if very modest income, although it was not the career envisaged by either mother or daughter.

While many daughters benefited greatly from the investments of their parents, they often cut short their educational ambitions due to unanticipated pregnancies. For them, as their mothers before them, marriage or a stable partnership was as important as continuing education. Alicia, living two doors down from Marta, was a female household head with nine children. Of her six daughters, Sylvia was the only one who completed high school, and while she talked of university, she was soon engaged to Jaime who did not want her to study further or work. Sylvia had four sons in quick succession, and when she and her partner split up she was reduced to doing washing work like her mother before her, and working in a local restaurant. So, despite her education, she repeated her mother's life course pattern of single parenthood, numerous children, and low-skilled employment. In direct contrast, living opposite Alicia was Carmen, whose eldest daughter Ana was one of a few of the second generation who completed tertiary education with a degree in public relations. By 2004 she was earning a considerable income, $700 a month, as a sales supervisor in one of Guayaquil's banks, and was living with her husband, a loan credit seller earning $400 per month, and one young son in a modern two-storey house away from Indio Guayas. As car owners, employing childcare, this household was one of the few that broke through the glass ceiling into professional jobs and a middle-class lifestyle.

Despite Ana's success, 'cultural norms' continued to be important intergenerational intermediary factors constraining women's agency (see Chapter 1). Table 3.4 summarises comparative levels of education, age at marriage, family planning knowledge, and male attitudes to work in Marta's family over three generations. It shows how slowly the options for young women in Guayaquil have changed. Even though the third-generation granddaughter was more educated

Table 3.4 Three-generation comparison of education, marriage age, family planning, and male attitudes to work, Indio Guayas 2004

Relationship	Level of education	Age at marriage	Family planning knowledge	Male partner's attitude to work
Mother	Primary Adult education secondary	14	No sex education or family planning before first child; use of coil after second daughter	Consensus working as a home-based dressmaker; conflict when community political leader
Daughter	Secondary	18	Limited sex education (from aunt) and no family planning until after first child	Passive husband, with wife earning most of the family income
Granddaughter	Still completing tertiary	Aged 19 and not married or engaged	Using family planning to allow sexual experimentation	Living at home until marries; balances university study with accounting job

and with knowledge of contraception, she was still expected to stay at home until she married and to go from the control of her father to that of a husband. She was not expected to live on her own, since this implied promiscuity, and still had the same pressures as her mother to marry as soon as possible, though in her case she was resisting it while completing her education. This highlights once again the importance of the relationship between women's agency around education and their individual empowerment.

Intergenerational financial-productive capital and growing aspirations

Linked to educational levels but also to labour market segmentation were employment-related issues of financial-productive capital. In 1978, only a small percentage of the male active labour force of Indio Guayas was absorbed into the stable wage sector, and competition between men and women existed in some informal sector activities. Where gender divisions of labour were rigid, such as in domestic service, 'women's work' remained protected, while in retail selling men and women competed with each other. The lack of a robustly developing formal industrial wage sector in the city meant that the service sector absorbed the largest proportion of the labour force, with the informal economy a particularly important part of the growth in services.

Employment security data, with its associated level of income stability, was one of the asset index categories. This shows that in 2004 women consistently found more stable employment than their male partners and kin. This had significant implications for women's access to, and autonomy and control over, resources since they were often the family breadwinners, and thus had more control over budget allocations for food and education as against alcohol – often prioritised by men. Furthermore, there was a dramatic increase in the numbers of women working in government employment, from nil in 1978 for mothers to just over one in five daughters in 2004. In contrast, few sons were employed in government service, with more than two-thirds engaged in a range of self-employed activities.

By 2004, when the third-generation granddaughters were completing education and looking for jobs, many identified that their most important priority was a job rather than a good relationship with a man. They aspired to professional careers and not the local informal-economy roles available to their grandmothers and mothers, such as dressmakers, sellers, washerwomen, domestic workers, cooks, and child minders. Third-generation young women's preferred 'professions' were as secretaries, engineers, or personnel in the navy. At one level, these young women were likely to do far better than their parents and grandparents. But while they had more education and better jobs, they still relied heavily on household social capital – evidenced by its increase over the 1992–2004 period. Family support structures were essential to get on, including the networks required to get jobs and finance to support their education. This limited their ability to make choices, with challenging gender or generational power relations still difficult to achieve.

Land ownership and empowerment

The search by women in Indio Guayas to be 'independent', understood as gaining more control over their lives, was partially achieved through work and accumulating associated economic resources. However, as widely recognised, they were not necessarily empowered by independent income (Cornwall *et al.* 2007, 15). Another important concrete empowerment measure related to land title ownership. In Indio Guayas, by 2004 both Marta, now a widow, and Alicia, still a female household head, were single titleholders, while Mercedes, Lidia, and Carmen, still in nominal or actual marriages, were joint holders with their male partners. In a context where people did not make wills, households were beginning to encounter the problem of the gendered nature of inheritance. As Mercedes' sister, Rosa, who was well aware of legal matters, commented:

> I don't have a will which states what belongs to each one. It's not a habit in our culture. Those inside the plot think it's going to be left to them when their parents die and that's how it will be.

How far was this tangible asset, acquired and accumulated by first-generation women, transferred to the next generations? In Indio Guayas, the second generation faced a very different housing situation from their parents in a context where the 'free' invasion land was no longer available. Cross-generational transfers to adult sons and daughters were therefore essential for the next generation's asset portfolio.

The story of Alicia, female household head of nine children, and her daughters illustrates the complexity of this intergenerational transfer. Her plot status, linked to the urbanisation stage when she came to Indio Guayas, meant that as an early invader she acquired her waterlogged plot free, obtaining her land title in the 1970s. The choice as to which offspring got space to 'nest' on her plot or to live in her house, let alone inherit it, was influenced by numerous factors. Rather than gender or birth order of offspring, these included getting on with in-laws, financial resources available to acquire a plot themselves, and the necessity of living close by for childcare assistance. Alicia clearly prioritised her daughters over her sons; while both sons rented with in-laws along with acquiring plots in the new peripheral hills of the expanded city, the daughters faced a more complex situation. Daughter number three, Sylvia, was adamant that as a single mother she had rights; she had refused to live with her mother-in-law as her ex-husband expected, wanting her independent home. Thus she built her own bamboo-cane-walled house 'nesting' at the back of her mother's plot. Youngest sister Joanna, a single mother with a third child on the way, still lived as a 'hidden household head' in her mother's house. In contrast, daughter number two, Lola, lived in her in-laws house; this had become poignant when her husband became involved with another woman, and Lola, with her children, had no option but to continue living in a house to which as a daughter-in-law she would never acquire title, while she could not return to her mother's over-crowded house. Thus while some second-generation children dealt with the complexities of this intergenerational asset transfer, others did not; the only person in this family whose decision had the potential to empower her was Sylvia, informally nesting on her mother's plot. However, with Alicia still on the plot, and no will in place, this lengthy narrative of asset transfer is still incomplete, indicating the need for longitudinal perspectives.

The transformative potential of community social capital as an asset

Above I summarised findings relating to the limited community social capital of female as against male household heads, while identifying the important participation of their female spouses in community mobilisation to contest and negotiate for community services. In addition, I identified the decline in community social capital along with the successful acquisition of such services. However, behind this succinct measurement of the accumulation and erosion of an asset is a complex anthropological narrative that illustrates the powerful transformative potential of collective action in achieving just, more equitable cities, while pointing also to the very real limitations of their sustainability.

The history of the formation of the Indio Guayas (IG) barrio committee in 1975 and its evolution over the past 30 years identifies the crucial importance of local community women at all stages of its existence, while noting differences between the leadership and members. In the 1970s, as newly arrived women neighbours, desperate about their living conditions, became aware of the importance of collective rather than individual action to mobilise for infrastructure, they joined the local barrio committee. Women were not automatic leaders but, as in Marta's case, moved into leadership positions when frustrated with incumbent male presidents. Life histories showed that women who had experienced difficult childhoods were more likely to get involved in residential struggle, determined that their children, particularly their daughters, should not suffer in a similar manner. Thus personal suffering was as important as external political struggle in developing consciousness of gender oppression. As shown by a 1978 mobilisation speech, Marta, as president of the committee, worked ceaselessly to encourage women's participation, well aware of their subordinate positions within their households.

> We must fight. Above all I want the women, the housewives, to help us, to come with us wherever we go to get the services we need. Why? Because you are the heart of your home. You are the ones who suffer the actions of your husbands. The woman is a slave in the home. The woman has to make ends meet.

The IG committee, with predominantly female members, had 'internal' responsibility to maintain social order in a peripheral area lacking a police station or any law-enforcement services, mediating and settling invasion disputes. Far more important, however, was its 'external' mobilisation responsibilities. As in other urban contexts, this was a highly complex reciprocal process that required committees to be co-opted by political parties that exchanged infrastructure in return for votes and political support. In Guayaquil the external driver of political change, associated with the move towards democracy, provided the opportunity to use the resurgence of political activity to mobilise for infrastructure. When a new political party, *Izquierda Democratica* (ID), sought to establish their political base in this new 'popular sector', the IG committee, together with 20 other local committees, showed remarkable 'urban savvy' to scale up their level of community social capital by constituting themselves as the Front for Suburbio Struggle (*Frente Lucha Suburbana* [Frente]), and then allowing their committees to be co-opted by the ID political party.

During the 1978–1985 period the IG committee under Marta's leadership, with other members of the Frente, embarked on a remarkable first-generation asset accumulation strategy in a reciprocal process in which infrastructure was provided for political votes, retaining its commitment to the same political party during this period. In this way, Indio Guayas first acquired patio and street infill. Community mobilisation did not stop with this success, but motivated them to undertake further lengthy rounds of negotiations over subsequent years with local officials and politicians to provide mains electricity and piped water, garbage services, and streetlights in a long list of prioritised basic needs. For a community starting life in Indio Guayas living on water entirely without services, such collective action was undoubtedly transformative, and by ensuring greater equality of services in the city's peripheral areas, contributed fundamentally to a more just city.

By the mid-1980s, to address the pressing problem of social infrastructure, community organisations moved beyond local political parties and the municipal level, with Marta and other Frente leaders negotiating with international donor and international non-governmental organisations (INGOs). In a further transformative process in terms of addressing social inequalities, the Frente committees embarked on health and pre-school education programmes with the United Nations Children's Fund (UNICEF), and then over an extensive period acquired an impressive range of social infrastructure through Plan's cross-sector community-based programme. As the community leader running both of these programmes, Marta welcomed them; not only was she frustrated by NGOs and politically aligned groups offering quick-fix solutions, but she also recognised the fragility of the IG committee, whose continued participation depended on rolling out new projects. By 1992, she astutely observed: 'If you want to keep the committee functioning, you have to keep looking for projects.'

While positive consequences of the INGO programme included the strengthening of the leadership capacity of community leaders, increased financial independence, and an associated 'empowerment' of local women from participation in the home-based childcare programme, there were also negative outcomes, particularly for community social capital. Acceptance of Plan's model of community participation was important to guarantee long-term service delivery. It also meant, however, that Plan's long-term presence created a welfarist dependency, such that when in 2002, after 25 years, it pulled out of Indio Guayas, the barrio committee's importance declined, and hence community social capital, as measured in the 2004 asset index, was reduced.

Throughout the life of the IG committee, its success depended on complex trust agreements both internally within the community as well as externally with a political party, and then INGOs. To sustain the IG committee required cohesion among neighbours despite gendered differences in participation. While family members might join the committee, it was the women who regularly attended and guaranteed its continuation. Male participation was unreliable; along with political leaders and officials, men living in IG all saw this as women's 'natural' work. As was widely stated, 'women have free time while men are out at work'. A convenient myth, this hid the fact that most women with both reproductive and productive activities made considerable sacrifices, risking jobs and neglecting children, in order to participate. In turn, women often justified committee work in terms of their gender-ascribed roles. Just as domestic work was their responsibility, so too was community mobilisation to improve family living conditions. Men allowed their wives to participate, as long as they saw family benefits and their domestic comforts were not disturbed. Tension often developed, however, especially when mobilisations involved women travelling outside the barrio, frequently at night. These internal tensions undoubtedly influenced the decline in the long-term participation of women members, especially once external agencies no longer provided financial support.

While daughters had watched their mothers participating in an IG committee, indeed often accompanying them to community meetings and citywide mobilisations, this did not translate into strong second-generation community social capital. Those second-generation households who no longer lived on their parents' plot had set up their own houses on the hills and agricultural land on the city's periphery. Although they repeated some of the struggles experienced by their parents – but living in muddy streets rather than over water – in a very different political and economic context, services had arrived far faster; by 2004, half had mains water connections and almost all had septic tanks. Despite the fact that three-quarters were tapping illegal electricity, second-generation households did not mobilise to acquire infrastructure, with significant implications in terms of community social capital. Only 14 per cent of the next generation, living away from their parents in Indio Guayas, was involved in community groups. At the same time, membership of sports clubs grew among the next generation, with around one-quarter of young men involved in some type of sporting activity. This longitudinal perspective indicates that although transformative collective action was critical for first-generation women to contribute to more just cities, this did not necessarily transform gender relations within households or communities, nor was it sustained. While the knowledge of the importance of community social capital was not transferred intergenerationally to daughters and granddaughters, it nevertheless made a difference in terms of a daughter's individual aspirations, such as to complete their education. Again this speaks to the relationship between different assets, in this case between social and human capital.

Turning back to the issue of the empowerment of first-generation local women leaders, such as Marta, while individually empowered through the popular and political process, there were nevertheless heavy costs at personal and professional levels. Individual positions of power distanced them from their female neighbours, and made them prone to criticism from their male partners, and local verbal abuse. To address this, women leaders behaved as scrupulously 'respectable', with kin or a woman friend accompanying them outside the community, and down-dressing unprovocatively. Publicly they justified their participation in terms of a concern for their children's needs rather than acknowledging personal ambition and power.

Did her daughters follow in her footsteps and was there an intergenerational transfer of this extraordinary capacity to generate community social capital? Over time they inevitably took on some of their mother's community responsibilities. Interestingly, in 2005, when her elder daughter, Adriana, visited Barcelona, she met women migrants from Indio Guayas with challenges around rights and responsibilities relating to the breakdown of marriage and the distribution of assets such as housing. Marta's neighbour, Carmen, who moved to Barcelona to earn resources to give her children a better home, needed to make a will and change her house title deed back in Guayaquil. Adriana, with an extensive knowledge of such issues, very quickly took on a leadership role in providing advice and offered to follow-up once back in Guayaquil. Just as her mother Marta had acted as community leader around first-generation assets such as physical and social infrastructure, so too her daughter took on a similar role, but this time around third-generation assets such as the range of rights women were contesting. For the second generation, it was this type of transnational community social capital linking Barcelona to Guayaquil that was now more important.

Conclusion

The fact that in Indio Guayas female-headed households do better than male-headed households in terms of income poverty, but worse in terms of asset accumulation, contributes to the debate contesting the generalisation that female-headed households are poorer than male-headed households through providing a longitudinal perspective that highlights the limitations of static 'snapshot' studies. More specifically, male-headed households accrued assets much faster than female-headed households and by 2004 had a larger asset portfolio than did female-headed households. The fact that the asset portfolios of female-headed households were smaller than those of males suggests differences in resource allocations between these different types of household.

Intra-household analyses of the accumulation of individual assets within households to the next generation showed that daughters were doing better than sons in terms of human capital, as well as in the job market, reflecting the lack of stable skilled work opportunities for young men in Guayaquil, despite their levels of education. However, the relationship between individual assets and women's empowerment or wider transformative processes was more complex in terms of intergenerational asset transfers; the dramatic increases in educational human capital of second- and third-generation girls has undoubtedly empowered them, if only in modest ways in relation to job choices, and an awareness of the need for greater control over their lives. Yet cultural norms around marriage and male partnerships remain strong, reinforced by earlier generations. Equally, access to housing presents the next generation with the greatest challenges.

Finally, the decline in community social capital is best understood within the framework of the complex lengthy history of collective action and political negotiation. While this certainly was transformative in terms of contributing to a more just city, it was the critical role of women, both as leaders and committee members, that achieved this – but neither fundamentally transformed gender relations within families, nor was measurably transferred to the next generation. However, this chapter has also shown that each generation of women contributes to the transformation of just cities in small ways. Therefore, it suggests we need to look for small steps in a long process rather than assume we can identify major visible processes of change on a large scale.

Acknowledgements

This chapter draws on a number of previous publications from 30 years of research in Indio Guayas, Guayaquil. Of particular importance is my longitudinal study, *Ordinary Families Extraordinary Lives: Intergenerational Asset Accumulation and Poverty Reduction in Indio Guayas, Guayaquil, Ecuador*

1978–2004 (2009), as well as an earlier co-edited chapter on gender and assets, written with Andrew Felton: 'The Gendered Nature of Asset Accumulation in Urban Contexts: Longitudinal Evidence from Guayaquil, Ecuador' (2010). My acknowledgements to Andy, and as ever, to all whose who made this earlier work possible. I would also like to thank Cathy McIlwaine and Sally Roever for their profound, incisive, and helpful reviews on an earlier version of this chapter.

Notes

1 This was a consequence of the 1990s international poverty alleviation/reduction debate – heavily influenced by Sen's (1981) work on famines and entitlements, assets, and capabilities, as well as those of Chambers (1992) and others on risk and vulnerability. This distinguished between poverty as a static concept and vulnerability as a dynamic one, as well as identifying the multi-dimensionality of poverty (see Moser 1998).
2 For a review of the similarities and differences between social protection, sustainable livelihoods, and asset accumulation approaches, see Moser (2008).
3 Male-headed households are also called couple- or joint-headed households. However, in this analysis I follow local perceptions of headship in which any household with an adult male partner or husband was perceived as the head of household. In all women-headed households there was an absence of male partner.
4 In 1978 a universe survey of 244 households was undertaken over the 11-block area; in 1992 a random sample survey of 263 households, undertaken in exactly the same spatial area, picked up 56 households that had also been in the 1978 universe survey. In 2004 these same 56 households were tracked, and 51 were re-interviewed (indicating a 9 per cent attrition rate). Caroline O.N. Moser undertook sociological surveys, together with researchers including Brian Moser, Peter Sollis and Alicia Herbert, as well as a trained team of community members comprising Lucy Zavalla, Rosa Vera, Carmita Naboa, and Angela Vinueza.
5 The Barcelona survey comprised 23 questionnaires and semi-structured interviews, using five adult members from three households from the panel data set, boosted by households from Calle K (located in the middle of the survey areas), as well as the community leader's daughter's network of local ex-schoolmates.
6 A fifth type of capital, natural capital, is used in the livelihoods literature. Natural capital includes the stocks of environmentally provided assets such as soil, atmosphere, forests, water, and wetlands. This capital is more generally used in rural research. In urban areas where land is linked to housing it is more frequently classified as productive capital, as is the case in this study. However, since all households lived on similar-sized plots when they arrived in 1978 this was not tracked in the data set.
7 See Moser and Felton (2007b) for an econometric description of the construction of an asset index.
8 See Moser (1996) for details on the construction of the poverty line.

References

Agarwal, B. (1994) *A Field of One's Own: Gender and Land Rights in South Asia*, Cambridge: Cambridge University Press.
Bebbington, A. (1999) 'Capitals and Capabilities: A Framework for Analysing Peasant Viability, Rural Livelihoods and Poverty'. *World Development* 27, 12: 2021–44.
Buvinic, M. and Youssef, N.H. (1978) *Women-Headed Households: The Ignored Factor in Development Planning*. Washington, DC: International Center for Research on Women.

Carter, M. and Barrett, C. (2006) 'The Economics of Poverty Traps and Persistent Poverty: An Asset-Based Approach'. *Journal of Development Studies* 42, 2: 178–99.

Carter, M, and May, J. (2001) 'One Kind of Freedom: Poverty Dynamics in Post-Apartheid South Africa'. *World Development* 29, 12: 1987–2006.

Chambers, R. (1992) *Poverty and Livelihoods: Whose Reality Counts?* Institute of Development Studies, Discussion Paper no 347.

Chant, S. (2008) 'The "Feminisation of Poverty" and the "Feminisation" of Anti-Programmes: Room for Revision?'. *Journal of Development Studies*, 44, 2: 165–97

Cornwall, A., Harrison, E., and Whitehead, A. (eds) (2007) *Feminisms in Development: Contradictions, Contestations and Challenges*, London: Zed Books.

de la Rocha, M (1994) *The Resources of Poverty: Women and Survival in a Mexican City*, Oxford: Blackwell.

Deere, C.D., Doss, C., and Grown, C. (2007) *Measuring Women's Assets: A Guide to Survey Development*. Paper presented at World Bank workshop on a project to collect data on individual assets, Washington DC, May.

DFID (2000) *Sustainable Livelihoods: Current Thinking and Practice*, London: DFID.

Elson, D. (1991) 'Male Bias in Macroeconomics: The Case of Structural Adjustment', in D. Elson (ed.), *Male Bias in the Development Process*, Manchester: Manchester University Press.

Filmer, D. and Pritchett, L. (2001) 'Estimating Wealth Effects without Expenditure Data – or Tears: An Application to Educational Enrollments in States of India'. *Demography* 38, 1: 115–32.

Gilbert, A. and Ward, P. (1978) 'Housing in Latin American Cities', in D. Herbert and R. Johnston (eds), *Geography and the Urban Environment*, New York: John Wiley.

Haddad, L., Hoddinott, J., and Alderman, H. (1997) *Intrahousehold Resource Allocation in Developing Countries: Models, Methods and Policies*, Baltimore, MD: Johns Hopkins Press.

Jackson, C. (1998) 'Rescuing Gender from the Poverty Trap', in C. Jackson and R. Pearson (eds), *Feminist Visions of Development: Gender Analysis and Policy*, London: Routledge.

Kabeer, N. (2005) 'Gender Equality and Women's Empowerment: A Critical Analysis of the Third Millennium Development Goal'. *Gender and Development*, 13, 1: 13–24.

Kanbur, R. (ed.) (2002) *Qual–Quant: Qualitative and Quantitative Methods of Poverty Appraisal*, Delhi: Permanent Black.

Moser, C. (1993) *Gender Planning and Development: Theory, Practice and Training*, New York and London: Routledge.

Moser, C. (1996) *Confronting Crisis: A Comparative Study of Household Responses to Poverty and Vulnerability in Four Poor Urban Communities*, Washington, DC: World Bank.

Moser, C. (1997) 'Household Responses to Poverty and Vulnerability, Volume 1: Confronting Crisis in Cisne Dos, Guayaquil, Ecuador'. Urban Management Program Policy Paper no. 21, World Bank.

Moser, C. (1998). 'The Asset Vulnerability Framework: Reassessing Urban Poverty Reduction Strategies'. *World Development*, 26, 1: 1–19.

Moser, C. (ed.) (2007) *Reducing Global Poverty: The Case for Asset Accumulation*, Washington, DC: Brookings Institution Press.

Moser, C. (2008) 'Assets and Livelihoods: A Framework for Asset-Based Social Policy', in C. Moser and A. Dani (eds)., *Assets, Livelihood and Social Policy*, Washington, DC: World Bank.

Moser, C. (2009) *Ordinary Families Extraordinary Lives: Intergenerational Asset Accumulation and Poverty Reduction in Indio Guayas, Guayaquil, Ecuador 1978–2004*, Washington, DC: Brookings Institution Press.

Moser, C. and Felton, A. (2007a) 'Intergenerational Asset Accumulation and Poverty Reduction in Guayaquil, Ecuador', in C. Moser (ed.) *Reducing Global Poverty*, Washington, DC: Brookings Institution Press.

Moser, C. and Felton, A. (2007b) 'The Construction of an Asset Index Measuring Asset Accumulation in Ecuador'. Working Paper 87, IDPM/Chronic Poverty Research Centre (CPRC).

Moser, C and Felton, A. (2010) 'The Gendered Nature of Asset Accumulation in Urban Contexts: Longitudinal Evidence from Guayaquil, Ecuador', in Jo Beall, Basudeb Guha-Khasnobis, and Ravi Kanbur (eds), *Beyond the Tipping Point: The Benefits and Challenges of Urbanisation*, Oxford: Oxford University Press.

Pearson, R. (2003) 'Feminist Responses to Economic Globalisation: Some Examples of Past and Future Practice', *Gender and Development*, 11: 25–34.

Sen, A. (1981). *Poverty and Famines: An Essay on Entitlement and Deprivation.* Oxford: Clarendon Press.

Sen, A. (1990) 'Gender and Cooperative Conflicts', in I. Tinker (ed.), *Persistent Inequalities*, New York: Oxford University Press.

Sen, P. (1999) 'Enhancing Women's Choices in Responding to Domestic Violence in Calcutta: A Comparison of Employment and Education', *The European Journal of Development Research*, 11, 2: 65–86.

Sollis, P. and Moser, C. (1991) 'A Methodological Framework for Analysing the Social Costs of Adjustment at the Micro Level: The Case of Guayaquil, Ecuador', *Bulletin of the Institute of Development Studies*, 22, 1: 23–30.

Villavicencio, G. (2003) 'Eje: Defensa de los Derechos'. Mesa: Informalidad y Economía Subterránea. Paper presented at 'Diálogo Nacional por la Unidad y el Desarrollo Capítulo Guayas', Guayaquil, 19–20 March.

World Bank (2000) *World Development Report 2000/01: Attacking Poverty*. Washington, DC: World Bank.

4 Key drivers of asset erosion and accumulation in informal employment

Findings from the Informal Economy Monitoring Study

Sally Roever

Introduction: the role of assets in informal livelihoods and just cities

In the past decade, two cross-cutting trends have placed urban employment at the centre of the development agenda. First, for the first time in history, the global population became predominantly urban (UN-HABITAT 2008). Second, the global economy experienced a financial crisis leading to sharp increases in unemployment and working poverty, both of which have persisted throughout the recovery period in many regions (ILO 2010; 2014). In that context, the ability of cities to generate quality employment[1] has become a major concern and is now widely recognised as a key pathway out of poverty (World Bank 2013).

A central part of the urban-employment challenge is the significant gender gap in access to, and quality of, remunerative work. In most regions of the developing world, informal employment – that is, employment arrangements that do not provide individuals with legal or social protection through their work (ILO and WIEGO 2013)[2] – comprises more than half of total non-agricultural employment, and accounts for a larger share of women's employment than men's (Vanek *et al.* 2014, 7–8).[3] The individual- and household-level constraints on earnings and productivity among women are well documented in studies of women's economic empowerment: they include limited access to formal employment, low education levels, household and care responsibilities, patriarchal community and household relations, and constraints on women's mobility (Folbre 2001; Kabeer 2011; 2013; Mahmud *et al.* 2012). The potential for women's ownership and control of assets to lead to greater economic opportunity, increase their bargaining power, respond to shocks, manage risk, and cope with vulnerability is also well documented (Doss *et al.* 2008, 2–4). But placed in the context of urban planning and city government practices, assets alone are insufficient: without effective protection of property and livelihood rights, assets can easily be eroded.

This chapter examines both the systemic constraints on the ability of informal workers in specific occupational groups to maintain and accumulate productive assets through their work, and the opportunities for accumulating assets over time. It approaches informal employment through the lens of occupational groups because different income-generating activities require different types of productive asset, and because some constraints are specific to, or more intense for, particular activities. The focus is mainly on street and market vendors, but the analysis also makes reference to home-based workers and waste pickers.[4]

The chapter begins with an analysis of access to credit and start-up capital, a common (but not universal) starting point for informal livelihood activities. It shows that differences between occupational groups are more significant than differences between men and women. It then drills down into the street-vending sector, examining how gender-related constraints on *sources* of capital relate to the work process and can embed informal vendors, especially women, in dependent relationships. These constraints are then linked to the ability of street vendors to access and claim urban public space as a collective asset. The chapter then assesses the impact of city government practices on vendors' most common asset – stock – in the context of their use of urban public space.

The analysis concludes by examining the role of membership-based organisations (MBOs) as transformative collective assets for informal workers. It compares the ways in which both large-scale, formally constituted MBOs and smaller-scale, informally constituted MBOs may contribute to both asset accumulation and to transformation in ways that fundamentally challenge power relations underlying exclusionary practices. The chapter thus makes two key contributions to debates on gender, assets, and just cities: first, it argues that *claimed livelihood assets*[5] such as urban public space are important to informal workers, particularly those with limited access to capital; and second, it demonstrates the role of *community social capital*[6] as a collective asset in the context of informal livelihoods.

Data, concepts, and methods

The chapter draws on data from the Informal Economy Monitoring Study (IEMS), a ten-city, three-sector study of key drivers that affect working conditions among home-based workers, street vendors, and waste pickers.[7] Quantitative data were collected through a survey questionnaire administered to approximately 150 respondents per city-sector ($n = 1,953$).[8] Qualitative data were collected through 15 structured focus groups, of about five persons each, per city-sector, using participatory research tools. Data collection took place in 2012. The cities, sectors, and local research partners – all MBOs of informal workers or local support non-governmental organisations (NGOs) – are presented in Table 4.1.

The IEMS data are based on samples of informal workers who are members, affiliates, or contacts of the MBO partners. In each city, the research team drew the most representative sample possible of the MBO membership. The findings are, therefore, not necessarily representative of the full population of informal workers in a city or locality; rather, they may be considered representative of the

Table 4.1 Study cities, partners, and occupational sectors

City	Partner	Occupational sector(s)
Accra	ISSER/StreetNet Ghana Alliance	Street vendors
Ahmedabad	Self-Employed Women's Association (SEWA)	Home-based workers, street vendors
Bangkok	HomeNet Thailand	Home-based workers
Belo Horizonte	INSEA	Waste pickers
Bogotá	Asociación de Recicladores de Bogotá (ARB)	Waste pickers
Durban	Asiye eTafuleni	Street vendors, waste pickers
Lahore	HomeNet Pakistan	Home-based workers
Lima	Federación Departamental de Vendedores Ambulantes de Lima (FEDEVAL)	Street vendors
Nakuru	Kenya National Alliance of Street Vendors and Informal Traders (KENASVIT)	Street vendors, waste pickers
Pune	Kagad Kach Patra Kashtakari Panchayat (KKPKP)	Waste pickers

population of MBO members and broadly indicative of conditions that prevail among informal workers more generally.

For this chapter, the quantitative data are used to present broad patterns of access to and sources of capital among workers in all three sectors, and to analyse one specific type of asset (stock) in the context of a single sector (street vending). The analysis of street vendors' stock permits both comparisons between men and women, and comparisons among vendors with different kinds of access to urban public space. The replacement value of street vendors' stock may be considered an indicator of their potential earnings, and is likely a more reliable indicator than earnings itself.[9]

The qualitative data are used to explore processes of asset accumulation and erosion. Focus groups were structured around ten participatory research tools that built on participatory urban appraisal methods (Moser and McIlwaine 2004) to complement the study's conceptual framework. The results were written up immediately afterward in reports of about 10–12 pages on average, and later coded by theme.[10] The results were then further coded according to the mechanisms linking each type of driver, its effect on workers' assets, and the consequences or livelihood implications thereof. The analysis was designed as a theory-generating exercise to help inform current debates on gender, informal work, and just cities. The chapter departs somewhat from existing definitions of assets (Ford Foundation 2002) in advocating for the inclusion of public goods, such as work sites in public space, as claimed livelihood assets, and for the inclusion of collective assets such as MBOs, both of which are important contributors to productivity and earnings among informal workers.

Gender and assets in the informal economy

The analysis begins with an examination of access to credit, the starting point for many livelihood activities. The growing literature on gender gaps in access to credit shows mixed results in relation to women's access to bank loans (Aterido *et al.* 2011), but many of these studies do not emphasise informal sources of loans and focus on enterprises with employees, rather than own-account workers and cooperative members.[11] Also, among informal workers it is important to ask whether start-up capital is needed to enter an activity, and if so, what sources of start-up capital are available.

Capital and access to credit

Just over 33 per cent of the full IEMS sample reported that they have taken out a loan of any kind. This finding is broadly consistent with other studies that have found generally low access to credit among informal enterprises as compared to formal enterprises. But the data also add nuance to those that have found a gender gap in access to credit: while there is almost no difference at all between men and women within each sector, there is an important difference between occupational sectors, where 38 per cent of street vendors access loans, as compared with 24 per cent of waste pickers.

Table 4.2 suggests that this is because street vendors have a greater need to borrow than waste pickers.[12] Many street vendors need not just start-up capital, but also working capital on a daily basis to purchase stock to sell (Roever 2014). The most common *sources* of start-up capital, however, differ considerably

Table 4.2 Source of start-up capital by sector and sex (%) (multiple response)

	Home-based workers	Street vendors		Waste pickers		Total
		Men	Women	Men	Women	
Did not need capital	44.07	3.38	4.68	58.28	50.59	32.87
Used my own capital	24.38	67.96	36.70	11.54	6.32	26.18
Used money from other household member(s)	6.26	9.66	22.66	0.59	1.17	9.01
Borrowed from friends	1.57	5.80	7.68	1.19	0.70	3.43
Borrowed from family	5.59	5.31	13.86	0.00	0.70	5.79
Personal loan from a private lender	1.57	0.48	8.80	0.89	0.47	3.07
Personal loan from a bank	3.13	3.86	3.75	0.89	0.00	2.30
Loan from a micro-finance institution	1.57	2.42	2.25	0.89	0.00	1.38
Took over family business	2.24	2.42	6.18	0.00	0.00	2.46
Other	6.49	7.25	7.68	2.96	0.23	4.92
N	447	207	534	338	427	1,953

Source: IEMS survey data (2012).

between male and female street vendors. Nearly twice as many men (nearly 70 per cent) as women (37 per cent) had their own capital to use to start up their street vending enterprises, a finding that is consistent with studies of gender-differentiated access to capital within the household.

The patterns of borrowing among men and women street vendors also suggest that women may be more embedded in socially dependent relationships than men. Women are far more likely to use money from other household members, borrow from family or friends, or take out a personal loan from a private non-bank (usually informal) lender – hardly any men or women said they took out loans from a bank or micro-finance institution. These results indicate that a higher share of women than men enter the activity in a relationship of dependence through borrowing from informal sources, while men are less likely to be embedded in such dependent relationships.

The qualitative data also show a pattern of borrowing through social networks and value chains, particularly among women street vendors.[13] In fact, resorting to debt in order to cope with various negative drivers was the single most common response among street vendors across the five cities where street vendors were studied: of 456 total responses to negative drivers documented in the focus groups, 18 per cent related to borrowing. These responses included taking out loans, buying goods from wholesalers or suppliers on credit, negotiating with creditors, and joining self-help loan schemes. Except for the latter, nearly all mentions of these coping strategies referred to borrowing from informal money lenders, and many mentioned abusive terms of borrowing, including exorbitant interest rates and weekly or daily repayment terms.

Although both men-only and women-only focus groups mentioned borrowing as a coping strategy, this was far more common among women, who mentioned borrowing 37 times, as against 14 times by men. In sum, the quantitative and qualitative data together suggest that women are less likely than men to have their own start-up capital, and therefore enter the activity in a relation of dependence; and once in the activity, women may be more likely to resort to borrowing as a coping strategy than men, compounding such relations of dependence via a reliance on wholesalers and informal money lenders – who are more likely to be men than women.

Putting capital to work: street vendors' stock

Once a source of capital is identified, street vendors must determine what type of stock and how much of it to purchase. The stock then becomes the vendor's most significant asset.[14] The replacement value of a street vendor's stock may be considered an indicator of the vendor's earnings potential: a higher replacement value indicates that the stock either has a higher per-unit value or there is a higher volume of it. In the four cities where both male and female vendors participated in the IEMS study, the average replacement value of stock among men ranges from 23 per cent higher than that of women (Nakuru) to 354 per cent higher than that of women (Durban).

The replacement value of stock is likely higher among men than women in part because women are less likely than men to have start-up capital of their own, and instead must borrow it, making it risky to invest in high volumes or valuable goods. But also, women in the sample are twice as likely as men to sell perishable goods (Roever 2014) whose replacement value-per-unit is low relative to other product categories. Both of these factors point to gender constraints that influence how women commonly enter the informal livelihood activity – with borrowed money, to sell perishable goods. These constraints are compounded, as the next section will suggest, by factors related to urban public space.

Urban public space as a productive asset for street vendors

For street vendors, capital is necessary to buy stock, while reliable access to a secure, viable workplace in public space represents a pathway to economic opportunity. These interdependent factors – capital for purchasing stock, the quality and quantity of the stock itself, and access to space from which to sell it – form the basis of a street-vending livelihood. A comparison of the replacement value of stock among male and female street vendors according to how they are located in urban public space helps illustrate this interdependency. Street and market vendors rely on access to a steady and reliable flow of customers, usually found in 'natural markets' – urban areas where sellers and buyers traditionally congregate, such as transport junctions.[15] Competition among vendors for strategic spots on the sidewalks and streets in natural markets is considerable, and conflict between vendors and city governments over which vendors can sell at which locations (and at which times) is common.

Vendors who are able to work at the same place every day, rather than moving constantly as itinerant vendors, can maintain a greater volume of stock than those who can sell only what they can carry. Those vendors with a fixed location reported a replacement value of stock twice as high as those who sell from different locations. The gender gap in stock value is far greater for those who have a fixed location from which to sell: men who sell from the same place every day have stock more than twice the value of women who sell from the same place every day, while the difference between men and women who work at different places is relatively small, given the common constraint on the quantity of stock they can carry. Thus, a fixed work location may be considered an essential asset for this occupational group.

Such locations, however, are rarely owned. Rather, vendors commonly gain access to them through formal systems such as licensing and permitting schemes or, more commonly, through informal agreements among vendors and between vendors and local officials. Though access to a fixed space clearly benefits both men and women, there are power dynamics involved in determinations of who gets the most lucrative sites, and in many localities those determinations also have a gender dimension.

Owning or controlling a space in a built market can be another pathway to regular clientele when the market is well located, designed, and operated.[16]

Among both men and women, vendors in built markets reported far higher stock value (about three times more on average) than those who work in the streets or other places. The focus group data suggest that the relationship between having a stall in a built market and having more valuable stock is a mutually reinforcing one: those who can afford to rent a stall in a built market have space to display and store a higher volume and variety of goods, which in turn attracts repeat customers and generates higher earnings, enabling further rent payments. The opportunity to benefit from this mutually reinforcing cycle is limited to those with enough capital to secure a built market stall, however.

A similar pattern exists among vendors with different types of work premises. Those with fixed stalls report a replacement value of stock double, or more, than those who sell from mobile stands, carts, and tables; and the latter reported significantly higher replacement value of stock than those who sell from a blanket or tarp on the ground.[17] Those who sell only what they carry have the least valuable stock of any category. And the gender gap appears larger near the bottom of the hierarchy: for example, men who sell from fixed stalls have stock worth about 1.7 times the stock among women in the same category, while men who sell from a blanket or tarp on the ground have stock worth more than four times the stock of women in the same category. The gender gap appears to narrow, in other words, as the workplace becomes more secure.[18] Moreover, women in fixed stalls have stock worth ten times that of women who carry their goods, compared to men with fixed stalls who have stock worth about five times that of itinerant male vendors.

The role of city government in asset erosion

The previous section located several gender gaps in street vending: in sources of start-up capital, patterns of informal borrowing, and replacement value of stock according to the vendor's work site in urban public space. This section examines the relationship between city government and the use of public space for street vending, focusing on practices that drive asset erosion. The evidence suggests that both men and women experience these practices, but they may affect women disproportionately depending on how they access capital and what kind of stock they sell.

The analysis centres on practices that affect street vendors' stock. Table 4.3 quantifies all focus group mentions of stock being confiscated, damaged, taken, stolen, or destroyed, and participants' comments about how they respond. The columns reflect somewhat different asset erosion pathways in each city. Participants in Accra and Nakuru reported fewer details about confiscations than participants in the other three cities. In Accra, the lower number of confiscations likely has to do with the sample there, which included a higher share of market traders than street vendors to reflect the make-up of the membership of the MBO partner (Anyidoho 2013). Market traders have fixed stalls and pay rent for their space, providing them with a more secure workplace than those in the streets. In Nakuru, though some groups mentioned confiscations, they also indicated that the city has a licensing system for street vendors, so confiscations were less common (Lubaale and Nyang'oro 2013).

Table 4.3 City government practices and asset erosion among street vendors (number of mentions in focus groups)

City government practices	Accra	A'bad	Durban	Lima	Nakuru
Confiscations (total)	10	30	31	42	11
Confiscations	9	25	19	39	9
Confiscations despite permit	0	0	9	0	0
Confiscations of permit	0	0	3	0	0
Confiscations of stall/cart	1	5	0	3	2
Police steal stock/stock goes missing/gets damaged/destroyed	4	26	14	11	8
Police non-response to complaints	0	0	12	1	0
Police charge/over-charge for return of confiscated goods	2	6	5	4	1
Total mentions	26	92	93	100	31

Source: IEMS focus groups (2012).

On the other hand, confiscations were quite common in Ahmedabad, Durban, and Lima, even though the latter two also have permitting (Durban) or licensing (Lima) systems.[19] The case of Durban, in particular, shows how the lack of legal and social protections for informal traders can form an asset erosion pathway related to loss of stock (see Figure 4.1). In that city, many participants said that they had paid for a permit, but still had their goods confiscated. 'Should they come to your table or stall while you are away at the toilet, they will ask for a permit; if others report that you are on your way back, they will simply confiscate your stock. This is so harsh, because it means that we cannot take a break, or go to have lunch' said one 37-year-old male trader (Durban focus group 2).

Many focus groups indicated that once police confiscate stock, it is very difficult to recover it. In some cases the vendor will go to the police station and pay the fine associated with the infraction. Even in those cases, once the fine is paid, 'sometimes we do not get our goods back, they keep it to themselves' (Durban focus group 6); and in other cases 'you find that the stock has been reduced' (Durban focus group 2). Or, 'when taking our goods, they do not pack it, they just throw it in their trucks; by the time you claim it back, it is destroyed' (Durban focus group 7).

Reporting missing stock does not always lead to its recovery: 'when you have paid, you ask them if you [can] count if they [the goods] are the same quantity as they were before, but they refuse and start fighting you' (Durban focus group 6). The focus groups had eight mentions of non-response to complaints about damaged or missing goods: 'We report the matter at the police station but nothing happens, as the very same police are the ones guilty of these wrongdoings!' (Durban focus group 11). The conclusion was that 'They do as they please' (Durban focus group 6). Several said they were forced to take out loans from informal moneylenders, referred to as 'loan sharks' by participants, at high interest rates in order to replenish stock lost to confiscation.

Durban Asset Erosion Pathways

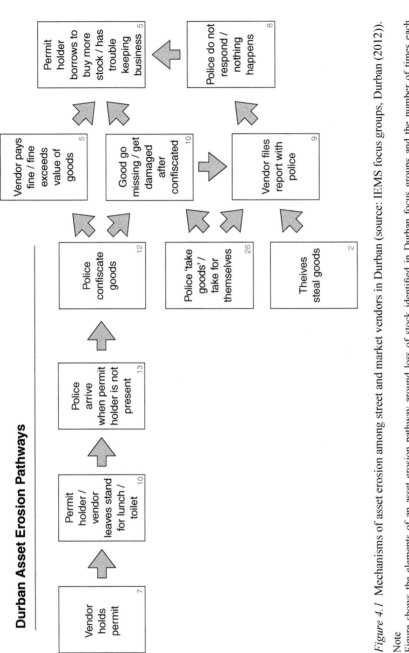

Figure 4.1 Mechanisms of asset erosion among street and market vendors in Durban (source: IEMS focus groups, Durban (2012)).

Note
Figure shows the elements of an asset erosion pathway around loss of stock identified in Durban focus groups and the number of times each element was mentioned across the 15 groups in that city.

Vendors in this city also said that at times police simply take goods for themselves, rather than going through the motions of a formal confiscation. It was not always possible to tell from the focus group reports whether 'police take our goods' meant that police confiscate goods, or that police simply take the goods, as in 'police eat our very stock that they confiscate from us' or 'some police take our stock that they confiscated to their houses' (Durban focus group 13). They also said thieves steal their goods, and even if the police come to take a report, 'they will act as if they are writing your problem down but once they are gone, they will never come back with the feedback' (Durban focus group 4).

It should be noted that other assets, besides stock, were also affected by city government practices in these cities. For example, participants in Ahmedabad indicated that police or city authorities also confiscate their carts or weighing scales during an eviction drive (Ahmedabad focus groups 10, 12, 13, 15). In Accra, vendors refer to similar acts as 'demolition exercises', meaning that their stalls, stands, or carts are demolished during a street-clearing operation. Vendors in Lima also said that in addition to their goods, city authorities take their carts and trays. Such operations constrain vendors' willingness to carry large quantities of stock: 'We can't buy large amounts of merchandise, because you don't know what will happen' (Lima focus group 10).

The asset erosion pathways identified through the qualitative data in Durban show how the lack of legal protections in informal work – specifically, protections of the rights to livelihood, property, and due process – interact with other constraints to limit the possibility for asset accumulation. Many vendors, especially women vendors, must borrow in order to purchase stock; they may have to limit the quantity of stock they purchase, either because of lack of capital or lack of a work space to accommodate it; and their stock may be confiscated or destroyed in the absence of legal protections against police abuse.[20] This is especially problematic for fruit and vegetable vendors, who in this sample are disproportionately women, because their stock gets eaten or goes rotten after being confiscated.

The role of membership-based organisations in transformation

The previous sections show the ways in which informal street vendors, especially women, are embedded in power relations that can undermine their livelihoods. Assets, too, 'exist within social processes, structures, and power relationships, all of which mediate access to them and the accumulation of their value' (Moser, Chapter 1 of this volume). From a policy standpoint, it is not hard to imagine how interventions designed to better protect these workers' economic rights could contribute to reducing asset erosion and increasing economic gains. But better protection of assets on its own would not necessarily have a transformative impact on the owners of these assets.

Rather, the focus group data support the notion that collective struggles 'have proven far more effective in challenging the structures of oppression than individual acts' (Moser, Chapter 1 of this volume). Indeed, interventions to better protect the economic rights of informal workers are unlikely to be designed in the first place without collective action among informal workers to demand them. This section examines the extent to which informal workers' organisations can themselves be understood as collective assets with transformational capacity. It departs to some extent from the previous sections in that it looks primarily at how informal workers' organisations challenge power relations based on class, rather than gender. The findings may, however, inform current thinking about the role of community social capital as a collective asset – particularly when formally constituted – in creating more just and inclusive cities.

Organisations in two city-sectors are compared: street vendors' organisations in Durban, following on from the previous section, and waste pickers' cooperatives in Bogotá, Colombia. The two-case comparison permits a contrast between an organisational environment in its early stages (Durban) versus one that is further developed and defined by formally constituted and networked MBOs (Bogotá).[21] In Durban, earlier attempts at organising self-employed women ran into challenges (Skinner and Devenish 2006), and organising efforts of both men and women in the street-vending sector are evolving. The study partner there, Asiye eTafuleni (AeT), is a non-profit organisation that supports some of these small-scale membership-based organisations. In Bogotá, the study partner, the Asociación de Recicladores de Bogotá (ARB), was founded in 1990 and is now a well-established, city-wide organisation with 17 affiliated cooperatives and 1,800 members (Acosta and Ortiz Olaya 2013); it is also affiliated with a national association (Asociación Nacional de Recicladores) and a Latin American regional network of waste picker associations (Red Lacre). The contrast reflects the extent to which MBOs can play a role in transforming power relations, both for individual members and for an informal working class.[22]

The first part of the analysis examines the ways in which MBOs in these two cities contribute to asset accumulation (Table 4.4). It considers contributions to four types of asset: financial capital (including earnings); human capital (including skills); physical capital (including productive resources); and social capital. The first two of these, financial capital and human capital, are realised at the individual level (left column); that is, individual members of the MBO accumulate earnings and skills as a result of the MBO's interventions. The second two of these, physical capital and social capital, are formed at the level of community – in other words, the cooperative membership as a collective. Examples from Bogotá and Durban are presented in the right-hand columns.

The second part of the analysis considers the question of how organisations contribute to transformation, understood as a process of challenging the underlying structures of discrimination, marginalisation, and exclusion. It examines contributions that are realised at the individual and community levels, but also includes processes and interventions that engage actors at the city, national, and global levels. Each of the contributions identified in the analysis (Table 4.5) challenges existing notions of power, whether those held by opponents of informal workers, other actors in the value chain, the general public, or the workers themselves.

Table 4.4 How membership-based organisations contribute to asset accumulation

Level	Contributions to asset accumulation	Bogotá	Durban
Individual	Financial capital/ earnings	Securing sources of recyclable materials	Reducing differential pricing
Individual	Human capital/skills	Capacity building workshops, training, courses	Skills development, awareness building, rights training
Community (cooperative membership)	Physical capital/ productive resources	Buy-back centre, trucks, sorting warehouses, collection routes	Safe trading space
Community (cooperative membership)	Social capital/ community	Building unity, solidarity	Communication

Table 4.5 How membership-based organisations contribute to transformation

Level	Contributions to transformation	Bogotá	Durban
Individual	Strengthening sense of professionalism in work	Training, awareness building	
Individual	Strengthening professional identity vis-à-vis others	Identity cards/professional accreditation, uniforms	
Community (cooperative membership)	Strengthening sense of agency in power relations	Negotiating with authorities, preparations for confrontations with authorities	Negotiating with authorities
City/national	Challenging efforts to eliminate informal waste recycling	Marches, demonstrations, protests, legal campaigns	
City/national/ international	Strengthening articulation with other organisations		

Source: IEMS focus groups, Bogotá and Durban (2012).

Asset accumulation

Financial capital and human capital are the assets most commonly mentioned as contributions of the MBO. For Bogotá's waste pickers, ARB's core contribution is to facilitate access to sources of recyclable material: hospitals, apartment buildings, supermarkets, and others that generate a high quantity of recyclable material and that will allow waste pickers to access it.[23] ARB may, for example, send a representative to convince a building administrator to allow waste pickers onto the property to collect waste and take it back to the warehouse for sorting. This mediating role is essential to waste pickers' earnings because 'some administrators allow you to collect if they see that you are organised and there is an organisation that can answer for us if need be' (Bogotá focus group 2). Gaining access to reliable sources of materials is especially important for women, whose average monthly turnover is lower than that of men (Acosta and Ortiz Olaya 2013). Fourteen of the 15 groups identified access to a source of recyclables as a key contribution of ARB and its base-level cooperatives.[24]

For Durban's emergent street vending organisations, direct contributions to earnings on the part of organisations were less frequent. One group mentioned an example in which the organisation had intervened in a situation of differential pricing. 'Before SAIWA [South African Informal Workers Association], pricing was different for Indians, whites and blacks. SAIWA has ensured that the difference in pricing was abolished' (Durban focus group 2). As a result of that intervention, the group said it was able to get better prices on stock, implying a better return on sales.

The extent of ARB's contributions to human capital is also substantial. All 15 focus groups from Bogotá said they had received some form of training or capacity building as a result of their membership, including basic skills training for literacy and numeracy – especially important for women, who are twice as likely as men to have no schooling (Acosta and Ortiz Olaya 2013). Female participants also mentioned a benefit that ARB provides to new mothers, an earlier effort to establish a childcare centre, and help they have received for calamities involving children (Bogotá focus group 3, 12, 13). Others discussed legal empowerment via training on waste pickers' legal rights. Many groups mentioned training that increased their technical knowledge of recycling, aimed not only at increasing their skills, but also distinguishing organised waste pickers as holders of a profession – something that contributes to the transformative dimension discussed below.

Three Durban focus groups named skills development, awareness-building workshops, and know-your-rights training as benefits of their membership. Several said that their organisations 'help when we have problems', implying that the organisation can play a troubleshooting role when crises arise, something a few Bogotá groups also mentioned. But the Durban organisations had not yet reached the point of devising strategies around building vendors' capacity to challenge others' perceptions (as well as their own) about the skills required to perform their job, which Bogotá's waste pickers had.

Contributions to physical and social capital were identified in fewer focus groups than financial and human capital in both cities. In Bogotá, three groups noted the importance of ARB's ownership of a buy-back centre and trucks that would come and transport waste to the sorting warehouse. They also identified ARB's management of a system of allocating collection routes to its members, designed to achieve a fair and equitable distribution of access to recyclables so that every member could make a living. For street vendors in Durban, the equivalent contribution of the organisations was the creation of a safe vending zone, mentioned in relation to one of the base associations in particular, Traders Against Crime. One member explained:

> The place where we operate our businesses was a no-go area for whites and Indians due to crime. We fought it and made that area to be safe for all. Indians and whites are coming in numbers to buy from us, this is because they feel safe.
>
> (Durban focus group 2)

In terms of social capital, seven of 15 focus groups in Bogotá said that a key contribution of the organisation was to build unity among the members. As the following section will suggest, unity appears as a necessary condition for challenging power relations. As one participant put it, 'The ARB creates unity, and unity creates strength' (Bogotá focus group 14). Some spoke of events held by the cooperative to integrate the various base organisations, such as sports and cultural events.

In Durban, one group of men mentioned that the organisation 'encourages communication among us' (focus group 2). However, the importance of solidarity as a source of empowerment was not lost on the traders who had less to say about their organisations per se. One group, like several others, had difficulty expressing any positive drivers that supported their sector. But then a female trader said:

> For me it makes my life better waking up in the morning knowing that I am going to other women, we are going to have funny conversations, laugh until the afternoon ... in that way even if I was in a bad mood when I arrived, later when I go back all that will be forgotten because of the other traders.

She went on, 'even if I have stress, they make me feel better, we are able to share our thoughts' (Durban focus group 8).

Transformation

The contrast between a nascent and an advanced organisational setting is more pronounced when the organisation's contributions to transformative actions are considered. In Bogotá, a key dimension of the ARB's transformative strategy is to combine capacity building with tactics for challenging underlying perceptions of waste pickers. Focus group participants said that because they are poor, the public sees waste pickers as 'thieves, drug addicts, criminals, vagrants and homeless people'. In response, the ARB complements the skills training mentioned above with an insistence on viewing recycling as a skilled profession. This tactic fosters self-respect among workers who spend their days handling waste, and it encourages them to insist that others treat them with respect. Members become committed to 'be respectful, wear a complete uniform, [carry] an identification card ... then the people place confidence in you' (Bogotá focus group 8). Members feel that they 'have to show that we are not like' the thieves and drug addicts with whom they are often confused (focus group 12).

ARB also emphasises the environmental role of waste pickers in developing their professional identity. As one participant said, 'We're helping the environment by decontaminating the world. I feel proud. We're finally being recognised and we're treated differently now.' Several also mentioned that the uniforms and identification cards given to members also help distinguish them from others. The sense of personal transformation that has emerged out of the efforts of the cooperatives to change public perceptions of waste pickers – from vagrants, criminals, and homeless people to professionals and environmental agents – is clear. 'All I know and all I talk about today is due to the ARB. If I had joined up with anyone else, believe me, I would never have learned all this', said one male participant (Bogotá focus group 10).

A second dimension of transformation visible in the Bogotá focus groups is a sense of agency brought to recyclers through the organisation's ability to negotiate on their behalf, serve as a representative body, and mediate between workers and the city authorities from a position of some leverage. The contrast with Durban is clear: in Durban, many focus groups indicated that vendors feel powerless in the face of harassment and merchandise confiscations, although a handful did note small-scale gains from their MBOs' negotiations. In Bogotá, though, waste pickers have a sense of being prepared, informed, and in a position to make gains. One participant, for example, said that often when they arrive at an event convened by ARB, they are met with 'counter-pamphlets' directing them to the wrong place, so they need to be well informed and prepared through an effective network of information sharing (Bogotá focus group 2). Several articulated the positive effect of having ARB and ANR 'to back us', or to 'fight on our behalf', to 'struggle and defend us', 'to fight for us on the national level'. Twelve of the focus groups in Bogotá and four in Durban identified the contribution of their organisations in negotiation and representation.

In an urban regulatory environment that is generally hostile to informal workers, organisations also manufacture leverage through marches, demonstrations, protests, and legal strategies that place pressure on authorities. Twelve of the 15 focus groups in Bogotá spoke about these actions in the context of defending the existence of their jobs. In the context of constant threats by multinational waste companies and politicians who want to eliminate informal recycling (Parra 2015), the marches and demonstrations help reinforce the sense of unity and agency generated through other actions.

Finally, six of the focus groups noted the extent of articulation between their base-level cooperatives, the ARB as a second-level organisation, and its connection to the national and Latin American regional movements, and/or its connection to other institutions at national, regional, or international levels. One man said that being networked 'helps us bring leaders from other places and allows us to know and share experiences. We are more empowered nationally because we are many groups fighting for the same cause' (focus group 10). Another in the same group said specifically of the Latin American Waste Pickers Network: 'It has served to let us hear experiences from other associates. It has made the recycling trade known throughout Latin America and has enabled us to know other experiences on a global scale.'

Taken as a whole, the role of organising in the process of transforming unequal power relations is evident in the case of Bogotá, where the organisation has the capacity to develop an articulated, self-reinforcing strategy through the development of a professional identity, solidarity, a sense of agency, and a basis for negotiation, representation, and institutional networking. In doing so it helps waste pickers overcome the stereotypes and prejudices that accompany poverty and limit agency and choice. Of course, there are internal challenges and constraints on unity and power – within the ARB as within other workers' organisations – as well as external constraints on organisations that are excluded from an institutionalised collective bargaining system. Nonetheless, the importance of community social capital formed through informal workers' MBOs to the security and dignity of these livelihoods is clear.

Conclusions

In the context of the significant urban divide in many cities (UN-HABITAT 2008), it is important to analyse poverty among informal workers in the context of power relations between social actors (Moser, Chapter 1 of this volume). Without legal and social protections through work, informal workers are particularly vulnerable to exploitation and exclusion by more powerful actors. Efforts to make cities more just and inclusive depend in part on creating a more supportive and enabling environment for those engaged in informal livelihoods. The evidence presented in this chapter suggests the following challenges.

First, both women and men in the informal economy enter economic activity with limited access to formal bank loans, but men are more likely to have their own capital to use to start up, while women are more likely to borrow. Second, among street vendors, women are more likely than men to resort to borrowing as a coping strategy, leaving them embedded in relations of dependence and debt. Third, both their source of capital and their insertion into urban public space contribute to lower average stock value among women than men. Fourth, both men and women are affected by city government practices that erode stock, but those practices likely affect women disproportionately because they are more likely to sell perishable goods and more likely to depend on informal money-lenders to replace lost stock.

Systemic improvements to the status of women in informal employment depend on a significant challenge to the unequal relations of power, both between women and men and between informal workers and the formal state regulatory regime. The contrast between workers' organisations in the cities of Bogotá and Durban suggest that collective struggles may prove more effective in challenging power structures than individual acts, but they are more likely to do so if those organisations reach scale and survive long enough to develop long-term strategies for strengthening livelihoods. It is therefore critical for cities to address the urban employment challenge in part by creating a more enabling environment for informal workers' representative organisations.

Acknowledgements

The author thanks Martha Chen, Sonia Dias, Caren Levy, and Caroline O.N. Moser for their helpful comments on earlier drafts of the chapter.

Notes

1 The term 'quality employment' is used to signal the acknowledged need for improvements in poor people's access to employment that can generate sufficient income for them to live with security and dignity. This approach to 'quality employment' is consistent with the notion of 'full employment' as conceived by the Self-Employed Women's Association in India (Chen 2005), and is distinguished here from 'formal employment', whose technical definition is more focused on engagement between workers and the state.
2 The chapter uses the term 'informal employment' as per the ICLS definition (outlined in ILO and WIEGO 2013) in presentations of official statistics, but prefers the term 'informal livelihoods' in discussions of the day-to-day income-generating activities of the urban poor. 'Livelihood' in this sense refers to the activities in which the urban working poor engage to generate income, while acknowledging that assets and capabilities are also components in the classic definitions of livelihood systems (Chambers and Conway 1992). Many workers in the study sample engage in more than one income-generating activity; most are own-account or sub-contracted workers in these activities; and many have multiple and fluid workplaces and ambiguous relations with contractors, middlemen and other types of intermediaries. Because assets and capabilities can interact with these different activities and employment relations in different ways, using 'livelihood' in the narrower sense of the income-generating activity in its context is clearer for the purposes of this chapter, and also more appropriate than the term 'job', which carries a formal employment connotation.
3 Estimates based on official statistics. 'Non-agricultural' employment is used as a proxy for urban employment. In three of six regions and in urban China, informal employment accounts for a greater share of non-agricultural employment among women than men, and in two of six regions the share is similar. Only in the Middle East and North Africa does informal employment account for a significantly larger share of men's than women's non-agricultural employment (Vanek *et al.* 2014).
4 For definitions of these worker group categories, see ILO and WIEGO (2013).
5 'Claimed livelihood assets' are livelihood assets that informal workers do not own but claim access to in contexts where such assets are essential to the livelihoods of a significant portion of the population, but ambiguously or inconsistently governed.
6 'Community social capital' is distinguished from 'household social capital' following Moser and Felton (2007).
7 The study was coordinated by WIEGO in collaboration with ten partner organisations as part of the Inclusive Cities project. The term 'sector' is used to refer to occupational groups. The three sectors included in the IEMS are home-based workers, street vendors, and waste pickers.
8 The study included a total of 13 city-sectors.

9 The IEMS did calculate earnings among these groups (see Roever and Chen 2014), but they are notoriously difficult to measure accurately and reliably, especially among informal own-account workers.

10 The thematic coding of a complete digital data set with 195 focus group reports from ten cities and three sectors represents a new frontier in qualitative data analysis, allowing both for further quantification of the qualitative data and innovative qualitative data analysis techniques such as that presented in Figure 4.1.

11 Over 97 per cent of street vendors in the IEMS are own-account workers, meaning self-employed workers with no employees. Among waste pickers, about two-thirds are own-account workers and one-third are cooperative members; fewer than one per cent of the two groups combined are employers.

12 Though waste pickers have less need than street vendors as individuals for start-up capital, their cooperatives need working capital to reduce their members' exposure to exploitative middlemen.

13 For street vendors, the value chain most directly involves wholesalers and other suppliers of stock, as well as the informal moneylenders who provide access to capital.

14 The exception is the case of vendors who offer services. In their case, equipment and machinery are more likely to be the most important asset.

15 The term 'natural markets' was coined in India as part of the campaign to pass a central law on street vending. Its formal definition can be found in the 2014 Street Vendors Act.

16 Many markets are not well located, well designed, or well operated, particularly failing to incorporate meaningful vendor participation in decision-making, and are more accessible to men than women in many (though not all) localities.

17 To some extent an overlap exists between market vendors and fixed stall vendors, but it is not complete – in the combined sample about 60 per cent of vendors with fixed stalls work in markets.

18 The larger difference between men and women who do not have stalls, stands, or kiosks relates to access to capital at entry into the activity; men are more likely to have their own capital and may therefore be in a better position to sell more valuable goods (such as durables) and services than women, even if they cannot afford a fixed stall.

19 A licensing system regulates the right to trade, while a permitting system regulates trading space (Horn, n.d.).

20 A handful of focus groups also mentioned sexual harassment of female vendors by police, although those mentions related such harassment to access to permits rather than the prevention of confiscations or the return of confiscated goods.

21 The two cases broadly represent the ends of a continuum of MBOs within the IEMS. At one end of the continuum, the street vendors' organisations in Durban reflect smaller-scale, less formally constituted organisations that focus mainly (though not exclusively) on troubleshooting urgent issues. At the other end, the ARB in Bogotá (as well as SEWA in India) reflect the larger-scale, more formally constituted organisations that have well-developed longer-term strategies in addition to addressing urgent issues.

22 The term '*an* informal working class' is used to signify the extent to which a collective identity characterises informal workers in specific occupational groups in certain localities. Waste pickers who are members of ARB in Bogotá exhibit a strong livelihood-based collective identity as waste pickers that locates them in the economic structure of the city and country, but also as agents of environmental protection.

23 Recyclable material is in a way analogous to urban public space for street vendors in that it is a claimed livelihood asset with ambiguous rules of ownership and access.

24 A key distinction between the two cities is that ARB is a 'second-level association', meaning it is an organisation to which base-level associations (cooperatives) affiliate. In Durban, there is no equivalent second-level association; there are several base organisations, and then a local non-profit organisation that supports them.

References

Acosta Táutiva, Angélica and Rovitzon Ortiz Olaya. 2013. *Estudio de Monitoreo de la Economía Informal: Recicladoras y Recicladores de Bogotá, Colombia*. Manchester: WIEGO.

Anyidoho, Nana Akua. 2013. *Informal Economy Monitoring Study: Street Vendors in Accra, Ghana*. Manchester: WIEGO.

Aterido, Reyes, Thorsten Beck, and Leonardo Iacovone. 2011. 'Gender and Finance in Sub-Saharan Africa: Are Women Disadvantaged?' World Bank Policy Research Working Paper no. 5571, World Bank.

Chambers, Robert and Gordon R. Conway. 1992. 'Sustainable Rural Livelihoods: Practical Concepts for the 21st Century'. IDS Discussion Paper No. 296, Institute of Development Studies.

Chen, Martha Alter with Ruchi Khurana and Nidhi Mirani. 2005. *Towards Economic Freedom: The Impact of SEWA*. Ahmedabad: SEWA.

Doss, Cheryl, Caren Grown, and Carmen Diana Deere. 2008. 'Gender and Asset Ownership: A Guide to Collecting Individual Level Data'. World Bank Policy Research Working Paper no. 4704, World Bank.

Folbre, Nancy. 2001. *The Invisible Heart: Economics and Family Values*. New York: New Press.

Ford Foundation. 2002. *Building Assets to Reduce Poverty and Injustice*. New York: Ford Foundation.

Horn, Pat. (n.d.) 'Street Traders and Regulation'. StreetNet International.

International Labour Organisation. 2010. *Global Employment Trends January 2010*. Geneva: ILO.

International Labour Organisation. 2014. *Global Employment Trends 2014: Risk of a Jobless Recovery?* Geneva: ILO.

International Labour Organisation and WIEGO. 2013. *Women and Men in the Informal Economy: A Statistical Picture*. 2nd edn. Geneva: ILO.

Kabeer, Naila. 2011. 'Between Affiliation and Autonomy: Navigating Pathways of Women's Empowerment and Gender Justice in Rural Bangladesh'. *Development and Change* 42, 2: 499–528.

Kabeer, Naila. 2013. *Paid Work, Women's Empowerment and Inclusive Growth: Transforming the Structures of Constraint*. New York: UN Women.

Lubaale, Grace and Owen Nyang'oro. 2013. *Informal Economy Monitoring Study: Street Vendors in Nakuru, Kenya*. Manchester: WIEGO.

Mahmud, Simeen, Nirali M. Shah, and Stan Becker. 2012. 'Measurement of Women's Empowerment in Rural Bangladesh'. *World Development* 40: 610–19.

Moser, Caroline and Andrew Felton. 2007. 'Intergenerational Asset Accumulation and Poverty Reduction in Guayaquil, Ecuador, 1978–2004', in Caroline O.N. Moser (ed.), *Reducing Global Poverty: The Case for Asset Accumulation*. Washington, DC: Brookings Institution Press.

Moser, Caroline and Cathy McIlwaine. 2004. *Encounters with Violence in Latin America: Urban Poor Perceptions from Colombia and Guatemala*. London: Routledge.

Parra, Federico. 2015. 'Reciclaje Sí, Pero Con Recicladores'. WIEGO Technical Brief No. 9, WIEGO.

Roever, Sally. 2014. *Informal Economy Monitoring Study Sector Report: Street Vendors*. Cambridge, MA: WIEGO.

Roever, Sally and Martha Alter Chen. 2014. 'Making Women's Self-Employment More Viable'. Background Paper for UN Women, Progress of the World's Women.

Skinner, Caroline and Annie Devenish. 2006. 'Collective Action for Those in the Informal Economy: The Case of the Self Employed Women's Union.' In R. Ballard, A. Habib, and I. Valodia (eds), *Voices of Protest: Social Movements in Post-Apartheid South Africa*. Durban: University of KwaZulu-Natal Press.

United Nations Human Settlements Programme (UN-HABITAT). 2008. *State of the World's Cities 2010/2011: Bridging the Urban Divide*. London: Earthscan.

Vanek, Joann, Martha Alter Chen, Françoise Carré, James Heintz, and Ralf Hussmanns. 2014. 'Statistics on the Informal Economy: Definitions, Regional Estimates & Challenges'. WIEGO Working Paper no. 2, WIEGO.

World Bank. 2013. *World Development Report: Jobs*. Washington, DC: World Bank.

5 Addressing gendered inequalities in access to land and housing

Carole Rakodi

Introduction

The well-being of urban residents depends on access to a suitable place to live, in a healthy environment, and within reach of work opportunities and services. To ensure that adequate housing is available and that it can fulfil its potential roles in tackling poverty and increasing prosperity, infrastructure, a flourishing urban economy, supportive social networks, and political voice are needed, as well as a house (a dwelling and the land on which it sits). While the availability of housing is determined by the market, policies, law, and practice, access to and control over it is unequally distributed between and within households. All are gendered. In particular, female heads of household are generally more disadvantaged than male heads, and women within families more disadvantaged than men, hindering the reduction of poverty and inequality overall.

Many factors influence the availability of adequate housing; among the most salient are the supply channels for plots and dwellings, how effective demand is exercised, and the laws governing land and housing. First, therefore, this chapter examines the extent to which women can access suitable housing through the main delivery channels typical in southern cities. This includes appraising whether policy interventions influencing supply or demand, while intended to improve the operation of such channels, have had a positive impact on women's access. Second, it assesses legal reforms intended to increase access to secure tenure, especially for women, and considers whether these have empowered them. Third, it discusses how laws relevant to housing delivery, as well as those governing marital relations and inheritance, affect households, and the men and women within them, and the ways these laws are influenced by social relations within and beyond the household.

To prepare the ground, this chapter discusses the roles housing can play in livelihood strategies, the promotion of ownership as the preferred way of strengthening tenure rights, and the anticipated benefits of improved access to and control over housing for women. In each instance, a simplistic understanding is inadequate, because the central concepts are complex; land and housing are related to many other dimensions of urban life, governance, and policy; and the characteristics of urban populations, governance arrangements, policies, and practices vary enormously from one country and city to another. The outcomes of attempts to improve women's access to and control over land and housing are both complex and varied. Unfortunately, there are few rigorous comparative gendered analyses of urban land and housing markets, the advantages and disadvantages of alternative forms of tenure for women, and the outcomes of interventions designed to improve women's access to suitable housing.[1] It is therefore necessary to exercise caution in generalising from the results of the limited evidence available. Nevertheless, this chapter assesses the available literature and identifies issues that require further gendered research.

Land and housing as assets

Dwellings – houses or apartments – and the sites on which they stand are significant assets for urban families, providing them with a place to live, enabling them to engage in income-generating activities, and to give their children a good start in life. Like other assets, land and housing constitute stocks of resources that generally appreciate in value (Moser 1998; Rakodi 1999). As well as providing a buffer against shocks and stresses, housing helps households to assemble livelihood activities that enable them to cope and ultimately prosper. Moreover, houses are not merely physical artefacts with practical functions and economic value, they also provide people with a sense of their own worth, enhance their sense of belonging, and empower them to act.

Most analyses of the roles housing plays in livelihood strategies focus on households. Problems arise when the concept of a 'household' is taken to be unproblematic. In practice, the composition of households, the allocation of paid and unpaid work, and responsibility for meeting household expenses, and the extent of income sharing and joint decision-making varies enormously between households, cities, and countries. In particular, the value placed on the potential benefits of household property, including real property – land and buildings – and control over its use and disposal as an asset to sell or bequeath is unequally distributed both among and within households. However, gender-blind housing studies and policies fail to recognise that men and women may prioritise different functions and aspects of housing, and that women's access to and control over housing depends on their position and roles within their households, families, and wider social networks. Patterns of social relations within and beyond the households in which people live are key to both understanding gender inequalities in access to and control over real property and explaining the outcomes of urban policies and legal reforms.

Strengthening property rights through promoting ownership

Efforts to improve the housing of poor urban residents have generally focused on promoting ownership of plots and dwellings, through increasing the supply of houses or serviced plots for sale and/or regularising informally settled areas, with 'ownership' meaning many things, depending on whether and how it is legally defined and documented.

The term 'property right' can refer to a holder's right to *use* a good (in this case real property) for consumption and/or income generation; to *transfer* it to another party in the form of a sale, gift, or bequest; and to *contract* with other parties by renting, pledging, mortgaging, or allowing use of it (Besley and Ghatak 2010, 4526). Rights can be bundled in different ways, giving rise to different tenure systems, which influence the scope for using land and property as assets and provide different levels of security, depending on holders' ability to claim rights, transfer them, and defend them against challenges (Payne and Durand-Lasserve 2013, p. 8). 'Ownership', implying an extensive bundle of rights to use and transfer property, is often considered to be the most desirable form of tenure, with a number of benefits over and above its use value in providing a place to live, as mentioned above.

Evidence shows that the practical and psychological benefits of ownership are valued by most poor households and by both women and men (see, for example, Loughhead and Rakodi 2002; Moser 1998, 2010; Moser and Felton 2010; Rakodi 1999). Ownership claims may be backed up by verbal agreements, social norms, social and political relationships, and/or various forms of documentation. In particular, legal ownership is associated with a 'title', the documentation and registration of statutory property rights, which typically provides for ownership to be long term – either time limited, as in a lease, or in perpetuity – transfers to be administered and registered by a state agency, rights to be defended in the courts, and sometimes for rights to be guaranteed by government. It also enables property to be used as collateral for a loan.

Conventionally, rights specified in state law are thought to be the most secure, but in practice people are not treated equally as legal persons: access to legal tenure and the court system is unavailable to many of the poor, and non-state law (customary or religious law) or social custom may trump state law. Thus property rights (who can do what with respect to a piece of property) and tenure (the means by which land is held) are not merely legal but are essentially relational.

In practice, many urban households cannot realistically aspire to 'ownership', as in most cities less and less land is available for free, the large-scale public production of serviced plots and/or dwellings is increasingly rare, buying or building a house is unaffordable, and institutional housing finance is unavailable to households with low and irregular incomes. Almost everywhere, many – and sometimes a majority – of poor households have no option but to rent. The production of housing for rent may be an important source of income for some owner households, but it is also important to consider whether and how rented housing can play a role in the livelihood strategies of tenants and how it is dealt with in policy and law. Rather than assuming that the concept of 'ownership' is self-evident, the main way in which housing is held and/or the most desirable form of tenure, a range of tenures need to be considered, especially in terms of their implications for women.

Empowering women by improving their access to and control over housing

Both women and men value home ownership, but commonly women prioritise the use value of the family home and the security it provides for them and their children over its value as a commercial asset, including its potential resale value. Housing-rights advocates focus on women's rights to own property in their own names, regardless of their marital status, have a veto over the sale of marital property, and retain rights to a share of the marital home following the end of a union, be it through separation, divorce or widowhood. Individual property ownership, or rights over marital property – especially joint tenure – are said to expand women's agency, increase their access to opportunities, and provide them with economic independence. This relates to their increased knowledge of their rights and their bargaining power in household decision-making, enabling them to prevent their husbands selling without their consent, increasing their self-esteem and respect from other family members, and increasing investment in household well-being, especially for daughters. In addition, such rights are said to reduce women's vulnerability to domestic violence or abandonment, to improve their exit options from abusive relationships and to enable them to avoid or postpone marriage (Datta 2006; World Bank 2014). Evidence on the nature and outcomes of changes to policies and laws designed to realise the benefits of ownership for poor households in general and women in particular is discussed below.

Improving women's access to land and housing assets by intervening in supply and demand

Women's access to and control over housing assets cannot be enhanced unless existing housing delivery channels provide adequate supplies of affordable and well-located serviced plots and houses, aided by well-designed and successfully implemented policies to increase supply and effective demand. However, for the most part, the delivery channels typical of Southern cities are neither capable of providing adequate low-cost housing nor are gender sensitive (Rakodi 2010). Therefore, it is important to identify attempts to tackle these problems and their outcomes for women, even though land and housing delivery channels vary between cities and over time, and are influenced not only by policy, but also by market forces, topography, and land administration arrangements. Demand, in turn, is influenced by economic trends, the income distribution and the availability of finance.

The supply of land and housing

Women's access to land and housing depends on the extent to which the available channels provide opportunities for both female- and male-headed households to access housing with security of tenure and an adequate standard of construction. This in turn depends on legal frameworks and the implementation of policies that seek to improve supply and ensure women's access. Both are influenced by social norms and relationships, which determine who within a family controls the use and transfer of houses.

Public provision of serviced plots and houses

Traditionally, land and housing policy designed to meet the needs of the urban poor focused on subdividing publicly owned land into serviced plots for 'self-help' house building or the construction of starter homes or complete dwellings. In earlier programmes, household heads in waged employment were allocated serviced plots and houses for rent or sale, mainly in their own names. Most beneficiaries were men, linked to their dominance of formal labour markets; joint titles were rare, and whether or not women and their children inherited the marital home following widowhood, divorce, or separation depended on the formal legal regime, government policy, customary laws and practices, and norms governing social relationships.

In the 1960s and 1970s, even large-scale programmes rarely, if ever, delivered sufficient numbers of plots and houses to meet the need, and the shortage of cheap plots and houses led to their leakage up the income distribution. Since the 1980s, with few exceptions, programmes have been drastically scaled back in response to state financial and managerial crises and economic liberalisation. One exception is South Africa, where the political settlement that ended apartheid in 1994 was accompanied by government commitment to a large-scale housing programme (see Meth in Chapter 6).

The privatisation of state-owned houses

In many countries, a second policy, associated with economic crisis and liberalisation, was the sale of publicly owned plots and houses. One of the few gendered assessments of the outcomes of housing privatisation was undertaken in Zambia, where the large stock of municipal and mine housing was transferred to 'sitting tenants'. Although ostensibly gender neutral, the policy had gendered effects. Most of the original tenants were employees, predominantly men, and where a tenant household still contained a man, the title was made out in his name alone. Although divorced or widowed women had been able to continue as tenants, when title was issued, they were vulnerable to eviction by their husband's relatives on the grounds that under customary law they were not entitled to inherit (Schlyter 2004a). Some men tried to avoid the dispossession of their widows by putting the house in the name of one or more of the children, but the effect was to make widows dependent on their children (Schlyter 2004b). Some women who could afford to do so invested in home improvements to strengthen their claim, but tenants also had to clear any payment arrears and if they could not afford to do so were expected to find another buyer or were evicted, a prospect more likely to be faced by poor women (Butcher 2009). Simultaneously, privatisation created a market that provided opportunities for some women with means to purchase houses.

In theory, programmes to privatise state housing and issue titles in former planned economies, for example in Eastern Europe and Central Asia or Vietnam, have been gender-equitable, but implementation was insufficiently gender sensitive to ensure that women benefited equally to men. In practice, local custom, culture, and tradition, as well as civil war and social dislocation, have exacerbated women's lower social status (Joireman 2013; Stanley *et al.* 2012; World Bank 2008).

Promotion of formal private subdivision and house construction

The formal private sector supplies a larger proportion of housing in middle-income than in low-income countries. Even in the former, however, prices exceed the capacity of many urban residents to pay. If women can afford to purchase property in this limited market, they often face fewer discriminatory attitudes and administrative practices than in other delivery channels (UN-HABITAT 2012, 28) and there is some evidence that the proportion of women who are acquiring property in this way is increasing – for example, in Kathmandu, Nepal (see Pandey 2010). However, women in general are still economically disadvantaged, subject to socially restrictive attitudes, and legally discriminated against, so relatively few can access privately produced formal housing.

Informal subdivision

In previous decades, low-income households in many cities in the South obtained access to free (or almost free) land through invasion, incremental squatting, or the allocation of plots by customary owners. Today, however, the proportion of households which can do so has diminished, along with the decline in availability of undeveloped publicly owned land. Remaining sites are often poorly located or environmentally risky, while private owners are more inclined to evict than tolerate informal occupiers as land values rise. In addition, although squatting is a cheap way of obtaining land, the physical hardships and level of vulnerability rule it out for many female household heads.

Where land is still held by customary owners, in African cities and elsewhere, informal subdivision can be an important source of land for housing. Under customary tenure, property transactions are regulated by traditional norms and practices modified by decades of socio-economic change. Within the relevant group – such as extended family, lineage, or clan – homestead land or rights in a family property are inherited by or allocated to those with entitlements, generally men upon marriage but rarely women in their own right. Women's property rights depend on their marital status and fulfilment of responsibilities for household maintenance and childcare. They are secure as long as the marriage is intact, but reliance on secondary rights reduces their bargaining power and makes them vulnerable to dispossession in the event of conjugal dissolution. In many African societies, widows are supposed to retain use rights while they remain unmarried and care for minor children, but the rising value of urban property often tempts their husbands' families to claim the property (Rakodi 2006). Sometimes widows may be entitled to land from their natal families, but more often they are forced to move into inferior and more insecure accommodation. In the past it was uncommon for non-homestead family land to be allocated to or inherited by women. Today, although this is still the case in many countries, there are signs of change in others, increasing women's access to land – for example in Maseru, Lesotho (Leduka 2004, 167–9).

Today, most land in private or customary ownership (and sometimes land in public ownership) is made available for construction through various processes of informal commercial subdivision. Such markets operate on the basis of informal social rules, although these may mimic and draw upon elements of the formal system to regulate standards and patterns of development or document transfers (Byamugisha 2013; Fernandes 2011; Rakodi 2006). They provide access to land for low- and middle-income households (although not to the poorest), including women who can both act independently and afford to purchase land. For example, in Kenya, companies are formed to legally purchase land, which is informally subdivided and allocated to the shareholders. In Eldoret, women were clear that the land-buying companies, in which most shareholders shared an ethnic identity, were all willing to accept female shareholders. However, social pressure to marry and the disadvantaged financial position of women meant that only 16 per cent of plot owners were women, of whom about 80 per cent had been married at the time they acquired the plot and only 20 per cent were never-married women who had obtained land in their own right, mainly through purchase (Musyoka 2004, 115–16).

Because such a large proportion of all urban low- and medium-cost accommodation is informal, policies have increasingly focused on regularising and upgrading informal settlements. Although there is an ongoing debate about the relative importance and sequencing of recognition, regularisation, infrastructure installation, and housing improvement, legal provisions to convey or strengthen property rights are central. They have significant implications for women, and so will be considered in some detail later.

Rental housing

In many cities in the Global South, most households have little choice but to rent. Some actively choose this option because of its flexibility, low cost, and locational advantages, such as women industrial workers in South-east Asia (Chant and McIlwaine 1995, 161). However, despite preferring a 'place of their own', others have limited options. Studies in Guadalajara and Mexico City, for instance, show that women, especially younger female heads with children, often prefer central locations to peripheral settlements where they might become home owners, because there are more income-earning opportunities and they can more easily combine paid work with childcare. In central locations, renting a room is generally the only option (Miraftab 1998; Wigle 2008). Generally, women's disadvantage in terms of education, income-earning capacity, and marital position means that they are disproportionately represented among renters (UN-HABITAT 2011, 16; 2012, 28; World Bank 2014, 132). Rental tenure is largely unregulated, insecure, and less suitable for livelihood activities than ownership: women tenants may be discriminated against by male landlords and are particularly vulnerable to bullying, violence, and arbitrary eviction (Baruah 2007; Chant 2013). In addition, landlords may not permit the use of rented dwellings for income generation or may prevent tenants from cultivating land around the house.

However, women also play a role in the rental market as landlords in their own right, or managing rental accommodation in which their husbands have invested, although in the latter case they are not necessarily regarded as joint owners and may not have control over the rental income (Kumar 2010). Indeed, in some serviced-plot schemes, the construction of additional rooms for rent is encouraged, to enable owners to repay loans and meet service costs, as well as increasing the supply of housing. Letting accommodation can be a prudent strategy for women, especially older women who are less able to access waged employment or pursue arduous informal sector activities. However, their ability to become landlords varies, depending on their ability to raise funds, social acceptance, and whether or not they inherit the marital home. In Gaborone, Botswana, for instance, where one-third of households are female-headed, gender-neutral government housing programmes have enabled many women to prioritise obtaining a plot and building a house. Not only do many married women manage rental dwellings in which their husbands have invested, but also half the landlords in low-income areas are female household heads. Remaining unmarried, becoming home owners, and investing in rental housing have, since the 1980s, been conscious strategies to achieve security, control their own lives, provide a good start for their children, and ensure continued support in their old age (Datta 1995; Larsson 1989; Kalabamu 2006). Similarly, as Gilbert and Varley (1991) note, in the inner city areas of Guadalajara and Puebla, Mexico, renting is often referred to as 'widow's business'. However, generally the production of rental housing is unsupported by official policies.

Translating need into effective demand

Households have to translate their housing needs into effective demand, since if their ability to buy or build is constrained by lack of resources, neither improved supply nor legal changes are likely to produce positive results. Attempts to increase effective demand have focused on reducing the standards and cost of housing intended for poor households, providing subsidies and improving the availability of finance. These potentially affect female-headed households directly and all women indirectly. For example, the proportion of female-headed households who could afford to build houses in Botswana's serviced-plot programme decreased following the introduction of increased standards and reduced subsidies in 1987 (Datta 1995).

Efforts to improve the availability of loans for house purchase, construction, and improvement have focused mainly on formal public or private housing-finance institutions. For example, nearly half of all titled households in a large-scale programme in Peru had applied for loans, almost all from the public sector Materials Bank. These applicants had lower socio-economic status than owners in regularised areas overall and included a greater number of female-headed house-holds (Field and Torero 2006, 14). More recently, some attention has been paid to the potential role of micro-finance in making credit available to poor people. The experience of national slum dwellers' federations shows that opportunities to save and obtain credit for investment in businesses or housing are both socially accept-able and particularly valued by women (see Mitlin in Chapter 7).

Legal reforms and gender equality

Good law is essential to enable women to access housing and protect their rights, although by itself it is insufficient. Not only does it provide a basis for gender-sensitive policies, it also enables women to hold property in their own right or as members of families, and to defend these rights in the courts. Both campaigning to change laws and the changes themselves can also influence social attitudes. Property law reforms have focused on improving and extending ownership rights during the privatisation of publicly provided plots and dwellings, the regularisa-tion of informal settlements, and new subdivisions. Changes in family law are also often required, as these govern how property rights are allocated between men and women on marriage, during marriage, and following divorce or widow-hood (UN-HABITAT 2007, 20–1). Both types of law are embodied in statutes, but in many countries state law co-exists with customary or religious law. Provi-sions within and between the different laws are often unclear or inconsistent, complicating the outcomes of legal reforms, including those intended to benefit women. For example, different bodies of law may govern legal (civil or reli-gious) marriage, customary marriage and consensual unions. In addition, reli-gious law, especially Sharia, is the main legal system in some countries and recognised as a source of personal law in many others, such as more than one-quarter of sub-Saharan African countries (Hallward-Driemeier and Hasan 2013). In theory, Sharia law permits women to retain control over their pre-marital property and wealth and entitles them to purchase property using their own resources (Sait and Lim 2006). However, its status and interpretation vary (see, for example, Sait's discussion of Sunni and Shia interpretations in different parts of Africa – Sait 2011). Both Sharia and customary law may be officially exempt from non-discriminatory principles embodied in statutory law.

Registration of ownership rights

The main benefit of property registration is the clarity it provides, which enables documented holders to defend their rights against challenges, encourages investment in construction, and enhances municipal revenue by integrating plots into the property tax system. Usually the focus is on title registration, although provision is often made for other property rights, such as use rights (Durand-Lasserve and Selod 2010). In India, for example, following the adoption by central government of a policy of regularising informal settlements ('slums') in the mid-1980s, various state governments introduced legislation permitting the granting of *pattas* (usually non-transferable leasehold rights, typically for 30 years) to squatters on suitable sites after five years of occupation (Banerjee 2002; 2004; Payne and Durand-Lasserve 2013). In Tanzania, the 1999 Land Act provided for the issue in unplanned settlements of both short-term renewable leases – non-transferable residential licences conveying the right to occupy land for two years – and longer-term titles – certificates of the right of occupancy (Kironde 2006).

Many countries have now enacted the legal and administrative reforms needed to roll out large-scale registration and titling and have adopted regularisation policies. In Latin America and the Caribbean this applies to at least 17 countries (Angel *et al.* 2006). One of the largest programmes is in Peru, where since the mid-1990s, titling of plots in informal subdivisions on the urban periphery has been possible because the land is publicly owned and barren (Calderón 2004; Field 2007). However, such large-scale registration and titling has been achieved in relatively few countries, with full legalisation of property rights proving complex and contentious. The focus on legalisation has also delayed linked measures to improve living conditions, such as infrastructure improvements, that may be an even higher priority for residents, especially women. As a result, many now advocate that existing settlements are recognised and upgraded prior to (or instead of) full titling, despite associated complexities. Such regularisation generally involves the recognition of use rights. In some contexts, despite evidence that full title is not necessarily required to realise the benefits of property ownership, households convert their use rights into titles. Female household heads in South Africa, for instance, prefer to convert their allocation documents into full titles (Marx and Rubin 2008; Payne *et al.* 2008).

However, registration does not give low-income people access to formal loans (Deininger and Feder 2009; Galiani and Schargrodsky 2004; Kironde 2006; van Gelder 2013; Varley 2007). Financial institutions are reluctant to accept low-cost houses as collateral because of the difficulty and cost of foreclosure, while low-income owners are unwilling to risk losing their only significant asset. Consequently, construction funds are usually incremental, coming primarily from income and savings. Moreover, regularisation and titling are not always entirely positive. For example, when registration in existing built-up areas is demand-driven, or if registration-of-use rights can be upgraded to a title, cumbersome procedures and cost may deter occupiers from proceeding. Registration of subsequent transfers of land (sales, inheritance, etc.) is deterred for the same reason, with the result that formalisation is often soon followed by de-formalisation. In Buenos Aires, for example, in a settlement study, 29 per cent of titled parcels had become de-registered because of the costs of formal divorce and re-registration (Galiani and Schargrodsky 2011).

For women, the balance between positive and negative regularisation outcomes depends on whether their rights are registered, whether they have a say in a decision to sell or use of the proceeds of sale, and whether they are able to defend their rights following changes in their circumstances. The outcomes vary between owners and renters. Ownership rights may be registered in individual, joint, or collective names. Traditionally, most registration has been in the names of individuals, typically household heads, and this continues to be the most common practice, disproportionately vesting ownership in the hands of men. However, the right of women to acquire, retain and register property in their own names is widely advocated because of the anticipated beneficial effects of ownership.

Most evidence of these effects comes from studies of rural areas. However, Agarwal and Panda's panel survey of married women in urban and rural areas of Thiruvanthapuram District, Kerala found that women's ownership of land or a house in their own names provides them with a greater say in decision-making relating to taking out loans, using contraceptives, and having sex with their husbands. It also significantly reduces their vulnerability to marital physical or psychological violence, both deterring violence and providing an escape if violence occurs. The study showed that 71 per cent of propertied women who had experienced long-term physical violence had left home, with few returning, compared to 19 per cent of property-less women – almost all went to live with their parents, with half then returning to their husbands. The results applied equally to urban and rural women (Agarwal and Panda 2007). In another example from Costa Rica, Chant (2009) partially attributes the rising proportion of poor female-headed households amongst the poor to the promotion of titling, as well as legal changes that grant them greater entitlements to conjugal assets and protection from domestic violence. This has strengthened their ability to live alone and made them wary of letting men get too involved in their lives, lest they lose control over their assets.

Joint tenure

Alongside legal recognition of women's individual property ownership, joint tenure is increasingly advocated as a way of safeguarding the position of spouses. Full or partial 'community of property', therefore, is generally considered the most gender-equitable marital property regime, especially for property acquired during a marriage. Consequently it is the mandatory default regime in increasing numbers of countries. It implies joint registration *and* administration of property and provides married women with protection against the unilateral sale or mortgaging of marital property by their husbands, and continued rights following widowhood, divorce, abandonment, or separation (UN-HABITAT 2005).

Generally, women welcome this initiative. For example, in the Peruvian titling programme almost two-thirds of beneficiaries were married couples with joint-named titles. However, with consensual unions not recognised in law, in these cases titles were issued in the name of the male household head (Field 2004). In Vietnam, where joint titling was made mandatory in 2003, 2.8 million Land Tenure Certificates (use rights which can be transferred, mortgaged, and later converted into titles) had been issued in urban areas by 2007. All the female respondents in a 2007–2008 study in three provinces favoured joint title (compared to 85 per cent of men), with urban women considering that the benefits of converting single into joint titles would outweigh the costs (World Bank 2008, 56). Female respondents in a study of married couples in Chandigarh, Punjab, based on three samples – one area where *pattas* had been issued in the husband's name, one in which they had been issued in joint names, and an unregularised settlement – found that women valued joint tenure for all the above suggested reasons (Datta 2006).

In principle, the apparent positive benefits of joint titling have been widely recognised; nevertheless, in practice many titles continue to be issued solely in the husband's name in countries such as Ghana (World Bank 2005, 520) and Tanzania (Kironde 2006). Interpretations vary: sometimes a woman's desire to have her name on the registration document is said to indicate that she distrusts her husband, and may be 'less than fully committed to the relationship' (Varley 2010, 91); in other cases that the marriage is in trouble (Rakodi 2006; Kalabamu 2006; 2009). In addition, adding a wife's name to an already-issued title may face social, bureaucratic, or pecuniary hurdles (e.g. in Ahmedabad – Baruah 2007).

A few studies have attempted to assess the claim that joint titling empowers women within their households by increasing their say in decision-making. The results are mixed, in part because women's empowerment cannot be attributed to property ownership alone. Field (2003 quoted in Deininger and Feder 2009, 249), for example, found that squatter households in Peru who were given titles experienced a 22 per cent reduction in fertility and that 'females who received joint title experienced twice the reduction in probability of having a child than those where the title was in one name only'. In Vietnam, the 2007–2008 study referred to above found that urban and rural women with joint title were more aware of legal issues, more likely to proactively seek a Land Tenure Certificate, had more of a say in the use and disposition of land, and were more likely to earn independent incomes (World Bank 2008).

However, joint tenure may not necessarily or straightforwardly empower women, with women's intra-household bargaining power also influenced by education and income (Doss 2013). Similarly, in Costa Rica, in contrast to Chant's positive findings, a study in Heredia reported that although joint title had given women more bargaining power during divorce, it also meant that couples were likely to stay in unhappy or violent relationships after they would otherwise have split up, since neither could afford to buy the other out (Blanco Rothe *et al.* 2002, quoted in Varley 2007, 1747).

Inheritance laws

The intergenerational transfer of property is important to both the immediate security of a deceased person's heirs and long-term wealth accumulation. While joint tenure may prevent the dispossession of widows, divorcees, and separated women, women's rights to property also depend on inheritance laws and related social norms and practices. Although the legal position has improved, statutory inheritance laws still differentiate between women and men in 28 of the 143 countries included in a newly created database (World Bank and International Finance Corporation 2014, 132). For example, in Sharia law inheritance rules (*mirath*) provide for a woman's (and daughter's) share of inherited property to generally be half that of a man (or son) in a similar situation (Sait and Lim 2006, 110; see also COHRE 2006) and intestate succession laws may exclude land held under customary tenure from the property a widow is entitled to inherit from her husband (Hallward-Driemeier and Hasan 2013).

Reforms to discriminatory inheritance laws can strengthen women's ability to retain marital assets (whether or not they re-marry), enable them to bequeath assets to recipients of their choice, reduce gendered differences in wealth and well-being within households, and level the playing field between sons and daughters (Deere *et al.* 2013). For example, amendments to the 1956 Hindu Succession Act, which governs inheritance for 80 per cent of India's population, specify that daughters and sons should inherit equal shares of joint family property. A 2011 survey of property owned by three generations of members of 7,894 Hindu and Muslim households in four cities in Karnataka, where the Act was amended in 1994, compared the share of total assets received by male and female siblings in the same household between households whose heads died before and after the amendment. The share of physical assets owned by Hindu women who were single before the reform, but whose fathers died after it, had increased, because they had received less separate but more joint property. In addition, girls enrolled in primary school after the reform had completed more years of education than those enrolled prior to it, demonstrating increased investment in daughters. However, the reform had not weakened the dowry system – fathers had also increased daughters' dowry despite their entitlement to an increased share of family property (Deininger *et al.* 2013). While inherited assets may in part account for gendered differences in wealth and well-being within families, as claimed by Deere *et al.* (2013), their significance varies.

Even where statutory inheritance law is non-discriminatory, gendered attitudes towards heirs are complex and patriarchal norms and practices often undermine its implementation and enforcement. For example in Guadalajara, Mexico, if an owner dies intestate, children are entitled to inherit equal shares of the property. However, the views of respondents varied. Many believed that their sons should come first, because they are expected to marry and become responsible for their own families, whereas others intended to favour their daughters because women are considered to be at a socio-economic disadvantage. On the whole, male householders favoured sons over daughters, while female householders were more likely to favour daughters over sons. However, there were indications that attitudes are changing: some believe that whichever of their children look after them in their old age should be favoured and younger people are more likely to think that children should inherit in equal shares (Varley 2010).

Attitudes to widows are equally complex: men's and women's views on their obligations to their spouses are influenced by, for example, the type of marital relationship, people's knowledge of and ability to claim their rights, and customary laws and social practices. Even if widows have the right to inherit or use marital property, their ability to exercise this right may depend on their relations with the deceased husband/partner's family and compliance with onerous and degrading practices and rituals – for example, levirate marriage where the brother of a deceased man is obliged to marry his brother's widow, and the widow is obliged to marry her deceased husband's brother (Chant 2013, 18; COHRE 2006; UN-HABITAT 2007). Widows may be disproportionately likely to be poor, depending on whether they are able to work, have their own or inherited property, are being supported by family members, and/or are expected to re-marry (Varley 2013). For example, in Malawi, where the vast majority of urban residents own their own houses, a recent study found that two-thirds of widows had been dispossessed (Ngwira n.d.). In most African countries, widows are expected to re-marry, reinforcing husbands' families' efforts to prevent them inheriting the marital home, whereas in India not only is re-marriage socially stigmatised, widows may have to support themselves, often by low-paid work (Vera-Sanso 2010).

Conclusion

House ownership is widely aspired to and plays an important role in the livelihood strategies and well-being of poor people. Women's ability to access suitable housing, influence decisions about its acquisition, use, and disposal within their households, and retain rights to their own and marital property following the end of a marriage depends on the volume and characteristics of housing supplied through the available housing delivery channels, legal provisions, the social relations in which they are embedded, and prevailing attitudes. Policies, legal reforms, and improved practices aimed at addressing gender inequality, in the course of ensuring that housing delivery channels can meet the need for well-located housing with secure tenure, have had mixed results. There is evidence to show that, as long as women retain control over their own property, have equal rights to marital property, and can assert their rights following separation, divorce, or widowhood, becoming a property owner and/or registering ownership of an existing house benefits them, providing a secure place to live, a greater say in household decision-making, protection following the end of a marriage, and enhanced livelihood opportunities. However, it is also clear that women's property rights are determined not only by policies and statutory laws, but also by religious and customary law and social custom. Moreover, many gender-equitable policies and legal reforms are not fully implemented in practice, and when they are, the outcomes for women are mixed.

Because of the complexity of outcomes, the scarcity of relevant studies, and the dearth of gendered data, many gaps remain in our knowledge of how best to enable women to acquire housing assets and exercise agency over their use and disposal, as well as the policies and laws that can most effectively reduce social and gender inequality and promote women's empowerment. A better understanding is needed of the gender asset gap at household level (Deere *et al.* 2013), how individual and joint ownership affect women's role in household decision-making, the relationships between marital arrangements and property rights, and the implications of changing patterns of wealth transfer through dowry, bride price, gifts, or bequests. Assessments are needed of the gendered outcomes of policies to increase the supply of serviced plots and houses to low- and middle-income households, register individual, joint, or collective owner- ship in and upgrade existing housing areas, improve access to institutional housing finance, and reform property and family laws. These should assess whether initiatives have improved security of tenure and control over property, increased gender equity in the ownership of material assets, empowered women within their households and families, and enhanced their voice and influence in urban civil and political society. They should also consider the effects of women's engagement in legal reform, policy-making, and programme design and implementation, through their own social mobilisation or by invitation. In addition, because of the importance of inheritance in wealth transfers, the need to maintain property registration following transfers, and the intergenerational transmission of well-being through investment in human and social as well as physical capital, long-term tracking is needed of the effects of new housing supply, privatisation of state housing, and laws requiring joint tenure or gender parity in inheritance. In addition to disaggregating the outcomes by gender, they need to be disaggregated by income/wealth and other dimensions of social difference to assess their overall contribution to equity and social justice at the city level.

Note

1 This chapter is based on a commissioned review (Rakodi 2014) prepared for the World Bank's follow-up to the 2012 World Development Report on *Gender, Equality and Development* (World Bank 2014). Time and language constraints hindered the inclu- sion of non-English language sources. While this influenced the geographical coverage of the report, feedback from researchers working in languages other than English and a range of countries confirmed the main findings.

References

Agarwal, Bina and Panda, Pradeep (2007) Toward freedom from domestic violence: the neglected obvious, *Journal of Human Development*, 8, 3, pp. 359–88.

Angel, S., Brown, E., Dimitrova, D., Ehrenberg, D., Heyes, J., Kusek, P., Marchesi, G., Orozco, V., Smith, L., and Vilchis, E. (2006) *Secure Tenure in Latin America and the Caribbean: Regularization of Informal Settlements in Peru, Mexico and Brazil,*

Princeton, NJ: Princeton University, Woodrow Wilson School of Public and International Affairs www.princeton.edu/research/final_reports/f05wws591g.pdf, accessed 7 June 2013.

Ayalew Ali, Daniel, Collin, M., Deininger, K., Dercon, S., Sandefur, J., and Zeitlin, A. (2014) *The Price of Empowerment: Experimental Evidence on Land Titling in Tanzania*, Washington, DC: Centre for Global Development.

Banerjee, Banashree (2002) Security of tenure in Indian cities, in Durand-Lasserve, Alain and Lauren Royston (eds), *Holding their Ground: Secure Land Tenure for the Urban Poor in Developing Countries*, London: Earthscan, pp. 37–58.

Banerjee, Banashree (2004) Maximising the impact of tenure and infrastructure programmes on housing conditions: the case of slums in Indian cities. Paper presented to the International Conference on Adequate and Affordable Housing, Toronto, 24–27 June.

Baruah, Bipasha (2007) Gendered realities: exploring property ownership and tenancy agreements in urban India, *World Development*, 35, 12, 2096–109.

Besley, Tim and Ghatak, Maitreesh (2010) Property rights and economic development, in Rodrik, Dani and Mark Rosenzweig (eds), *Handbook of Development Economics*, Vol. 5, North-Holland: Elsevier, pp. 4526–95.

Butcher, Sian (2009) Lived experiences of privatization in Lusaka and Cape Town: women and state rental housing. University of Cape Town, Faculty of the Humanities, MA dissertation.

Byamugisha, Frank F.K. (2013) *Securing Africa's Land for Shared Prosperity*, Washington, DC: World Bank.

Calderón, Julio (2004) The formalisation of property in Peru 2001–2002: the case of Lima, *Habitat International*, 28, 2, pp. 289–300.

Chant, Sylvia (2009) The 'feminisation of poverty' in Costa Rica: to what extent a conundrum? *Bulletin of Latin American Research*, 28, 1, pp. 19–44.

Chant, Sylvia (2013) Cities through a 'gender lens': a golden 'urban age' for women in the global South? *Environment and Urbanization*, 25, 9, pp. 9–29.

Chant, Sylvia and McIlwaine, Cathy (1995) *Women of a Lesser Cost: Female Labour, Foreign Exchange and Philippine Development*, London: Pluto.

COHRE (2006) *In Search of Equality: A Survey of Law and Practice Related to Women's Inheritance Rights in the Middle East and North Africa (MENA) Region*, Geneva: Centre on Housing Rights and Evictions.

Datta, Kavita (1995) Strategies for urban survival? Women landlords in Gaborone, Botswana, *Habitat International*, 19, 1, pp. 1–12.

Datta, Namita (2006) Joint titling: a win–win policy? Gender and property rights in urban informal settlements in India, *Feminist Economics*, 12, 1–2, pp. 271–98.

Deere, Carmen Diana, Oduro, A.D., Swaminathan, H., and Doss, C. (2013) Property rights and the gender distribution of wealth in Ecuador, Ghana and India, *Journal of Economic Inequality*, 11, 2, pp. 249–65.

Deininger, Klaus and Feder, Gershon (2009) Land registration, governance, and development: evidence and implications for policy, *World Bank Research Observer*, 24, 2, pp. 233–66.

Deininger, K., Songqing Jin, Nagarajan, H.K., and Fang Xia (2013) Does inheritance law reform improve women's access to capital? Evidence from urban India. Paper presented to the Annual World Bank Conference on Land and Poverty, Washington, DC, 8–11 April. www.irma.ac.in/institute/others/rbi/wp2.pdf, accessed 1 June 2015.

Doss, Cheryl (2013) *Intrahousehold Bargaining and Resource Allocation in Developing Countries*, Washington, DC: World Bank.

Durand-Lasserve, Alain and Selod, Harris (2010) The formalization of urban informal land tenure, in Lall, S.V., Freire, M., Yuen, B., Rajack, R., and Helluin, J.-J. (eds), *Urban Land Markets: Improving Land Management for Successful Urbanization*, Dordrecht: Springer Verlag, pp. 101–32.

Fernandes, Edesio (2011) *Regularisation of Informal Settlements in Latin America*, Washington, DC: Lincoln Institute for Land Policy.

Field, Erica (2004) Property rights, community public goods, and household time allocation in urban squatter communities: evidence from Peru, *William and Mary Law Review*, 45, 3, pp. 837–87.

Field, Erica (2007) Entitled to work: urban property rights and labor supply in Peru, *The Quarterly Journal of Economics*, 122, 4, pp. 1561–602.

Field, Erica and Torero, Maximo (2006) Do property titles increase credit access among the urban poor? Evidence from a nationwide titling program, Harvard University, Department of Economics, mimeo.

Galiani, Sebastian and Schargrodsky, Ernesto (2004) Effects of land titling on child health, *Economics and Human Biology*, 2, pp. 353–72.

Galiani, Sebastian and Schargrodsky, Ernesto (2011) *The Dynamics of Land Titling Regularization and Market Development*, Helsinki: UNU-WIDER.

Gilbert, A. and Varley, A. (1991) *Landlord and Tenant: Housing the Poor in Urban Mexico*, London: Routledge.

Hallward-Driemeier, Mary and Hasan, Tazeen (2013) *Empowering Women: Legal Rights and Economic Opportunities in Africa*, Washington, DC: World Bank, Africa Development Forum.

Joireman, Sandra F. (2013) Securing property rights for women (and men) in Kosovo. Paper presented to the World Bank Conference on Land and Poverty, 8–11 April.

Kalabamu, Faustin T. (2006) Changing gender contract in self-help housing construction in Botswana: the case of Lobatse, in Stifel, D.C., Vanessa Watson, and H. Acselrad (eds), *Dialogues in Urban and Regional Planning*, Vol. 2, London: Routledge.

Kalabamu, Faustin T. (2009) Towards egalitarian inheritance rights in Botswana: the case of Tlokweng, *Development Southern Africa*, 26, 2, pp. 209–23.

Kironde, J.M. Lusagga (2006) Issuing of residential licences to landowners in unplanned settlements in Dar es Salaam, Tanzania. Consultancy report for UN-HABITAT, Shelter Branch, Land and Tenure Section.

Kumar, Sunil (2010) Gender, livelihoods and rental housing markets in the Global South, in Chant, S. (ed.), *The International Handbook of Gender and Poverty*, Cheltenham: Edward Elgar, pp. 367–72.

Larsson, Anita (1989) *Women Householders and Housing Strategies: The Case of Gaborone*, Botswana, Gävle: National Swedish Institute for Building Research.

Leduka, R. Clement (2004) *Informal Land Delivery Processes and Access to Land for the Poor in Maseru, Lesotho*, Birmingham: University of Birmingham.

Loughhead, Susan and Rakodi, Carole (2002) Reducing urban poverty in India: lessons from projects supported by DFID, in Rakodi, Carole with Tony Lloyd-Jones (eds), *Urban Livelihoods: A People-Centred Approach to Reducing Poverty*, London: Earthscan, pp. 225–36.

Marx, Colin and Rubin, Margot (2008) *The Social and Economic Impact of Land Titling in Selected Settlements in Ekurhuleni Metropolitan Area*, Johannesburg: University of the Witwatersrand, Centre for Urban and Built Environment Studies.

Miraftab, Faranak (1998) Complexities of the margin: housing decisions by female householders in Mexico, *Environment and Planning D: Society and Space*, 16, 289–310.

Moser, Caroline (1998) The asset vulnerability framework: reassessing urban poverty reduction strategies, *World Development*, 26, 1, pp. 1–19.

Moser, Caroline (2010) Moving beyond gender and poverty to asset accumulation: Guayaquil, Ecuador, in Chant, Sylvia (ed.), *The International Handbook of Gender and Poverty*, Cheltenham: Edward Elgar, pp. 391–8.

Moser, Caroline and Felton, Andrew (2010) *The Gendered Nature of Asset Accumulation in Urban Contexts: Longitudinal results from Guayaquil, Ecuador*, Helsinki: UNU-WIDER.

Musyoka, Rose (2004) *Informal Land Delivery Processes and Access to Land for the Poor in Eldoret, Kenya*, Birmingham: University of Birmingham.

Ngwira, Naomi (n.d.) *Women's Property and Inheritance Rights and the Land Reform Process in Malawi*, Blantyre: Institute for Policy Research and Analysis for Dialogue for USAID.

Pandey, Shanta (2010) Rising property ownership among women in Kathmandu, Nepal: an exploration of causes and consequences, *International Journal of Social Welfare*, 19, pp. 281–92.

Payne, Geoffrey and Durand-Lasserve, Alain (2013) Holding on: security of tenure – types, policies, practices and challenges. Office of the High Commissioner for Human Rights, research paper commissioned by the Special Rapporteur on the right to an adequate standard of living for an Expert Group Meeting on Security of Tenure, 22–23 October http://direitoamoradia.org/wp-content/uploads/2013/03/Payne-Durand-Lasserve-BackgroundPaper-JAN2013-FINAL-1.pdf, accessed 24 May 2013.

Payne, Geoffrey, Durand-Lasserve, Alain, and Rakodi, Carole (2008) *Social and Economic Impacts of Land Titling Programmes in Urban and Peri-urban Areas: International Experience and Case Studies of Senegal and South Africa*, London: Geoffrey Payne Associates.

Rakodi, Carole (1999) A capital assets framework for analysing household livelihood strategies, *Development Policy Review*, 17, 3, pp. 315–42.

Rakodi, Carole (2006) Social agency and state authority in land delivery processes in African cities: compliance, conflict and cooperation, *International Development Planning Review*, 28, 2, 263–85.

Rakodi, Carole (2010) Gender, poverty and access to land in cities of the South, in Chant, Sylvia (ed.), *The International Handbook of Gender and Poverty*, Cheltenham: Edward Elgar, pp. 353–9.

Rakodi, Carole (2014) *Expanding Women's Access to Land and Housing in Urban Areas*, Washington, DC: World Bank.

Sait, Siraj (2011) Not just another 'custom': Islamic influences on African land laws, in Home, Robert (ed.), *Essays in African Land Law*, Pretoria: Pretoria University Law Press, pp. 91–112.

Sait, Siraj and Lim, Hilary (2006) *Land, Law and Islam: Property and Human Rights in the Muslim World*, Nairobi and London: UN-HABITAT and Zed Books.

Schlyter, Ann (2004a) Gender issues in housing privatization: intricacies of property transfer in Zambia, *Trialog*, 1, pp. 18–23.

Schlyter, Ann (2004b) *Privatisation of Council Housing in Lusaka, Zambia*, London: RICS Foundation.

Stanley, Victoria, Lamb, Tony, and De Martino, Samantha (2012) *Gender and Land Administration: Issues and Responses*, Washington, DC: World Bank. www-wds.

worldbank.org/external/default/WDSContentServer/WDSP/IB/2012/08/07/000333038 _20120807015300/Rendered/PDF/714070BRI0Box30IC00KB530Gender0Land.pdf, accessed 1 June 2015.

UN-HABITAT (2005) *Shared Tenure Options for Women: A Global Overview*, Nairobi: UN-HABITAT.

UN-HABITAT (2007) *Policy Makers' Guide to Women's Land, Property and Housing Rights across the World*, Nairobi: UN-HABITAT.

UN-HABITAT (2011) *A Policy Guide to Rental Housing in Developing Countries*, Nairobi: UN-HABITAT.

UN-HABITAT (2012) *State of Women in Cities 2012–2013: Gender and the Prosperity of Cities*, Nairobi: UN-HABITAT.

van Gelder, Jean-Louis (2013) Then I'll huff, and I'll puff, and I'll … : a natural experiment on property titling, housing improvement and the psychology of tenure security, *International Journal of Urban and Regional Research*, 37, 2, pp. 734–49.

Varley, Ann (2007) Gender and property formalisation: conventional and alternative approaches, *World Development*, 35, 10, pp. 1739–58.

Varley, Ann (2010) Modest expectations: gender and property rights in urban Mexico, *Law and Society Review*, 44, 1, pp. 67–99.

Varley, Ann (2013) Feminist perspectives on urban poverty: de-essentialising difference, in Peake, Linda and Rieker, Martina (eds), *Rethinking Feminist Interventions into the Urban*, London: Taylor and Francis.

Vera-Sanso, Penny (2010) Gender, urban poverty and ageing in India: conceptual and policy issues, in Chant, Sylvia (ed.), *The International Handbook of Gender and Poverty*, Cheltenham: Edward Elgar, pp. 220–5.

Wigle, Jill (2008) Shelter, location and livelihoods: exploring the linkages in Mexico City, *International Planning Studies*, 13, 3, pp. 197–222.

World Bank (2005) *Gender Issues and Best Practices in Land Administration Projects: A Synthesis Report*, Washington, DC: World Bank.

World Bank (2008) *Analysis of the Impact of Land Tenure Certificates with both the Names of Wife and Husband in Vietnam*, Hanoi: World Bank.

World Bank (2014) *Voice and Agency: Empowering Women and Girls for Shared Prosperity*, Washington, DC: World Bank.

World Bank and International Finance Corporation (2014) *Women, Business and the Law 2014: Removing Restrictions to Enhance Gender Equality*, London: Bloomsbury Publishing.

6 The gendered contradictions in South Africa's state housing

Accumulation alongside an undermining of assets through housing

Paula Meth

Introduction

This chapter has two aims. The first is to examine the mass-subsidy housing pro-gramme in South Africa from a gendered perspective, focusing largely, but not exclusively, on particular positive social outcomes of the programme. The second aim is to highlight the ways in which the housing programme is less positive, revealing negative outcomes for residents, some of which are distinctly gendered. As such, the chapter contributes to wider debates on asset accumula-tion by offering an analysis of the contradictions of housing as a gendered asset by examining the lived experiences of housing beneficiaries, in order to support feminist scholarship on the challenges of 'women's access to and control over housing' (Rakodi 2014, 2). Its focus is South Africa where, since the fall of apartheid, the state at the scale of the city has adopted a mix of developmental policies alongside policies that support existing capital, state, and traditional elite interests (Parnell and Robinson 2012). 'Developmental' policies refer to those interventions which are progressive and which focus on universal basic needs and engendering citizen participation, and result in actions which are redistribu-tive (after Parnell and Robinson 2012). This wider policy context includes increasing formal housing supply, implementing welfare policies, improving schooling and health care, and broadening political inclusion, and is actively shaping the urban spaces of South African cities, with the housing programme transforming large swathes of cities, particularly their peripheries. Arguably these developmental interventions contribute to forms of gendered asset accu-mulations, as would be expected from progressive structural change. Recogni-tion of state-led interventions in shaping assets accumulations is important, and contributes to a broadening of the debate beyond bottom-up practices to consoli-date and acquire assets (see Moser in Chapter 1).

The South African mass-subsidised housing programme is the topic of much research (see Cross *et al.* 2013; Zack and Charlton 2003; Tissington 2011; Huchzermeyer 2011) and some of this is discussed below. Despite this research, work exploring the social outcomes or the lived experiences of 'delivered housing' is relatively patchy but growing (see Charlton 2014). Furthermore, there is limited work on the gendered outcomes of state housing per se (although see Chenwi and McLean 2009 on gender and housing inadequacy). However, research by Charlton (2004, 2014), Venter and Marais (2006), and myself (Meth 2014b) provides evidence that receiving a home is very positive for many women, but that negative outcomes are evident too. It is these contradictory outcomes that form the focus of this chapter.

The chapter briefly outlines the mass-subsidised housing programme in South Africa before analysing at the micro-scale the home and the gains and losses of the housing programme, including those which are gendered. It concludes by considering how the housing programme can contribute to gendered asset accumulation through social changes in particular, as well as exploring the implications of the analysis for the production of a transformative and just city.

The mass housing programme in South Africa: context and outcomes

Since 1994 the South African state's mass housing programme has provided just over three million Reconstruction and Development Programme (RDP, a colloquial term for state housing) formal houses to low-income residents. Many of these beneficiaries were previously living in informal settlements. In some cases, such as Cato Crest in Durban, formal housing was built on site, following the removal of informal housing. More commonly, this new state housing is built on greenfield land, often on the peripheries of South African cities. House size has shifted over the course of the programme, from its original intention of providing a starter home including the site and basic services with a small house (Charlton and Kihato 2006), to a subsequent 30 m² then 40 m² as the minimum for the gross floor area. This upper limit was stipulated in the 2007 revision to the National Norms and Standards of the Housing Act (Tissington 2011) and includes two bedrooms, a separate bathroom, and combined kitchen and living area. This shift was in response to criticism about the small-sized housing being delivered by the post-apartheid state, with direct unfavourable comparisons made with housing delivered during the apartheid era (Charlton and Kihato 2006, 267). Housing designs are generally standardised: detached and single storey. There are variations, sometimes determined by regional topographical requirements, but also in response to local design innovations.

To qualify for this housing benefit, beneficiaries must be South African citizens or have a Permanent Residency Permit, they must be over the age of 21, be married or have financial dependants, and earn between zero and 3,500 rand per month (Tissington 2011, 22–3). These criteria (particularly the requirement for dependants and the earnings limit) have enhanced the likelihood of women gaining access to housing and the ownership of a key asset. Indeed, Pieterse (2014) claims that more than 50 per cent of these houses have gone to female beneficiaries. Housing gained under this programme is subject to specific regulations around resale, and beneficiaries are not permitted to sell their houses within eight years of acquisition. This limits the use of this housing asset for financial gain in the medium term, although there is evidence of illegal sale and purchase of state housing, with mixed outcomes for beneficiaries in terms of sale prices achieved (see Tissington 2011).

The capacity to extend the house for either personal use or to provide for rental is mixed. Beneficiaries of new housing have pointed to the costs of home ownership, which preclude extending their homes (see Charlton and Kihato 2006; Tissington 2011). Furthermore, settlements with new formal housing are subject to planning regulations for extensions, which illegalise informal extensions (such as backyard shacks) or present prohibitive costs. Informal acceptance or outright rejection of informal extensions by urban authorities varies geographically.

This brief overview of South Africa's mass housing programme suggests that asset accumulation for the poor has been achieved through a structural national intervention, although debates continue over the contribution of such an asset to poverty-reduction (see Charlton and Kihato 2006; Tissington 2011; Cross *et al.* 2013). Nonetheless, housing ministers emphasise both the quantitative achievements as well as the wider impacts of this programme on beneficiaries:

> Through the national subsidy scheme we have housed around 11 million people since 1994.... We have ... made an enormous difference to the lives of those families who now live in their own properties, receive services and have access to social and economic amenities.
>
> (Kota-Fredericks 2013)

The state has consistently focused on the production of 'decent' housing for poor residents. Their original mission incorporated a clear agenda for social change, reinforced by Kota-Fredericks' claims above: '[We must] create a country where slums are eradicated and in their place, decent, secure communities are created where our children can grow up in dignity' (Sisulu 2008).

The housing programme: social outcomes and a gendered analysis

The social changes of the housing programme loosely outlined by these ministers, be they amenities, creation of communities, or the enhancement of dignity are of central importance to this chapter as they point to the accumulation of outcomes which are more than 'bricks and mortar' (as expressed by the South African Constitutional Court cited in Tissington 2011, 27). In examining the experiences of men and women of the housing programme, this chapter uses its empirical material to focus primarily on certain social outcomes in relation to asset accumulation, but also briefly considers material and economic outcomes. Social outcomes, in line with those spelled out above, are those which relate to society more broadly, and include health and well-being, community, welfare, education, relationships, and safety. This chapter focuses specifically on social outcomes relating to family relations, identity formation, as well as interpersonal violence.

As the aim of the chapter is to examine the gendered dimensions of beneficiaries' experiences, before turning to a clarification of methods, it discusses the focus on gender adopted. The uneven relationship between men and women is a central concern and, where feasible, it explores both their experiences of the housing intervention, bearing in mind the locus of the house as a predominantly female space. In doing so, the chapter also examines the role of a (new) home for men, and how this change in housing shapes their sense of identity and self-worth. This recognises that for many men the ideal of daily employment beyond the home is not met, forcing them to spend long periods of time around the home or in the neighbourhood (Meth 2014a). Based on a review of the available literature, however, there is no particular evidence on the accumulative or undermining impacts of the housing programme on men in particular. This is a notable absence, and this chapter begins to address this below, but ultimately focuses more on women's experiences. More substantive empirical work on men's experiences is required to strengthen such an analysis and the subsequent discussion of methodology points to the partial evidence gained on this matter.

Methodology and case study: Cato Crest

This chapter draws on findings from several sources, including empirical and secondary. With regard to the former, five related but distinct projects have been conducted in Cato Crest between 2001 and 2013 focusing on the following themes: women's experiences of violence; men living informally and violence; governance in a formalising settlement; parenting and formalisation; and domestic violence and housing. All projects adopted a qualitative approach variously employing mixed methods: diaries, interviews, focus groups, photography, and some drawing with men and women living in this settlement (Meth 2003; Meth and McClymont 2009). This chapter is informed by data from all these projects but draws specifically on the two most recent (both of which were pilot projects), which between them carried out six focus groups with men and women (five residents per group), two interviews with local police, an interview with the Area Committee, a representative of Durban Municipal Housing, and a regional housing representative based in Pietermaritzburg. Most of the data were collected by Zulu-speaking researchers, conducted in Zulu, and later translated into English. This chapter also draws on other sources on Cato Crest, as well as studies across South Africa to produce a broader insight into housing as a gendered asset.

The particular neighbourhood of Cato Crest is part of the wider Cato Manor settlement, in the city of Durban, a large city on the east coast of South Africa. Located within 7 km of the city centre, the area was originally an Indian residential area (with some African residents) until apartheid policies of segregation forcibly removed all Indians and Africans from the area in the 1960s and 1970s. In the 1980s, as apartheid was crumbling and the urbanisation of Africans to cities was rapidly rising, Cato Manor became informally settled, with residents self-building shacks constructed from basic materials such as wood, mud, and scrap metal. The area was also a popular choice owing to its good location in relation to wealthier parts of the city of Durban, which for many presented employment opportunities. Since the late 1990s, this site was earmarked as a massive redevelopment programme, of which the mass housing programme was part. Redevelopment has been slow, and is ongoing with areas of shack housing still evident in Cato Crest in 2015, but with gradual formalisation occurring. Formal houses are usually detached, but some semi-detached were experimented with.

For men and women living in Cato Crest, the overall assessment is that accessing formal housing has meant gaining the asset of a home – both a physical and financial asset. But such asset accumulation has also been accompanied by the potential for their benefits to be undermined by the various challenges of this housing programme (poor quality, new costs, etc.), as well as wider structural and cultural inequalities. In turning to a specific analysis of the gendered experiences of asset accumulation through housing, this chapter first identifies the positive experiences and then turns to the contradictory outcomes.

Positive experiences of gendered accumulation of housing

The acquisition of a house for individuals and their families represents the accumulation of an asset. This asset has economic, social, and material value for the owner and occupants. The production of a settlement consisting of owner-occupied housing has had significant benefits for many women. Importantly, the scale of the housing programme has meant that high proportions of women have gained access to and ownership of a formal state house. This is likely to be particularly beneficial for female-headed households who were a dominant household category in Cato Crest prior to formalisation. As detailed earlier, South African Housing Ministers have emphasised the social gains they hope to see arise out of the housing programme. Specific social outcomes include improvements in safety and security, gains in privacy, reductions in domestic tension and violence, and re-defined identities. These are significant in shaping an accumulation of gendered assets despite being relatively intangible and, at times, contradictory.

Safety and security

The impact of the housing programme on experiences of crime is generally positive, but is also mixed. In Cato Crest, crime certainly appeared to have been reduced as a consequence of housing formalisation, although explanations were complex. Home ownership positively affects community knowledge and residents explained that knowing who lives in particular houses meant that they could check for criminals trying to enter and hide in the area; this was impossible in the former shack settlement as 'people who were renting keep changing and we saw new faces all the time' (Bolina, female focus group 2011). This knowledge also related to the labelling of the housing. Male residents explained that because the new houses had numbers on them 'if we saw the criminals we are able to tell the police which house is for the criminal' (Bongani, male focus group 2011).

> The development comes with change, in term of crime it is decrease. At *mjondolo*[1] people come and look [to rent] shacks and we don't know where that person is coming from and also the reason to move to Cato Crest. The crime was increasing because some people were the criminals and coming to hide at Cato Crest. In the RDP houses we know all neighbours and even a person who's visiting a neighbour is easy to know.
>
> (Didiza, male focus group 2 2013)

Improved legibility was also a function of house spacing, with defined mobility spaces and lighting making it easier to spot criminals: 'We have got the street light, even the passages are clear to walk [along], even at night ... there is no place for criminals to hide. All people who live in this area belong to this area' (female focus group 2011).

The de-densification and orderliness of the settlement also positively affected crime. In Cato Crest around 500 shacks were replaced by 200 houses, meaning that around 300 households were not rehoused in the same area because of additional space requirements associated with formalisation (roads, footpaths, etc.) (interview with housing manager, Durban, 2011). De-densification reduced the number of residents living in the settlement and, since in principle only those officially allocated housing were able to access the housing, residents felt greater confidence in the more-controlled nature of residential habitation: 'The houses are for the families now not criminals' (female focus group 1, 2013).

Privacy, decency, and domestic violence

The empirical evidence illustrates a relationship between an improved living space and a reduction in domestic violence, hence the accumulation of housing as an asset does indeed intersect with an accumulation of other assets, specifically freedom from violence. Through an analysis of everyday stories of socialising, cleaning, living, and sleeping, it is clear that gains in privacy were significant, and that these impacted on men and women's abilities to live and perform 'decency' because of their access to a bigger or differently laid out home.

> There is privacy because there is a bedroom for the parents and bedroom for the children. People are less stressed in [these] houses because there is a kitchen for cooking and place for sleeping. The small space creates violence.
>
> (Interview Area Committee 2013)

> Yes the new houses decrease the domestic violence.... In the informal settlement if the relatives want to visit, [it] was creating problems as

everything was in one room. If my partner wants to bath the relative have to go outside until my partner is finished dressing. Another example, if the pastor of my church visit [he] has a place to sit, in the informal settlement the pastor sit together with me on my bed and people interpret wrong and create violence.

(Siyanda, female focus group 2 2013)

Significant spatial gains were acquired, with legible divisions of space contributing to privacy and residents' ability to live decently. The size of housing (mostly around 40 m^2) meant less tension is produced through daily living: '[M]ore allegations of domestic violence [are from] the people still living at *mjondolo* and at transit [camps] because [these] are crowded and have small space' (Interview Area Committee 2013).

Positive impact on parenting and identity

Housing security, and ownership, were revealed to be significant for men's and women's identities and also their experiences of parenting. All residents discussed the challenges of living informally for raising a family, both in terms of practical issues such as protecting children from the elements, but also in terms of the social challenges of living informally relating to crime.

I do have my room to think with my problem while the children have their own room to make noise. We have space for cooking and the children [are] able to ... study in their room. If I'm thinking back in the informal settlement it was difficult if the rain comes we were sleeping in one bed with girls and boys because we did not have the space. I appreciate what government did to us.

(Siyanda, female focus group 1 2013)

As a parent I feel happy now ... there is a big difference, we smell the fresh air not that smell of the toilet, rubbish and mud. The sickness is decreased especially TB ... you can clean and stay clean.

(Nester, female focus group 2011)

Previous research with residents who lived informally (Meth, 2009) emphasised the negative emotions residents attached to living in informal conditions. A repeated concern was that it was the equivalent to living like an animal and this affected residents' sense of self-worth, their identity and their association with non-informal residents. These concerns shaped residents' abilities to engage with their wider family, particularly relatives who lived away from the informal settlement and who were suspicious or negative about such an environment. Residents now described feelings of relief and joy at being able to host relatives in dignity: 'My status has changed now I feel less stressed ... my sister [used to describe my shack as] the place of the animals not for the person who is alive.

My status is changed because of the new house' (Fikile, female focus group 2011).

Men's stories and concerns about living in their informal homes in Cato Crest also directly contributed to their feelings of marginalisation (Meth 2009). In 2011 men who had received houses claimed that it was much easier to be a parent in their new house. They felt that it was hard to get their children to listen in the shack settlements because 'we were living with good and bad people and it was crowded, children were getting confused by different people' (Felokwa-khe, male focus group 2011). Bongani reinforced the positive impacts on their identity since the housing change: 'the status has changed. People who looked down on us, they asked now to come and find them the place to live' (Bongani, male focus group 2011).

Thus, it is evident that a number of significant positive social changes occurred for residents living in new state housing. These changes have produced gendered asset accumulations across concerns such as safety and security, to privacy and domestic violence as well as residents' identities, particularly as parents. These gains are returned to later in this chapter as their role in shaping a more just and transformed city is considered. These asset accumulations are important and must not be sidelined in policy critiques. They contribute to some elements of Moser's (1989) criteria regarding gender planning, which considers practical versus strategic gender needs. Arguably, many of the positives outlined above satisfy practical gender needs (basic needs for shelter and security) but some also contribute to meeting strategic gender needs. These might be through the entitlement of women to a housing asset which affords them legal and finan-cial security, but also arguably to the improvement of poor men's and women's status within the wider city, as they shift from 'feeling like animals' to home-owners or citizens. Gendered identities in this sense have been redefined, both between men and women, but also between residents within this settlement in contrast to those of the wider city.

Despite this, the provision of formal housing also raises a number of other contradictory outcomes, and these are discussed in order to illustrate the ways in which accumulated assets can also be undermined.

Downsides: the undermining of accumulated assets

The receipt, occupation, and use of formal housing can simultaneously work to negatively impact on women in particular, but at times, both men and women. This relates to housing construction quality, location, cost, as well as impacts on social processes, such as the rise of different forms of violence over the receipt of assets, and community decline as a result of the housing asset.

Poor construction and the limitations of an incremental build

Poor construction quality of new housing is well documented in South Africa (Zack and Charlton 2003; Charlton and Kihato 2006; Tissington 2011) and invariably challenges residents who cannot finance repairs. Residents in Cato Crest pointed to poorly built window casements, doors, and cracked walls and floors. Furthermore, various houses were incomplete, with services still not connected (including water and electricity) despite houses being occupied by beneficiaries. Poor quality was blamed on poorly skilled contractors as well as corrupt practices within the building sector. More broadly, the notion of providing a starter home whereby residents incrementally build and transform their house was problematic for women in particular. Venter and Marais (2006) explain that women lacked the funding as well as the skills to build their own houses and to extend or repair as necessary: 'the physical attributes and flaws of the low-income houses are more severely and negatively experienced by respondents from female-headed households' (2006, 77). None of the residents interviewed in Cato Crest had extended their houses due to lack of financial resources, prohibiting the purchase of building materials and the payment of formal planning applications.

Location

The positive location of Cato Crest was emphasised earlier as the reason for its rapid settlement in the late 1980s and onwards. Residents remarked on this benefit and although valuations were not available, it is highly likely that Cato Crest's location will in the future positively impact on the financial value of the housing asset, bearing in mind the prevention of sale by law for the first eight years of occupation. This benefit is, however, atypical, as the vast majority of houses delivered under this programme are on poorly located sites, often on the edge of African townships, which themselves are located on cities' peripheries. This spatial marginalisation has thus resulted in multiple complaints and critiques of residents' inaccessibility to jobs and services and the difficulties of poor and costly transportation links (Charlton 2004, 11; Tissington 2011).

There is limited research on the gendered significance of poor location in South Africa, although Cross *et al.* (2013) offer a detailed investigation of the links between location, city 'shape', and the capacity for housing to act as a poverty reduction measure. Questions of location are highly complex and seemingly intractable, challenged by stubborn housing markets, land prices, and poor transportation links, but point to the significance of what might be termed 'spatial assets' which can be undermined by such factors.

Livelihoods

Related to the issue of location, the evidence on whether the housing programme positively or negatively impacts on livelihoods is very mixed, and depends on a range of factors, often at the scale of the individual household. Potential impacts on livelihoods relate to a range of 'financial capital assets', including wages, income from rentals, and business activities. Arguably there is a connection between poor location and difficulties of securing a livelihood (Cross *et al.* 2013,

243, 244) simply due to a lack of market and poor access to goods and services, and employment more generally. For some, however, livelihoods have been positively enhanced through the housing programme as access to electricity allows residents to expand their informal trading practices. The impact on livelihoods is critical for women who suffer from far higher rates of unemployment and are more dependent on informal employment, often located close to the home environment because of child-caring responsibilities. The new housing also has cost implications for water and electricity, which residents struggle to fund. The poor feasibility and inflexibility of residents' plots and homes to facilitate livelihoods practices, a critical natural asset, compounds these costs. This relates to the size, relative location, and material adaptability of home, as well as local restrictions on informal economic practices. In Cato Crest, women identified builders' rubble as a barrier to subsistence gardening.

Moving from the micro-scale of the home to the broader-scale national perspective, an evaluation of the impact of the housing programme on livelihoods requires consideration of the relationship between new housing and poverty reduction – and the evidence in relation to this is mixed. Work by Cross *et al.* (2013), Charlton and Kihato (2006), and Tissington (2011) appears to conclude somewhat negatively on this matter: 'Housing delivery has had a limited impact on poverty alleviation and houses have not become the financial, social and economic assets as envisioned in the early 1990s' (Tissington 2011, 61). This particular outcome requires continued detailed analysis. The capacity for the housing programme to achieve poverty reduction is hampered by its lack of integration with other national policies, employment in particular.

Tensions over competing claims to assets

The housing offer from the state is a one-off subsidy, which residents can claim once in their lives. Female beneficiaries have received more than 50 per cent of state houses (Pieterse, 2014). These facts, alongside extensive waiting times (ten years and upwards) shape the attitudes of those who are waiting for a house, or who do not qualify or meet the criteria. Research in 2013 revealed that a number of women were now reporting new forms of violence (usually from male relatives) who were claiming ownership of the woman's new housing asset. This signifies a direct undermining of a gendered asset accumulation. Women do not necessarily lose their homes (the housing asset), but rather they suffer violence:

> The violence I experience now is that my brother beat my daughter.... The house I received in 2005 I gave it to my mother because that time I was not married.... My brother beat my mother because he wants to take the house. When my mother passed away, the house was left with my daughter and he starts to beat my daughter and he said the house is for his mother. The case is in the court.
>
> (Lethiwe, female focus group 1 2013)

In this case, resentment over the provision of a house to a woman has led to violence from her brother; other cases point to violence from sons and other male relatives. Research at this stage is preliminary, but the evidence invariably raises questions about the nature of the allocation process as well as the procedures around beneficiary suitability and criteria satisfaction. Clearly there is a shortage of suitable and affordable housing in the area, irresolvable through the housing programme. This reality fosters tension. Indeed, Bähre (2007), in an exploration of the ways in which conflict and violence are at the heart of urban development in South Africa, argues that 'development cannot be expected to take place within, or create, a parallel universe in which violence is not crucial' (2007, 99) and he points to 'fierce struggles over resources ... [as being] ... at the core of development in South Africa' (2007, 99). The evidence here reveals that this needs to be understood in gendered terms.

Changing household composition may also shape these particular tensions over new assets. Patel (2012, 112), in relation to a case study in Gauteng (Doornkop, Soweto), argues that around 49 per cent of surveyed households were composed of woman caregivers with children and extended family all living in the same space. Patel explains, beyond her case study, that nuclear and single-parent households appear to have decreased and that this trend towards households with single parents and other relatives is increasing (Patel, 2012, 112 after Bureau for Market Research [BMR] 2007). BMR (2007 cited in Patel 2012, 112) suggest that this might be caused by a need to pool resources and to share care responsibilities. Whatever the reasons, the impact of these housing compositions on tensions over housing assets is an area for further investigation, including the identification of its gendered nature.

Injustices can be 'hidden' by new housing

Injustices against women can by hidden by their new housing due to the material changes of formal housing. The building materials of concrete blocks and the individual plot layout produces housing that is more soundproof, private, and separate from neighbouring houses and can be celebrated as a form of physical capital, an asset. Arguably, domestic violence is less evident in such a material space and is thus hidden through better built form. Thus, formal housing has the capacity to reinforce the silences of domestic violence. This finding is not absolute, as various residents complained about the fact that they can still hear their neighbours, but many participants pointed to the ways in which formal housing means there is less likelihood of neighbours attending to a domestic violence incidence: 'If there is misunderstanding for partners in the house they close the room and talk not in front of the children, and neighbours will not hear anything' (Nothando, female focus group 2 2013).

Women were now dependent on neighbours asking for help, as they no longer knew what was happening within the formal houses. Support was not available for those who remained within their homes during and following times of violence.

This finding does not point to the erosion of housing as a gendered asset; rather it points to the complex ways in which a gendered asset can be undermined during the lived experience of that asset. The finding of women's heightened vulnerability to violence and potential loss of neighbourly support does not critique the housing programme, but rather critiques society and its structures of patriarchy and inequality that allow gender violence to persist. It is relevant to the housing programme, however, because the provision of formal housing was assumed to impact positively on social processes including safety and community relations, as specified by housing ministers. Such positive social outcomes arguably require effective integration between various government interventions (including crime and justice, policing, employment, and social welfare) in order for structural changes to lead to transformation.

Declining communal bonds

Injustices within homes can also be hidden by declining communal practices. With the receipt of formal housing, there is evidence of subsequent changes to notions of community and residents' senses of responsibility in relation to their fellow neighbours. Living informally, where life is desperate, can mean that communal ties are necessarily very strong, forged through shared experiences of daily challenges, and this is certainly how residents of Cato Crest now describe their former communities of informal residencies. This point must not be over-romanticised. There is ample evidence of the neighbourly tensions present in squatter settlements, often as a result of poverty and crime, shaping mistrust and a lack of cohesion. Nonetheless, residents' comments in the newly upgraded Cato Crest provide evidence of communal change. Prior to formalisation, in situations of domestic violence neighbours often responded and assisted where feasible. This has changed:

> It is changed because at *mjondolo* people were crowded and if anything happen was easy to spread to everybody. In the RDP house a person [will only] know your story [if] you go to that particular person and discuss. If you are sitting in your [RDP house] no one will know your problems.
>
> (Babavana female focus group 2 2013)

This shift is partly a function of spatial changes (more privacy, more soundproofing, less communal ways of living) but may also prove to be a function of social changes to ideas of community that ally living 'decently' with more individualistic styles of living. In the past residents relied heavily on their neighbours for food, advice, and support in times of crisis (including protection): 'we were very close with neighbours while we were living in the *mjondolo* and now that united-as-neighbours [has] disappeared.... We are not sharing food and talking as we do at *mjondolo*' (Lethiwe, female focus group 2 2013).

This communal shift supports the argument of Davy and Pellissery that 'the everyday social contract of informality forges a bond between the members of a local community that cannot be replaced by formalisation easily' (Davy and Pellissery 2013, s80–1). Arguably, such communal ties take time to develop, and Cato Crest has certainly not been communally coherent since the first land invasions in the late 1980s. But it raises questions about what replaces the particular social contracts of informality. Again this evidence is not a critique of the housing programme, rather it points to intangible outcomes of the housing intervention which work to undermine some of the benefits gained through the housing asset.

The housing programme, integration, and the accumulation of gendered assets

The discussion above points to a number of contradictory outcomes of the housing programme which are directly and indirectly government-driven. Bearing in mind the relative rarity of the significant rise in ownership and shelter for millions of women in particular, the capacity for such a programme to positively build gendered assets through housing is now considered, focusing in particular on the idea of integration before turning to an examination of how these gendered assets contribute to both enhancing but also undermining goals for a just city.

The housing programme in South Africa was explicitly intended to reduce poverty and contribute towards socio-economic change (Charlton and Kihato 2006, 256), including building communities, fostering decency, improving safety and so on. Such aims were embedded in policy rhetoric and some were articulated in terms of gender in the early specifications of the housing programme as well as in subsequent reviews of the housing programme (see also the commissioned Council for Scientific and Industrial Research [CSIR] report in 2003). The need to 'support the role of women in the housing delivery process' was identified in the white paper on housing (Venter and Marais 2006, 72 after Republic of South Africa, 1994, 21) and '[f]rom a gender perspective, it seems as if the housing policy, with its subsidy scheme objectives, promotes gender equality – no policy-related obstacle prevents women from becoming homeowners' (Venter and Marais 2006, 72). Yet despite these commitments to gender equality, the actual implementation of the housing programme has not benefited substantially from a gender agenda: '[a]n evaluation of the housing subsidy scheme indicated that housing policy directives specifically focusing on gender equity are largely neglected in most provinces' (Venter and Marais 2006, 72 after Public Service Commission, 2003, 58). Furthermore, Charlton (2004) notes that housing policy has concentrated on women's involvement in housing construction, not occupation; policy has failed to appreciate wider legal and social inequities between men and women which might shape women's control over the housing asset, the specific needs of vulnerable abused women are not championed, and the policy does not address gender concerns after the subsidy has been allocated (Charlton 2004: 18–19). Furthermore, an additional concern is the failure to provide housing for women under the age of 21 with dependants, given that they arguably account for half of all pregnancies (Venter and Marais 2006,

72 after Parnell, cited in Marx 2003). Despite these concerns, it is evident that housing delivery has yielded progressive outcomes for many women, but arguably achieving more transformative social changes through what is effectively a singular or sectoral programme of intervention requires integration with other interventions.

The housing programme's capacity to meet wider social goals is hampered by the poor integration of the housing programme with other socio-economic programmes, particularly employment creation, and safety and security initiatives. Furthermore, despite the rhetoric, the housing programme has not been produced or enabled through participation (neither communal nor political) (Cross *et al.* 2013, 243). The challenges of producing integrated settlements is recognised more widely within reviews of the housing scheme at the national level (see Charlton 2004, 13), where despite clear policy commitments to integration, the outcomes are argued to be 'partial' (Venter and Marais 2006, 77). On the ground, housing managers responsible for delivering the national programme also struggle with meeting social outcomes. Here, a housing manager in Msunduzi explains that national government rhetoric is not matched in delivery:

> Most of the things which the national government talks about are not happening at the lower level because of the funds.... It is nice to do the speeches and the policy but the money to do this is not available.
>
> (Interview with Msunduzi Housing Officer 2011)

Substantive social changes are not deliverable through a housing programme alone, as despite contributing to gendered asset accumulations, the programme is unable to counter the simultaneous undermining of these assets.

Forging urban transformation and just cities

There is widespread disagreement over the extent to which the South African state is achieving just outcomes though its policy measures. Parnell and Robinson (2012) point to the dramatic increase in the post-1994 era of social safety nets in South Africa, supporting Surender's observations of a wider shift to pro-poor policy instruments (including micro-financing, conditional cash transfers, social pensions, and public works programmes) across many developing countries (Surender 2013). Parnell and Robinson claim that 'South African cities, notoriously unequal places, are fairer now than 20 years ago because of this policy position' (Parnell and Robinson 2012, 604). This chapter argues that the housing programme is arguably key to this reduction in inequality, and importantly that these urban development and welfare programmes are producing social and spatial justice across South African cities. Despite Tissington's cautionary analysis of the failed impact of the housing programme on poverty reduction (2011), South African cities are visibly transformed, as large areas of formerly squatter settlements have been replaced with safe, durable, valuable, legally secure housing.

This insight is critical for accounting for some of the gender gains outlined earlier, evidence of gendered asset accumulation through structurally directed change. But it must also be understood alongside everyday experiences of urban change, at the micro-scale, especially when these are contradictory, recognising that the impacts of the accumulation of housing as an asset may indeed be limited.

Although South Africa has experienced a reduction in extreme poverty (through these welfare programmes), unemployment levels have largely remained static (Meth, personal communication 2014) and indeed are highly gendered. Patel argues that 'the unemployment rate was 39 per cent for women and 22 per cent for men based on recent national data' (Patel 2012, 107 after Ranchod 2010) and that the poverty share for African women has actually risen over the 15-year period from 1993 to 2008. This critical work highlights the differentiated nature of current poverty levels in South Africa, and points very clearly to the challenges facing urban African women. These persisting inequalities undermine transformative efforts.

Conclusion

This chapter has argued that a gendered analysis, sensitive to men's experiences as well as a focus on the home, contributes to a complex interrogation of housing as a gendered asset. Examining the contradictory outcomes of progressive interventions for the urban poor (including women), it raises questions about the capacity for the state to achieve particular social goals through its housing programme and points to the ways in which gendered assets can be simultaneously accumulated but also undermined. Access to shelter and security of tenure are critical gendered assets, yet the ability to secure a livelihood, live in safety, and to thrive requires wider interventions, beyond the scope of the housing programme. This recognition of the contradictory nature of gendered assets points to the challenges of achieving practical alongside strategic gender needs (Moser 1989), invariably requiring wide-scale gender equity informed by political-economic equality.

There is a need thus to theorise the intersection of these urban development programmes with the wider failure to reduce poverty alongside the persistence of patriarchal violence because these are intimately interconnected and their co-production or at least co-continuance must be understood. Analyses of hidden injustices can be productively explored through an engagement with wider socio-political changes, even when these are theorised as 'progressive' (cf. Parnell and Robinson 2012) and it is evident that these wider developmental interventions struggle to challenge entrenched cultural notions of gendered inequality.

Acknowledgement

I would like to thank both Dr Tamlynn Fleetwood and Mrs Sibongile Buthelezi for RA work in Durban, SA (pilot project), which took place in June/July 2013, as well as work conducted by Mrs Buthelezi in March 2011.

Note

1 Local term for a shack house.

References

Bähre, E. (2007). Beyond Legibility: Violence, Conflict and Development in a South African Township, *African Studies*, vol. 66: 1, pp. 79–102.

Bureau for Market Research (BMR) (2007). Population and household projections for South Africa by province and population group, 2001–2021. Research report no. 364. Bureau for Market Research, UNISA, Pretoria, South Africa.

Charlton, Sarah (2004). An Overview of the Housing Policy and Debates, Particularly in Relation to Women (or Vulnerable Groupings). Research report written for the Centre for the Study of Violence and Reconciliation.

Charlton, Sarah (2014). State Ambitions and People's Practices: An Exploration of RDP Housing in Johannesburg. Doctoral thesis, University of Sheffield and Wits.

Charlton, S. and Kihato, C. (2006). Reaching the Poor: An Analysis of the Influences on the Evolution of South Africa's Housing Programme. In Udesh Pillay *et al.* (eds), *Democracy and Delivery: Urban Policy in South Africa*, Cape Town, HSRC Press.

Chenwi, Lilian and McLean, Kirsty (2009). 'A Woman's Home is Her Castle?' Poor Women and Housing Inadequacy in South Africa, *South African Journal on Human Rights*, vol. 25: 3, pp. 517–45.

Cross, C., Nyamnjoh, F., Jansen, J., Hagg, G., and Pillay, U. (2013). Delivering Human Settlements as an Anti-poverty Strategy: Spatial Paradigms. In *State of the Nation: South Africa: 2012–2013*, Pretoria, HSRC.

CSIR (2003). Integrating Gender in Housing and Human Settlements. Report for the National Department of Housing.

Davy, B. and Pellisery, S. (2013). The Citizenship Promise (Un)fulfilled: The Right to Housing in Informal Settings, *International Journal of Social Welfare*, vol. 22: S1, pp. S68–S84.

Huchzermeyer, M. (2011). *Cities with Slums: From Informal Settlement Eradication to a Right to the City in Africa*, Claremont, UCT Press.

Kota-Fredericks, Zou (2013). National Informal Settlement Upgrading Summit, 2 July, Keynote Address by Ms Zou Kota-Fredericks, Deputy Minister of Human Settlements, www.dhs.gov.za/uploads/DM_Address_National_Upgrading_Summit.pdf, accessed 18 July 2013.

Meth, P. (2003). Entries and Omissions: Using Solicited Diaries in Geographical Research, *Area*, vol. 35: 2, pp. 195–205.

Meth, P. (2009). Marginalised Emotions: Men, Emotions, Politics and Place, *Geoforum*, vol. 40: 5, pp. 853–63.

Meth, P. (2014a). Violence and Men in Urban South Africa: The Significance of Home. In Gorman-Murray, A. and Hopkins, P. (eds), *Masculinities and Place*, Farnham, Ashgate.

Meth, P. (2014b). Producing 'Decent' Cities: Gender and Urban Upgrading. Seminar at UCT (ACC and Geography), March 2014.

Meth, P. and McClymont, K. (2009). Researching Men: The Politics and Possibilities of a Qualitative Mixed Methods Approach, *Social and Cultural Geography*, vol. 10: 8, pp. 909–25.

Moser, Caroline (1989). Gender Planning in the Third World: Meeting Practical and Strategic Gender Needs, *World Development*, vol. 17: 11, pp. 1799–825.

Parnell, Susan and Robinson, Jennifer (2012). (Re)Theorizing Cities from the Global South: Looking Beyond Neoliberalism, *Urban Geography*, vol. 33: 4, pp. 593–617.

Patel, Leila (2012) Poverty, Gender and Social Protection: Child Support Grants in Soweto, South Africa, *Journal of Policy Practice*, vol. 11: 1–2, pp. 106–20.

Pieterse, E. (2014). The Case of South Africa. In Moser, C. and Stein, A. (eds), *New Formal Housing Policies: Building Just Cities?* Briefing paper for the networking event World Urban Forum (WUF7).

Rakodi, Carole (2014). *Expanding Women's Access to Land and Housing in Urban Areas*, Washington, DC: World Bank.

Ranchod, V. (2010). Labour Force Participation and Employment in South Africa: Evidence from Wave 1 of the National Income Dynamics Study, *Journal for Studies in Economics and Econometrics*, vol. 34: 3, pp. 111–27.

Sisulu, L. (2008). Speech by the Minister of Housing at the occasion of tabling of the budget vote for the Department of Housing for the financial year 2008/09, http://lowcosthousing.blogspot.com/2008/06/l-sisulu-housing-dept-budget-vote.html, accessed 18 July 2011.

Surender, R. (2013). The Role of Historical Contexts in Shaping Social Policy in the Global South. In Surender, R. and Walker, R. (eds), *Social Policy in a Developing World*, Cheltenham, Edward Elgar.

Tissington, K. (2011). A Resource Guide to Housing in South Africa 1994–2010: Legislation, Policy, Programmes and Practice. SERI, Socio-economic Rights Institute of South Africa.

Venter, Anita and Marais, Lochner (2006). Gender and Housing Policy in South Africa: Policy and Practice in Bloemfontein, *Journal of Family Ecology and Consumer Sciences*, vol. 34, n.p.

Zack, T. and Charlton, S. (2003). Better Off But … Beneficiaries' Perceptions of the Government's Housing Subsidy Scheme. Housing Finance Resource Programme, occasional paper 12.

7 'The devil is in the detail'

Understanding how housing assets contribute to gender-just cities

Beth Chitekwe-Biti and Diana Mitlin

Introduction

Over one billion people live in informal settlements in towns and cities of the Global South. Many of them are women and many of them are living in unsafe and insecure housing. Finding new options that are effective at scale for these populations is central to addressing the challenge of achieving gender-just cities. This chapter reflects on the experiences of one social movement seeking to support such a transformation, namely Shack/Slum Dwellers International (SDI). It elaborates on SDI's goals and introduces their work to address the interests and needs of some of the most vulnerable and disadvantaged urban citizens. It elaborates on the evolution of their strategies as some of the first attempts to secure gender justice proved limited, particularly in relation to getting to scale. To illustrate the experiences, we describe and analyse events in Zimbabwe, where the partnership of the Zimbabwe Homeless People's Federation and Dialogue on Shelter (referred to below as the Zimbabwe Alliance) is actively taking up and using SDI approaches.

SDI is a transnational network of homeless and landless people's federations set up to 1996 to 'unite and empower the urban poor to articulate their own aspirations for change and develop their capacity, from the local to the global, to become critical women-led actors in the transformation of their cities'.[1] SDI is currently working with grassroots organisations in over 30 countries in the Global South and activities primarily focus on informal settlements. As elaborated below, SDI's processes of capacity development are centred on practical interventions that nurture experiential knowledge. These interventions are intended to improve access to assets for the households that are involved; however, as important for SDI and its affiliates is that they instigate learning and relationship-building to enable the development of further generations of implementation strategies that work better, are larger-scale, more holistic, and more effective in addressing citizen needs. As we show below, results are mixed. Limitations emerge because efforts are necessarily embedded within current understanding and actions that emerge from existing anti-poor practices and hence at best are only 'steps' (i.e. a small movement) towards just cities. However, they are progressive both in representing a collective intent and agreement as to how

SDI and affiliates can contribute to the transformation of urban policy and programming towards more inclusive and equitable towns and cities, and because they are a source for collective learning and reflection.

As SDI and affiliates move into their second decade, the development of collective capabilities that enable assets to be secured and used in ways that are consistent with the values and mission of the network has emerged as key. At the city scale, such capabilities include the management of relationships instigated by SDI affiliates with their local authorities (and other state agencies and utilities) and with other community groups and civil society organisations (see Mitlin and Mogaladi (2013) for an illustration from Durban, South Africa). Such capabilities also have to support the institutional changes needed for asset accumulation strategies to support the needs of diverse groups of citizens. Tilly (2004) and Mosse (2010) both argue that changes in such relationships are key to reducing discriminatory and exclusionary patterns of development.

The following section explains SDI's organising approach and its intervention tools, and their relationship to gender transformations and just cities. It describes a transition within SDI's own strategies for strengthening collective capabilities to manage relationships and acquire assets. To illustrate what transition means in practice, the third section introduces Zimbabwe and elaborates on the SDI experience in this context. The fourth section concludes.

How does SDI perceive gender justice, and hence how does it design its process?

SDI seeks to support development processes that are relevant to the most disadvantaged, and are effective at scale. SDI emerged from collective action by pavement dwellers in Mumbai, among women who were seeking to address their needs and those of their families. Menon (2010) describes the realities faced by these women, and their placelessness and invisibility. The gendered realities of these pavement dwellers helped to produce new insights and capacities. The women came together to form *Mahila Milan* (a network of newly formed women's savings groups),[2] which then established a partnership with two further agencies: first, the Society for the Promotion of Area Resource Centres (SPARC), a non-governmental organisation (NGO) seeking to be relevant to the needs of the urban poor in Mumbai, with staff engaged with these women to learn about their realities and collectively develop strategies to address their development needs; and second, the National Federation of Slum Dwellers (NSDF), that had been fighting evictions in Mumbai and other Indian cities with limited success. The male leadership of NSDF was looking for new alliances and approaches that would address the constraints they faced, and build new, more powerful aggregations of citizens. Following their agreement to collaborate, these three organisations became known as the Indian Alliance.

Since women faced many problems because of their inability to accumulate monetary assets, daily saving was identified as one particularly effective tool to improve their lives. With savings, addressing immediate needs became easier;

they could pay their husbands' fines, afford school and hospitals bills, and invest in enterprises. Some savings were kept within local neighbourhoods so that households could cope with emergencies, but other money, including savings for housing, was deposited at the bank. Evidence showed that savings helped to bring women together, as well as to build relations with local authorities – partly because owning financial capital meant politicians and officials treated groups differently (McFarlane 2004). The members of *Mahila Milan* were adamant that savings collectors should work every day, collecting loan repayments and offering opportunities for savings. This did not mean that women were required to save every day, rather that there was the potential. Daily savings practice offered regular interaction between members of savings groups, challenging the isolation that many women experienced. Through such interactions, local savings groups could identify needs and support women, whatever difficulties they faced, be it their own poor health, domestic violence, or other family crises. Savings led to strong, deep relationships between individuals, and helped women to strengthen their relationships with their families.

In addition to savings, other tools were developed to strengthen local community organisations and enable them to be more effective; these included household surveys to gather basic data (enumerations); mapping of shacks, plots, and services; and the development of exemplary projects to show how to address needs (precedents). Settlement profiling collected basic data about all the informal settlements in a district or city; the data include estimated populations, size and tenure status of land, provision of services, and living conditions.

Women leaders from the pavement communities began to visit other settlements, making links through programmes of community exchanges that offered repeated engagements as a way of developing a common understanding of problems, building confidence, sharing skills and addressing constraints. Such exchanges strengthened and extended *Mahila Milan*, with the network helping to create a necessary safe space in which women could find voice and confidence in addressing day-to-day challenges, removed from everyday gendered expectations fostered by patriarchal societies. Small, often incremental successes at the local level (for instance, securing improvements to water supplies) built solidarity and confidence to address 'bigger' issues. Savings brought a further benefit when women's money, scarce as it was, was offered for collateral finance in development projects. Governments began to treat women differently when they were able to offer money, even if only a small percentage of the total requirement. Over time women leaders gained skills to negotiate, solve problems, and mobilise others to accentuate their voice – all important capabilities in dealing with the state (Appadurai 2001; McFarlane 2004). As they developed their capabilities as leaders, and had more of a public profile, their families began to treat them with greater respect

The triple burden faced by women has been widely recognised, as identified in Chapter 1, and this reality was very much part of life on the pavements. Women were expected to contribute to livelihoods (sometimes as the sole income earner). At the same time, they were expected to provide for dependants, taking care of children, old people, and others with particular needs. They were frequently engaged in service provision, providing support to community improvements. Despite this burden, the leadership of women's savings groups was not interested solely in women's needs. From *Mahila Milan's* earliest days, their leaders believed that women's vulnerabilities would increase if they were isolated from their families. They identified that men also had needs; both men and women were more likely to be better off if these were addressed and not ignored (Patel and Mitlin 2010).

From neighbourhood to city

While the immediate attention of the Indian Alliance was focused on the women living on the pavements and others in informal settlements, there were many more in need of attention in Mumbai and beyond. The one billion living in informal settlements in the Global South are without safe and secure homes, and adequate access to basic services (Mitlin and Satterthwaite 2013). Many live in shacks, and a considerable proportion rent one or two rooms for their families. Pit latrines and septic tanks predominate in terms of sanitation. With water rarely provided 24/7, and alternative water suppliers costly if available, households frequently depend on shallow wells. Adequate drainage, pathways, and health and education services are all lacking. Inadequate city-scale investments and poor governance compound problems at the settlement level; transport services are expensive in peripheral locations while informal vending is at best tolerated and frequently restricted or criminalised (see Roever in Chapter 4 of this volume). Few formal employment opportunities exist in most locations, and educated men mainly take those available.

Aware of this context in urban informal settlements across the Global South, the Indian Alliance started to link up with groups in other countries. In 1996, six sister federations that had emerged during the previous five years came together to form SDI and support savings-based organising and other associated modalities of community organising. Across different cultures women found savings helpful in improving their lives, for reasons similar to those identified above (Mitlin *et al.* 2011; d'Cruz *et al.* 2014). In addition to accumulating cash, they benefited from learning new skills and capabilities, including managing collective money, formal financial accounting, and confidence in financial reporting. Further tools were refined and developed, most notably settlement profiling, mapping (increasingly with GIS) and enumeration (see *Environment and Urbanization* volume 24 of 2012, dedicated to the theme of mapping, enumerating and surveying informal settlements and cities). These tools provided information about the living conditions in informal settlements (including location, services, demography), and the situation of households. Financial capital, human capital, knowledge capital and social capital were all strengthened through SDI organising. Groups were successful in acquiring tenure security, land and housing, and infrastructure improvements. In their discussion of the achievements of the network, Satterthwaite and Mitlin (2014) identified that over 200,000 had secured formal tenure and some level of service upgrading, with 102 formal agreements with local authorities. Mumbai exemplifies success at scale; here, *Mahila Milan* groups have supported the construction and management of over 500 community-managed toilet blocks.[3]

As the SDI network grew, so did the diversity of contexts within which affiliates worked. However, in order to develop alternative and more effective solutions to development needs, SDI affiliates were working with a consistent set of agencies; local authorities and central governments (and in some cases parastatal agencies) were all key groups with whom federations needed to establish links and gain legitimacy. The portfolio of physical development projects or precedents was also comparable. This included greenfield development, informal settlement upgrading, service improvements, and the re-blocking of informal settlement plots and shacks to facilitate the easier installation of services. In the early years the SDI network prioritised greenfield development, as well as housing financed by both savings and donors. Loans were offered to local residents at a subsidised interest rate. In this case local authorities provided land either free of charge, or at a very low, affordable cost, while SDI groups (whose members were previously tenants) acquired land and undertook development. This model arose both because of local authority willingness to allocate land, and because of savings scheme members' conviction that it was easier to move to a new place than argue with their neighbours (many of whom had been sceptical about their savings activities) or try to negotiate tenure with landowners. In this model local authorities favoured new concrete-block houses within planned estates rather than incremental improvement of shacks in existing informal areas.

However, it became evident to SDI groups that success brought new challenges. These included a pattern of asset accumulation that favoured existing power relations and patterns of social stratification, rather than the radical transformative processes initially conceptualised by SDI's leadership.[4] Greenfield developments left behind those most in need, and resulted in high costs unaffordable to the many whose participation was originally intended. Large loans resulted in difficulties in repayment, and managing this took up much of the leaders' time.[5] Moreover, even when collective land ownership was introduced, along with collective service management through shared water meters, government agencies and some households pressed to individualise tenure. SDI affiliates were rightly concerned that individual titles would lead the most vulnerable households to sell their housing assets if facing an emergency and needing to raise funds.[6] As a result, the social dynamics within groups transferred from local and horizontal forms of engagement to more vertical forms of leadership, even though many of the groups continued to be led by women (Robins 2008). In some contexts, the potential to acquire housing assets meant that federation members compromised values of accountability and representation to secure access to a house.

Simultaneously, SDI groups looked more systematically at the upgrading of informal settlements through efforts to secure tenure, access infrastructure improvements, and improve housing incrementally. As noted above, this had been practised by many affiliates, but only on a small scale. As the problems with greenfield development became more evident, the interest in these strategies increased.

Time for a rethink

Although asset accumulation in housing enhanced opportunities for some, SDI affiliates recognised it was also problematic to change culture and institutions as this is a slow process that requires strong social movements to sustain the pressure that is needed to achieve this. They realised that they were at risk of reinforcing anti-poor patterns of development that disadvantaged the lowest-income households, many of which were headed by women. In response, the SDI network began to invest in collective capabilities and develop new processes to change norms and values, consistent with their initial intent. Table 7.1 summarises these changes.

While Table 7.1 illustrates changes in the ways in which SDI federations have sought to secure assets for their members, it is at risk of over-simplifying a complex reality in which there is an interrelationship between different assets. At the centre of the SDI process are skilled members of savings schemes, with individual and collective capabilities to change patterns of urban development, and their associated social stratification. Specific capabilities are recognised as central. Affiliates identify and support a range of leaders able to work together to address core problems faced by low-income and disadvantaged individuals, households, and groups. While savings create financial assets and strengthen links between neighbours, data collection strengthens knowledge associated with human capital assets, building relations with new groups in low-income areas and local authorities. Housing improvements may result in an income-earning potential through renting rooms, and establishing small shops and services such as hairdressing. Tenure security solutions that include tenants as well as landowners have been prioritised. Weru (2004), for example, describes the negotiation between structure owners and tenants in Nairobi that, in return for legal tenure, resulted in land sharing. These activities strengthen the knowledge-related human capital of individuals (for example, construction skills) and groups (for example, procurement practices and associated negotiations with suppliers). Activities such as savings, data collection, and physical improvements in low-income neighbourhoods increase the legitimacy of groups and enhance their reputation with state agencies and local authorities. The following section looks in detail at this changing strategy in one SDI affiliate country, that of Zimbabwe, with the final section concluding with a discussion about what this means for gender justice in cities.

The experience from Zimbabwe

The ability of SDI strategies to secure transformative changes has been rigorously examined in the difficult economic and political context of Zimbabwe. We first summarise this context and then discuss the changing approaches of SDI's Zimbabwe Alliance, one of the second generation of SDI affiliates. Zimbabwe is particularly notable for experiencing continuing political contestation and acute economic crisis; otherwise its context is similar to that elsewhere in the network where there is no provision for state subsidy finance to support upgrading and housing development. Only in Brazil, India, and South Africa are there substantive subsidy funds.

The challenges facing Zimbabwe's urban poor

In 2002, 38 per cent of Zimbabwe's 12.5 million people lived in urban areas. Over the past decade, many urban dwellers have faced increasing difficulties due to a multiplicity of factors rooted in Zimbabwe's urban history, paternalistic housing policy, and the political and economic context (Kamete 2006; Chitekwe-Biti 2009). In 2011, with a Human Development Index of 0.397 (lower than the sub-Saharan African average of 0.475), 72 per cent of Zimbabweans lived in poverty and 22 per cent in extreme poverty (ZimStat 2013). A key catalyst for recent difficulties has been the first spontaneous and then regularised land invasions that began in 2000 and that affected commercial farms in the peri-urban areas (Kamete 2006). Subsequent political instability, a collapse in the production of many agricultural crops, and economic mismanagement including hyperinflation from 2003 onwards compounded the situation. Between 2009 and 2013, a period of considerable political violence was followed by a negotiated settlement and the Government of National Unity taking up office with Zimbabwe African National Union – Patriotic Front (ZANU-PF) and Movement for Democratic Change (MDC) politicians sharing Cabinet posts. 'Dollarisation' of the economy stopped inflation and helped to secure a return to economic growth between 2009 and 2011 (Zimstat 2013, 9–10). The 2013 general election returned ZANU-PF to power and recent reports suggest an economic downturn (Hawkins 2014). Throughout this period, local authorities have been underfunded and unable to provide local populations with an adequate quality and quantity of services.

Low-income households in urban areas have faced and continue to face multiple difficulties. Migration to urban areas increased following independence in 1980, although local authorities lacked the resources to cater for the growing scale of needs. By 2007, the Ministry of National Housing and Urban Development estimated that the national housing backlog had increased to 1.2 million units.[7] The City of Harare confirmed 70,000 households on its housing waiting list. Even though the housing waiting list system does not deliver houses to the low-income families, people continue to register as a way to 'hedge their bets'. Waiting periods in Harare average up to 12 years in informal settlement surveys

Table 7.1 Changing strategies to ensure that asset accumulation is more transformative

Strategy	Original strategy	New strategy	Asset focus
Savings-based organising	**Strategy**: Savings groups that practise daily savings at the very local (lane) neighbourhood level **Results**: Favours women's engagement – builds stronger relations between women frequently isolated and denied public roles	**Strategy**: Savings-based organising continues. Strengthening links between savings groups and other residents' associations by emphasis on developing informal settlement network **Results**: Broad-based fora with range of other groups, generally more traditional and with a male leadership. Links assisted by data-collection activities (*see below*)	Social capital, financial capital
Lending activities	**Strategy**: Loan finance provision to improve affordability and inclusion **Results**: Lending for emergencies; group lending for income generation; housing investments	**Strategy**: Local emergency lending to continue. Less emphasis on income-generation lending. Shift from complete house loans to those for services and incremental housing development **Results**: More investments in basic services and upgrading of informal settlements, slower housing development with smaller, more affordable loans	Financial capital, physical capital
Engagement with local authorities	**Strategy**: Strong engagement with focus on strengthening voice of savings-scheme members **Results**: Local authorities offer access to greenfield sites to members of saving schemes	**Strategy**: Sharing of data collection information showing informal settlement conditions. Working with informal settlement organisations, identifying neighbourhood priorities, to present to the local authority **Results**: Greater emphasis on the coproduction of communal services. Policy reforms to reduce shelter costs such as low-cost fired earth bricks, smaller plot sizes. Discussions directed at addressing the neighbourhood needs as part of city-wide solutions	Social capital, physical capital

Documenting the potential and the problems	**Strategy**: Settlement level enumerations that outline problems and potentials. **Results**: Help to substantiate individual claims to citizenship and related entitlements	**Strategy**: Emphasis on citywide profiling as a tool to mobilise communities **Results**: Documentation used to legitimate community voice with the local authority, producing knowledge capital required for city-wide planning and upgrading informal settlements	Knowledge capital, bonding social capital
Physical improvements in living conditions	**Strategy**: Secure land for housing improvements from local authorities **Results**: Greenfield developments with local authorities constructing modern housing within a limited time scale. Local group emphasis on the acquisition of subsidised land	**Strategy**: Focus on informal settlement upgrading. Negotiations for tenure security (not individual purchase). Greater emphasis on water and sanitation. Small housing-improvement loans **Results**: Larger numbers of residents reached. Tenants benefit as well as landowners. Some support from local authorities. Some self-help solutions such as borehole water	Physical assets
Collective capabilities with capacitated leaders	**Strategy**: Emerging leaders of women-led savings schemes identified and supported to work with other groups **Results**: Experimentation with democratic practices to support new leadership based on participation	**Strategy**: Stronger accountability to members by leaders of women-led savings schemes and federations, narrative and financial reporting of activities. Rotation of leaders **Results**: Leadership rotation underway. Increased reflection on leadership styles	Social capital, knowledge capital

carried out by the Zimbabwe Homeless People's Federation. The waiting list system is perceived to be inherently corrupt and ineffective. However, there have been few options. The stringent enforcement of zoning and land ownership meant that there have been relatively few informal settlements, and those that did form were quickly eradicated. At best, those evicted were placed in 'holding camps' 20–30 km from the city centre and far from livelihood opportunities. People began to seek alternative ways of housing themselves and this manifested itself in increased occupancy levels within the existing housing stock. As many as 18 households per residential unit were recorded in some of Harare's high-density residential neighbourhoods.[8] The construction of backyard shacks for rental has long been an income-generation option for those living in low-income formal neighbourhoods.

In 2005 the national government responded to continuing political support for the opposition party, the MDC, with a move to remove and intimidate urban populations. Operation Murambatsvina (Drive Out Filth) demolished any shacks and brick buildings that allegedly did not conform to building regulations. Operation Murambatsvina left more than 700,000 people homeless and affected a further two million through the loss of their livelihoods (Tibaijuka 2005).

For women, Zimbabwe's socio-legal context presents particular difficulties. Post-independence legislative reforms include the enactment of the Legal Age of Majority Act in the post-1980 independence period which stipulates that upon attaining the age of 18 both men and women are legal adults capable of making independent decisions. Previously, women were viewed as perpetual minors for whom decisions were taken on their behalf by their fathers or male relatives, with responsibility passing to their husbands. There is now a government minis-try responsible for gender issues, with a gender policy and strategy. Zimbabwe is a signatory to all United Nations (UN) conventions that seek to protect the rights of women, such as the Convention on the Elimination of All Forms of Discrimination against Women. Property rights are dependent on the type of marriage parties have entered into; the civil marriage or Marriage Act chapter 5.11 provides the most protection and equal rights to both spouses in the event of divorce or death.

Despite such provision, significant discrimination against women continues, particularly relating to inheritance and property rights. Relations within both registered and unregistered customary unions are based on cultural norms and definitions of rights. Property is generally considered to belong to the men in the family, with the husband passing on their rights to their male children. Land and related legal documents such as Agreements of Sale and Title Deeds are usually registered in the men's names, putting married women at a disadvantage. Women are often dispossessed of their property when their partner dies, and are only granted rights to 'female' property such as kitchen utensils. Legal require-ments for formal housing discriminate against women (particularly those not for-mally married) as the authorities demanded demonstration of gainful employment through production of a pay slip or employment letter, as well as birth or marriage certificates as proof of dependence. Informal settlement on the urban periphery (with risk of eviction) is often the only option of accommodation available for unmarried, widowed, single, or separated women heading their households.

Official and legal processes in Zimbabwe are fraught with bureaucracy and are intimidating and complex; hence it is difficult for women to claim their rights. Surveys by the Zimbabwe Alliance have found that there is little available information for their members on the laws and processes in place to protect women's rights. Even with information, women find it difficult to navigate the processes required to bring a property dispute to the courts. Men resist these efforts, which many judge to take away their dignity and authority. In 2011, research carried out by the Alliance found that men thought that assets such as land and housing should belong to men to 'guarantee' that the asset remained within the family.[9] Customary unions are the most common form of marriage; 68 per cent of married women in communities where the federation has secured legal tenure rights to land and housing are in customary union marriages. Regarded as unregistered under current Zimbabwean marriage laws, these unions favour men in cases of property disputes.

The work of the Zimbabwe Homeless People's Federation

The Zimbabwe Homeless People's Federation, together with their support NGO, Dialogue on Shelter, was established in the late 1990s. The federation grew from community exchanges with a federation in South Africa (which emerged following exchanges with *Mahila Milan* in India) and subsequently from the realisation by low-income women living in informal settlements that only they could change their circumstances. Despite persistent and regular evictions, informal settlements had managed to remain in the peri-urban environs of large cities such as Harare and Bulawayo. By 1999, settlements such as Epworth, Dzivarasekwa Extension, Porta Farm and Hatcliffe Extension in Harare and Killarney and Ngozi Mine in Bulawayo were home to an estimated 70,000 households.[10] Years of evictions and subservient tenancy arrangements in rented rooms led the newly organised women to prioritise secure homes.

The Zimbabwe Federation has now grown to 1,300 saving collectives in 53 cities, towns, and urban centres, with a membership of over 53,000 households. Saving collectives organised at the neighbourhood level on a voluntary basis bring together residents who wish to save in order to address a variety of daily needs. While men are not excluded, up to 80 per cent of the members are women. Over 12,000 families have secured tenure as a result of federation activities. Such tenure rights include individual and communal land titles and upgrading rights in informal settlements. Since 2009, the movement has collectively saved over US$1 million, and leveraged an additional US$10 million to support investments in land, housing, and infrastructure assets.[11]

The Zimbabwe Alliance and asset accumulation

Asset accumulation strategies of the Zimbabwe Alliance have followed the trajectory outlined in Table 7.1. In addition to accumulating money, savings schemes have negotiated with city and government authorities to secure land allocations with the requirement to develop and upgrade housing. In 1999, savings schemes in Harare and the border town of Beitbridge were the first to negotiate successfully for land. Generally beneficiaries for local government land allocation are selected by the local authority, but in Beitbridge the saving scheme was given permission to select its own 56 beneficiary families. The savings scheme members prioritised those in need in combination with adherence to 'federation rituals', meaning beneficiaries had to be scheme members who were saving regularly, attending meetings and participating in exchanges and other activities. Elderly women-headed households were given preference to access land and loans from the recently established federation's Urban Poor Fund. The Harare group was made up of 100 families who had been evicted from an informal settlement; land was allocated by the Ministry of Local Government. The ministry's allocation was based on the individual family's repayment capacity. The federation offered building loans to all families to strengthen relations with the state and demonstrate their capacity to finance and manage housing construction. Families in both schemes received a Z$17,500 (US$450) federation loan sufficient to construct a two-roomed 24-square-metre house. The loans were payable over a ten-year period at an annual interest rate of 12 per cent.

These and other early projects were important in building a sense of self-confidence within the emerging federation, and demonstrating capacity to the state (in addition to addressing individual households' immediate needs). Social capital accrued to the movement at large as a result of demonstrated capacity to construct housing. Federation groups in other cities built upon the success of these early projects and secured land from their own local authorities. Through exposing their local authorities to these initial projects, members gained credibility and legitimacy. Subsequent housing projects were larger, with the movement being allowed to take on a bigger role in the planning as well as installation of services. For example, in Victoria Falls and Mutare, the federation was allocated land for 500 and 1,500 households, respectively.

These large projects in Victoria Falls and Mutare, begun in 2002 and 2003 respectively, tested the capacity of the federation to deliver and provoked introspection about the trajectory the federation had adopted and its implications for the broader objectives of the movement to address tenure issues equitably and at scale. It was evident to the Zimbabwe Alliance that the benefits of the land and housing projects tended to accrue to better-off members. In Victoria Falls, for example, after the community completed the installation of services they divided the costs proportionately to the size of the plot. The larger plots cost more and only members who demonstrated they could pay for these larger plots and the associated loans secured access. Predictably, these were households with someone in regular employment, and 80 per cent of these households were headed by men. The national committee of the federation worked out that these households had received twice the benefit of the average family included in the project. (Moreover, the relatively large loan amount per family meant that the federation's Urban Poor Fund had to turn down other loan applications due to limited capital.) The federation recognised that some members could not afford to participate at all.

The Alliance reached this conclusion at a time in 2005 when Zimbabwe faced immense challenges. The economic policies of the Mugabe-led government created acute difficulties, which affected the federation's members in numerous ways. Rising prices for food, shelter, education, and health care hit the urban poor the hardest. Additional problems were the loss of family breadwinners in part as a result of HIV/AIDS, high medical and funeral bills, and growing numbers of AIDS orphans who often had to be taken care of by the extended family.[12] High inflation eroded the value of savings and loans. The federation responded by indexing their loans to the cost of a bag of cement to maintain the real value of loan repayments. At the same time, they introduced new lending priorities to reduce the inequities observed in the early projects. The federation prioritised lending to groups to secure tenure and provide incremental services. Housing loans were still available but were limited to the construction of a two-room 24-square-metre shell unit.[13] The federation's leadership believed that these decisions would benefit the lowest-income families.

As they pursued this strategy through 2008–2009, the Zimbabwe Federation began to reflect further on their mobilising strategies and focus on savings scheme 'membership'. Exchange visits with other SDI affiliates such as the Kenyan Alliance of Pamoja Trust and Muungano had illustrated the potential of engaging local authorities through city-wide processes that began with profiling all informal settlements. While the Zimbabwe Federation had been collecting socio-economic data in informal settlements since 1999, it was only in 2010 that they begin to systematise this process, aiming at achieving city-wide scale – i.e. ensuring that all informal settlements in a given local authority area had been profiled and mapped. The mobilisation processes around the collection of this data enabled the federation to work with a wider aggregation of local organisations, important in the highly politically contested context of Zimbabwe. Data collection enabled all organisations within a given settlement to discuss their needs and reach consensus on the developmental priorities to be presented to their local authority.

Meanwhile, the economic crisis faced by municipalities combined with the residual effects of the 2005 Operation Murambatsvina created intense difficulties with much insecurity for low-income families living in towns and cities. Operation Murambatsvina had resulted in the demolition of many shacks in formal areas and hence considerable overcrowding as families squeezed into the rooms that remained. Over time and in the period leading to the 2008 general election, informal settlements began to re-emerge and spread. This was encouraged by residents re-occupying the settlements from which they had been evicted in

2005, and by occupations on state-owned land by ZANU PF-linked housing groups. In some areas, these occupations were tacitly and even overtly encouraged by national-level politicians (Muzondidya 2007). By 2013, the federation had documented 62 such areas in Harare alone. Lack of state finance resulted in a crisis in service delivery, with water shortages and the continuing absence of adequate sanitation. The growth in informal settlements meant that upgrading became a significant priority. This further encouraged the federation's leadership to focus on informal settlement upgrading and service delivery.

A range of activities has since taken place. In Harare, the federation entered into a memorandum of agreement to partner with the city in developing a slum upgrading strategy. This was secured in 2011 together with a fund to finance upgrading. The upgrading of Dzivarasekwa Extension (an informal settlement home to 480 families) has taken place. This upgrading has enabled a number of new precedents in service provision to be tested, including shared eco-sanitation and incremental housing development. Other innovations for the city's planning department that have previously been explored have included the sharing of plots to significantly reduce land costs. In 2014, the City of Harare approved the voluntary relocation of 120 families from Gunhill informal settlement. In Epworth, approval for an upgrading and tenure plan for 7,000 households has also been secured. Five cities are involved in a programme to spread the work in Harare to other local authorities. Settlement profiling and enumeration have taken place in Kariba and Bulawayo, although upgrading has not yet begun.

Conclusion

Transforming gender relations and achieving just cities are central to SDI's vision, strategies, and activities. The women-led savings groups that are its base organisations place a high priority on shelter, and as women articulate their aspirations for urban transformation, then tenure security, basic services, and housing all become important. What has SDI learned from its experience that will help to guide future strategies, both in general and specifically in respect of Zimbabwe?

SDI strategies have been closely aligned to asset accumulation approaches, with recognition that assets play a critical role in advancing the needs and interests of the lowest-income and most-disadvantaged groups. In the first-generation strategies, greenfield housing-development affiliates emphasised including disadvantaged women within the beneficiaries. As illustrated above in the case of Zimbabwe, this meant an emphasis on those renting in formal areas, and often on the elderly and others in particular need. What has become evident in both Zimbabwe and across the network is that the first generation of housing investments reinforced practices that disadvantaged low-income households (including those headed by women). These outcomes have occurred because of preference for complete housing and larger plots by better-off federation members and local authorities. Whatever the intention, high costs meant that it was hard for the lowest-income households to be included. Moreover the emphasis on savings means that both some community leaders and external agencies encourage local practices more akin to micro-finance and financial market inclusion, rather than using savings as a political tool to build collective practices and greater movement autonomy. Greenfield developments became an end in themselves rather than a strategy to build scale and inclusion.

However, important gains were achieved and significant capabilities developed. For example, the Zimbabwe Alliance has sought to challenge existing practices and protect the rights of women and children around property. The wide gap between policy and practice, and the provision of information to savings schemes applying for land or living-in settlements to be upgraded, has empowered married women (in customary or civil unions) to register with local authorities and put their names on allocation lists, or register jointly with their spouses. In federation-associated dwellings the rights of both female and male dependants have been protected. Participants are required to register their spouse and dependants as beneficiaries of their land and housing asset. In cases where individual members have died intestate, the local federation community supports the spouse and children to formally inherit property rights to the land and/or housing.

Reflections on the outcomes of greenfield developments enabled the alliance to re-orientate its work. Along with other SDI affiliates, activities in the last five years have sought to broaden the reach of the Zimbabwe Alliance. Affiliates have strengthened relations with a wider group of civil society organisations (both formal and informal) seeking to address the needs and interests of low-income urban citizens. Information collection such as the profiling of 62 low-income settlements in Harare has emerged as a central tool to advance such alliance-building. The emphasis has shifted from greenfield development to the upgrading of existing low-income settlements, both formal and informal in the case of Zimbabwe. Rather than a small number of households receiving a large asset such as a house, a much larger number of households are reached with an incremental model of upgrading. This is more affordable to low-income households as the required investments in improving living conditions are smaller. However, what is not yet clear is if upgrading will protect the claims of tenants. Zimbabwe has yet to secure the agreement made in Nairobi (discussed above) in which tenants also benefited from land allocations. This practice has been replicated in Nelson Mandela (Port Elizabeth), South Africa,[14] but it is far from consolidated across SDI affiliates.

With respect to both informal settlement upgrading and greenfield development, SDI affiliates recognise that making agreements with local authorities that require rapid housing consolidation is likely to be disadvantageous to the lowest-income groups. The situation in Namibia, where households are offered seven years to construct, is more favourable than that in Zimbabwe, where housing consolidation on greenfield developments is required within two years. In terms of informal settlement upgrading, protocols in Zimbabwe are still being established and the Zimbabwe Alliance is optimistic that additional time can be secured. SDI's experience in Kenya suggests that as households gain tenure, security, and services, they have been able to provide themselves with housing, upgrading one wall at a time. But local authorities in Zimbabwe are unhappy with the idea that housing will not be provided.

Finally, internal governance questions, reflecting the nature of relational power within the network, have been the focus of low-level and continuing discussions. Both in Zimbabwe and beyond there has been a reflection on the nature and practices of representation and accountability between leaders and members (in addition to similar reflections on accountabilities between citizens and the state).

Reflection on the positioning of SDI strategies in respect of the conceptual framework (Figure 1.1) in Chapter 1 helps to highlight the changes. In its earlier years, SDI affiliates placed more emphasis on accumulating the assets within the box in the centre of the framework. SDI affiliates now seek to nurture new patterns of social relations able to transform the impact of the 'driving forces' and minimise exclusionary anti-poor urban practices and outcomes. Affiliates (supported by the network) do this through developing the collective capabilities of grassroots organisations to both change access to assets – i.e. through enabling low income individuals, households, and communities to acquire and use assets – and to manage associated relations and resources. However, as evident from the discussion here, one of the core problems the SDI process has faced is that the strength of existing norms and values creates patterns of behaviour that weakens transformative intent and reinforces existing exclusions and disadvantages. In this context, SDI affiliates now place emphasis on three processes included within this framework. First, they seek to change cultural norms. Savings-based organising is favoured because it creates new roles for women, demonstrating their abilities to contribute to collective assets through improving neighbourhoods, strengthening their ability to stand up to coercion through collectives. What is evident is that as women gain confidence and capabilities, their standing within their own households changes. Other cultural norms that need to be transformed include leadership behaviour (i.e. from dominant to accountable leaders) and elite behaviours (e.g. challenging the exclusion of low-income citizens from meetings). Second, as illustrated above in the case of Zimbabwe, SDI affiliates seek to secure changes in institutionalised patterns of professional urban development such as city planning, such that planning processes and associated practices are affordable for low-income households. High costs will exclude low-income households while lower cost options will be more inclusive. Other important institutional practices secured by SDI affiliates relate to greater state–citizen interaction and more participatory governance with, for example, joint community and local authority committees within municipalities to plan the upgrading of informal settlements. Third, affiliates nurture 'feedback loops' to enable processes of empowerment to build the collective capabilities that are able to change cultural norms and institutional practices such that processes of asset accumulation are better attuned to just and equitable cities. SDI strategies are progressive both in representing a collective intent and agreement as to how SDI and affiliates can contribute to the transformation of urban policy and programming towards more inclusive and equitable towns and cities, and in being a source for collective learning and reflection.

In conclusion, assets are important but the accumulation of assets even for disadvantaged groups is not sufficient for a transformative urban future. Greater attention needs to be given to the form of assets, and processes of collective reflection that enable societal goals to be established that are equitable and just; realising such goals will require the development of new collective capabilities both within the social movement and within the state. SDI's international leadership considers the city federations as key learning agencies able to reflect on experiences and inculcate new practices of action and reflection among collectives of the urban poor. As discussed by Menon (2010) in the context of the pavement dwellers in Mumbai, the task of this network must be as much to 'unsettle' existing categories and the processes by which they are established as it is to use them to advance the needs and interests of the urban poor. Progress towards such a visionary goal as just cities is necessarily slow and SDI is conscious that its activities are works in progress; the experiential learning by organised communities moves forward step-by-step as achievements are secured and failures reflected on. Achieving social justice remains an ideal, rather than a fully formed design.

Notes

1 SDI's strategy plan 2013–2017.
2 The savings groups emerged from discussions with SPARC staff about what was going to reduce their vulnerabilities and help them address their needs.
3 SPARC, Samudaya Nirman Sahayak, Annual Review 2013–2014.
4 See Bolnick (1993) for an elaboration of this agenda in the context of South Africa. Bolnick went on to become one of the key network coordinators.
5 Concern about this trend was evident in 2005 in Namibia, when leaders expressed worries to one author that they were becoming a federation of debt collectors.
6 In South Africa a further challenge emerged when the generous state-housing subsidy resulted in households joining the federation to increase the likelihood of securing a financial contribution of upwards of US$1,000. Some of these households had higher incomes and had little interest in collective action to reduce vulnerabilities.
7 Speech by the Minister of Housing, quoted in *The Herald*, 6 April 2007.
8 Zimbabwe Homeless People's Federation Enumeration Survey of Mbare, Harare, April 1999.
9 Dialogue on Shelter and the Zimbabwe Homeless People's Federation, Status of Women Property Rights and Inheritance, Crowborough North and Dzivarasekwa Extension Survey Report, 2011.
10 Dialogue on Shelter, Consolidated Enumeration Survey Reports, 1997–2003.
11 Dialogue on Shelter, Annual Report, December 2013.
12 UNAIDS estimates that there were 890,000 children orphaned due to HIV/AIDS deaths: www.unaids.org/en/regionscountries/countries/zimbabwe.
13 Housing unit without finishes and in some cases without internal partitions.
14 Personal communication to one of the authors, CORC, April 2013.

References

Appadurai, A. (2001). 'Deep democracy: urban governmentality and the horizon of politics'. *Environment and Urbanization* 13(2): 23–43.

Bolnick, J. (1993). 'The People's Dialogue on land and shelter: community driven networking in South Africa's informal settlements'. *Environment and Urbanization* 5(1): 91–110.

Chitekwe-Biti, B. (2009). 'Struggles for urban land by the Zimbabwe Homeless People's Federation'. *Environment and Urbanization* 21(2): 347–66.

d'Cruz, C., S. Cadornigara Fadrigo, and David Satterthwaite (2014). *Tools for Inclusive Cities: The Roles of Community-Based Engagement and Monitoring in Reducing Poverty.* London, International Institute for Environment and Development.

Hawkins, T. (2014). 'Gucci Grace' Mugabe steps into Zimbabwe politics. *Financial Times* 5 November. www.ft.com/cms/s/0/428926d4-6435-11e4-bac8-00144feabdc0.html# axzz3JnS1D89E, accessed 21 November 2014.

Kamete, A.Y. (2006). 'Revisiting the urban housing crisis in Zimbabwe: some forgotten dimensions?' *Habitat International* 30: 981–95.

McFarlane, C. (2004). 'Geographical imaginations and spaces of political engagements: examples from the Indian Alliance'. *Antipode* 36(5): 890–916.

Menon, G. (2010). Recoveries of space and subjectivity: the clandestine politics of pavement dwellers in Mumbai. *Contesting Development: Critical Struggles for Social Change.* London, Routledge.

Mitlin, D. and J. Mogaladi (2013). 'Social movements and the struggle for shelter: a case study of eThekwini (Durban)'. *Progress in Planning* 84: 1–39.

Mitlin, D. and D. Satterthwaite (2013). *Urban Poverty in the Global South: Scale and Nature.* London and New York, Routledge.

Mitlin, D., D. Satterthwaite, and S. Bartlett (2011). Capital, capacities and collaboration: the multiple roles of community savings in addressing urban poverty. IIED Poverty Reduction in Urban Areas, Working Paper 34, IIED.

Mosse, D. (2010). 'A relational approach to durable poverty, inequality and power'. *Journal of Development Studies* 46(7): 1156–78.

Muzondidya, J. (2007). 'Ideological ambiguities in the politics of land and resource ownership in Zimbabwe'. *Journal of Southern African Studies* 33(2): 325–41

Patel, S. and D. Mitlin (2010). 'Gender issues and slum/shack dweller federations'. In *The International Handbook on Gender and Poverty*, ed. S. Chant. Cheltenham, Edward Edgar Publishing, pp. 379–84.

Robins, S. (2008). *From Revolution to Rights in South Africa.* Woodbridge and Pietermaritzburg, James Currey and University of KwaZulu-Natal Press.

Satterthwaite, D. and Mitlin, D. (2014). *Reducing Urban Poverty in the Global South.* Abingdon: Routledge.

Tibaijuka, A.K. (2005). *Report of the Fact-Finding Mission to Zimbabwe to Assess the Scope and Impact of Operation Murambatsvina by the UN Special Envoy on Human Settlements Issues in Zimbabwe.* Nairobi, UN-HABITAT.

Tilly, C. (2004). *Social Movements 1768–2004.* Boulder, CO, Paradigm Publishers.

Weru, J. (2004). 'Community federations and city upgrading: the work of Pamoja Trust and Muungano in Kenya'. *Environment and Urbanization* 16(1): 47–62.

ZimStat (2013). *Poverty and Poverty Datum Line Analysis in Zimbabwe.* Harare, Zimbabwe National Statistics Agency.

8 Routes to the just city

Towards gender equality in transport planning

Caren Levy

Introduction

Transport has a unique capacity to provide a simultaneous perspective on the (re)production of cities, as well as a window onto the daily lives of diverse women and men, girls and boys in those cities. This chapter explores the relationships between gender, transport, and planning in the context of urban development. This involves consideration of mobility in two senses, physical movement in the geography of the city as well as socio-economic mobility in the context of social structure. Because of the intersection of gender relations and the production of the built environment, spatial and social mobilities are deeply intertwined in the reproduction of both spatial and gender inequalities in the city and society (Levy 2013a). Responding to the framing of this book, in the unfolding arguments the chapter explores a gendered approach to urban transport, its interaction with asset accumulation, and how this might be articulated in the just city.

Sen has argued that

> the question of gender inequality ... can be understood much better by comparing those things that intrinsically matter (such as functionings and capabilities), rather than just the means [to achieve them] like ... resources. The issue of gender inequality is ultimately one of disparate freedoms.
>
> (Sen 1992, 125 in Robeyns 2003, 62)

While Sen does not choose to define more specific capabilities to assess inequalities, others have taken this up and freedom of movement is proposed as a core capability in the context of gender equality (Nussbaum 1995; Robeyns 2003; Kronlid 2008). This chapter seeks to show that in practice exercising this capability in cities and fast-growing urban areas is fraught with difficulty, and is differently and unequally experienced by women and men on the basis of their intersecting social relations of class, gender, ethnicity, religion, age, sexuality, and physical and mental ability (as appropriate to the context). Highlighting the articulation of an intersectional understanding of gender woven into these relationships and their implications for inequality (Levy 2009), the chapter acknowledges that because of the diverse social identities of transport users, movement in cities is also implicated in different and unequal access to and control over resources and the accumulation of assets.

Focusing on transport as the movement of people (not goods), it is argued that the travel patterns of transport users do not reflect the optimal 'travel choice' assumed by traditional transport planning. Far from being based on equal opportunities and felt needs, instead travel patterns reflect decisions that are made by diverse women and men in the context of problematic assumptions about transport users, the contested public space character of transport, and a false separation of decision-making in the public and private spheres (Levy 2013a). Thus an exploration of routes to the just city through a gender and transport lens demands a fundamental questioning of traditional transport planning.

The chapter is structured around the following sections. First, a tripartite definition of the just city is presented and its implications for transport discussed. This serves as a framework to explore the notion of the just city through a transport lens. The subsequent three sections explore three critical entry points in the transport system that are accessibility, mobility, and political participation, examining the dynamics of the everyday movement of diverse women and men, girls and boys, who negotiate social and spatial inequalities in cities. Each entry point is viewed through the lens of relations of power and social identity, exploring the different pathways to asset accumulation that transport offers to women and men at individual, household, and collective levels. In a concluding section, the transformative potential of transport to address the rights and needs of urban citizens, and to build routes to the just city is assessed (Levy 2013a).

Framing just cities through a gender and transport lens

What would a more transformative urban transport planning agenda for contemporary cities look like? Building on earlier work (Allan and Apsan Frediani 2013; Levy and Dávila forthcoming; Levy *et al.* forthcoming) that is based on the debates between Iris Marion Young (1990, 1998) and Nancy Fraser (1996, 1998a, 1998b) about social justice, it is argued that a just city embraces three intersecting principles: *redistribution, reciprocal recognition*, and *parity political participation*. Positing this as a framework to assess the relationship between transport and the just city, this section explores each principle in turn from the perspective of gender equality and transport.

At a macro-level, the domain of material *redistribution* is embedded in the relationship between social identity, urbanisation, and capital accumulation in the process of capitalist development. The intersection of these historical processes results in women's and men's differential access to and control over resources, which find their spatial expression in the structure of cities. In their critique of previously class-based explanations of the (re)production of the built environment, feminist geographers remind us that the intersection of different social identities (in early writings these related to gender and class in particular) are implicated in the construction of inequalities in cities, in which 'socio-economic, political and environmental processes create, reproduce and transform not only the places in which we live, but also the social relations between women and men in these places' (Little *et al.*, 1988, 1–2). They do so by demonstrating how the increasing separation between home and work under capitalist urbanisation is deeply gendered because of the problematic dichotomous separation and association of private space with women, reproduction, and consumption, and public space with men, politics, and production.

Transport and its interaction with land uses and land markets is strongly integrated into these processes, through the access transport affords to activities in the city both physically and socio-economically, and the mobility it supports in the public spaces associated with transport modes, routes, and hubs. Understanding transport in this way, reflects

> an approach that recognises 'deep distribution' [which] builds the foundation for an understanding of transport based on the articulation of power relations in public and private space at the level of the household, community and society that generate the structural inequality and dominance relations under which decisions about 'travel choice' are made.
>
> (Levy 2013a, 52)

The domain of *reciprocal recognition* in the just city concerns the two-way relationships between the recognition of difference in institutions, policies, and daily urban practices, and the recognition by oppressed women and men themselves of their own rights. In this sense, reciprocal recognition reflects a linking of individual and collective political consciousness with Fraser's notion of recognition (1996) and Young's notion of self development, that is, 'developing and exercising one's capacities and expressing one's experience' (Young 1990, 37). In the context of capitalist development, confronting the articulation of patriarchy with classist and other identity-driven conceptual and ethical frames, reciprocal recognition is essentially ideological in character. The 'politics of recognition' (Fraser 1996) is as much about the recognition of difference in the conceptual frames of institutional practices, as about the changed consciousness of oppressed women and men and their recognition of their right to demand more socially just treatment. Such reciprocal recognition has both material and symbolic implications for accessibility and mobility in transport and transport planning. This is powerfully demonstrated in two aspects of transport: in the questionable underlying gendered assumptions in traditional transport planning which have implications for women and men's accessibility, and in the approach taken by traditional transport planning to the public space character of transport which, combined with attitudes of discrimination in large sections of society, have implications for the mobility of diverse women and men.

The third principle of the just city is the right to exercise citizenship by participating in decision-making that affects one's life. While Young refers to this as self-determination or 'participating in determining one's action and the conditions of one's action' (see Young 1979 in Young 1990, 37), Fraser emphasises the 'parity' dimension of this participation, or 'social arrangements that permit all (adult) members of society to interact with one another as peers' (Fraser 1996, 30). In this chapter these two notions will be referred to as *parity political participation* in transport planning, the right to participate in transport planning decisions, which by their very nature have medium- and long-term impacts on the structure of cities and therefore on the travel experiences of urban citizens.

As implied above, when considering urban transport practices, the three domains of social justice have implications for accessibility and mobility in cities, and for decision-making in transport policy and planning. Transport practices are defined here as 'made up of the daily transport movements of diverse women and men, girls and boys, as well as by the transport system, including its planning and daily functioning' (Levy 2014, 1). In examining respectively the accessibility and mobility afforded by urban transport practices, as well as those related to decision-making, the following sections also explore the intersection of gender, transport, and asset accumulation, together with their relationship with the principles of the just city.

Clearly there is interdependence among *redistribution, reciprocal recognition*, and *parity political participation*, the three domains of social justice. This implies a complex process of transformation in institutions as well as in urban citizens themselves, both individually and collectively. Putting in place policies and practices that challenge inequality in gender relations, asset accumulation, and urban transport systems, will inevitably encounter a degree of fixity, often constituted as resistance to change. This is manifest in the power relations embedded in gender and class and their intersection with other social relations, as well as in the built nature of transport infrastructure in the city. The final section of this chapter will discuss selected strategies that seek to create, support, and sustain more socially just trajectories of change.

Gender relations in transport practices: accessibility

Accessibility is at the heart of questions of justice in any transport system. Although there is much debate about the definition and measurement of accessibility in the mainstream transport field (Bocarejo and Oviedo 2012), accessibility is generally defined as 'the ease of reaching desired destinations given a number of available opportunities and intrinsic impedance to the resources used to travel from the origin to the destination' (Bocarejo and Oviedo 2012, 143). Consequently, transport planners might use a combination of measures related to the transport system itself, its interaction with land use, and how people experience travel. This section focuses on the latter, but understood in the context of its linkages to the interaction between transport and the distribution of activities in the city. In addressing this focus from a gender perspective, the significance of the previously discussed principles of the just city for transport accessibility is highlighted.

Travel patterns reflect the *actual* access that diverse women and men, girls and boys have to different activities in the city – for example, work, school, hospital, shopping, leisure – and therefore to resources which contribute to the accumulation of financial, physical, productive, human, and social capital. In this sense, transport is a means to accessing activities that both generate and require particular assets, for example, financial assets; as well as for those who have particular accessibility needs, perhaps also physical assets, for its use.

Processes of contemporary urbanisation and urban development have resulted in most cases in the spatial separation of residence from production and from individual and collective consumption-related activities – for example, the separation of home from work (social and productive capital assets), health and education facilities (i.e. access to human capital assets). Transport then becomes critical in addressing the spatial distance between urban activities, and therefore in accessing asset-generating activities. However, transport accessibility is predicated not only on the spatial structure of cities but also on the social position of transport users. As argued in the previous section, framing transport in a feminist understanding of capitalist urbanisation highlights the importance of the social position of transport users, reflected in their simultaneous identities of class, gender, ethnicity, religion, age, sexuality, and mental/physical ability. In deepening our understanding of transport accessibility and the implications of its distributive character on asset accumulation and the just city, a number of issues are critical to note.

First, urban travel patterns reflect the gender division of labour. 'Transport accessibility ... has an integrative dimension in people's lives, enabling them to balance – or orchestrate – activities on a daily basis' (Levy 2013b, 24). Thus the space–time dimension of transport accessibility enables women and men to time manage activities embedded in the gender division of labour. For women this often involves balancing domestic duties, paid work, and in some cases family health and/or community-related activities. Where travel is necessary to carry out these activities, like getting to work, for example, the availability and frequency of transport, and the length of the trip will all be essential parts of the time-management equation for transport users. Given the gendered construction of the city, women and men also access different parts of the city; for example, women and men tend to work in different productive activities, which are also spatially located in different parts of the city. Although still limited in cities of the Global South, the analysis of gender-differentiated travel patterns and their implications for gender equality has been a growing field of research (for more recent research, see, for example, Salon and Gulyani 2010, on Nairobi, Kenya; Tran and Schlyter 2010, on Xian and Hanoi, China and Vietnam; Venter *et al.* 2007, on Durban, South Africa; Anand and Tiwari 2006, on Delhi, India; Srinivasan and Rogers 2005, on Chennai, India). While it is important to acknowledge the importance of context, this and similar research shows that 'based on their different social position, the purposes, modes and experiences of women's travel tend to differ from that of men' (Levy 2013a), as do the temporal and spatial patterns of their trips. With increasing numbers of women moving into work in the last 50 years, travel to work accounts for the highest proportion of both women and men's trips. However, men do proportionately more work trips than women, and thus comparatively more trips at peak hours. Women tend to do more domestic-related trips than men, for example, shopping, taking children to schools and family members to health facilities. These are often combined with other trips, so that women tend to do more multi-purpose trips than men, and also tend to do more off-peak travelling, when transport services are less frequent. Women also tend to use cheaper modes of transport than men. For example, research shows that while poor women and men tend to walk more than those with higher incomes, poor women walk the most. In many cities, women are more likely to use public transport than men. Even where there is a car in the household, unequal access to a driver's licence and the priority that is often given to the male journey to work results in fewer women than men car drivers in many cities (Levy 1992, 2013a, 2013b).

Second, because transport access also involves cost in addition to time and distance, women and men also face different constraints in their appropriation of the city, in part because of their differential access to and control over resources by virtue of their social position. This is particularly so for male and female workers for whom transport is a recurrent daily cost, but it is also relevant for transport access to other facilities like health, which as indicated above tends to be undertaken mainly by women. Indeed, for most household members and particularly for low-income women and men, there is a trade-off between the cost of transport and expenditure on other essential items like housing, food, and health. This results in a complex interrelationship between transport access and asset accumulation.

This relationship is particularly acute for workers in informal employment. In a recent report on 47 developing countries and economies in transition, 'in more than half of the countries, this share exceeds 50 per cent and in about one-third informal employment accounts for at least 67 per cent of non-agricultural employment' (ILO 2013, xi). In three-quarters of the countries with available data, the proportion of women in informal non-agricultural employment is higher than for men (ILO 2013). Given the scale of informal employment in contemporary cities, consideration of transport costs for this group of workers has significant implications for poverty and inequality. For example, among some of the most vulnerable informally employed workers, 63 per cent of waste pickers identified the cost of transport as a problem (IEMS 2014). Even for home-based workers, the majority of whom are women,

> the distance between the market/contractor and the home-cum-workplace as well as the time and money spent in commuting and transporting goods are of critical importance to the productivity and earnings of the workers.
>
> (Chen 2014, 16)

Representing about 30 per cent of total expenditure, '(S)ignificantly, about one quarter of the home-based workers who spend money on transport operate at a loss' (Chen 2014, 46). This implies a close relationship between the cost of transport and the accumulation of productive capital. It also implies a critical relationship between transport costs and the physical capital of housing. Where housing costs exceed 30 per cent of household income, this is generally considered a 'cost burden', with implications for other essential expenditure, including transport (Burnham and Theodore 2012).

This picture is further complicated when considering the differential access to and control over income by women and men within the household, a key dimension of gender inequality. Thus, transport accessibility, in all its dimensions, implies different pathways to asset accumulation for diverse women and men, and at the same time asset accumulation has implications for their transport accessibility. For example, addressing the cost of transport in policy and planning can have a major impact on the redistribution of opportunities and assets. Similarly, poor access to transport 'is a key constraint to poor women's ability to accumulate assets and reduce their vulnerability' (Venter *et al.* 2007, 657). Thus, relations of distribution are deeply embedded in this interrelationship. This focus on *informal* employment is particularly significant in the context of traditional transport planning, in which, while the journey to work has been the primary consideration, this has largely focused on *formal* employment.

Finally, although travel patterns reflect intersecting social relations, it would be problematic to equate them with the actual travel needs of women and men. A closer examination of the assumptions underpinning traditional transport planning reveals 'Western', gender, and middle-class stereotypes about transport users. These are embodied in the intersection of gendered assumptions relating to the structure of the household, the division of labour in households, and the control of resources and decision-making in households (Moser 1989), with class-based transport biases which focus on the (male) journey to work and on motorised transport, in particular the private car (Levy 1992, 2013a). Research has shown that these assumptions do not represent the everyday lives of most urban populations, and also contain within them the ideological foundations of gender inequality. Thus in most urban contexts the assumed norm of households as nuclear is not the only significant household structure. Similarly, the assumed gender division of labour – that the man of the household is the breadwinner and the women is the housewife – is also confounded by the increasing proportion of women who work. Finally, the treatment of the household as a unit because decision-making within it is assumed to be equal, masks the articulation of patriarchal power within households, which leads to an unequal distribution of resources in the household – for example, of cash, food, and education. The intersection of these gender and class biases results in the 'mal-recognition' of diverse women and men travelling in the city, and ultimately in a transport system that does not recognise their diverse felt needs. This is a primary reason why traditional transport planning contributes to distorted transport accessibility and the (re)production of urban inequality.

Gender practices in transport practices: mobility

In traditional transport planning, mobility is linked to physical movement manifest in actual travel or trips. In arguing for a fairer distribution of wealth in cities, an early critique of this in traditional transport planning in the 1970s to 1980s is still an issue in contemporary planning. It highlighted how mobility and the focus on movement in itself, in particular mobility as embodied in motorised transport, has taken precedence over the notion of accessibility. In this sense, influenced by the engineering aspect of transport planning, mobility is 'a very limited concept for transport policy analysis because it does not indicate why and how mobility is exercised (or not)' (Vasconcellos 2001, 54). This concern leads to statements like '(T)he unresolved dilemma in the Indian planning scenario is on where good mobility is seen as a sufficient condition for accessibility' (Murthy 2011, 122), a statement made in the context of Indian cities that lack much affordable public and public–private transport provision.

In contemporary social science debates, a different notion of mobility has emerged that recognises its importance in relation to globalisation, technologies, and urban space in everyday life. In this respect it is useful to make the distinction between accessibility, or what Ernste *et al.* (2012) refer to as 'transport mobility', and 'practice mobility' that is 'approaching mobility as a transformative power opposing the fixity and boundedness of space and place' (Ernste *et al.* 2012, 509). This so-called 'mobility turn' is as much about the positive potentials of modernity as it is about the control of movement (Cresswell and Uteng 2008; Law 1999), which recognises that mobility is "implicated in the production of power and relations of domination" (Cresswell 2010, 20). From a gender perspective, 'practice mobility' is not only about challenging spatial fixity but also the fixity of social relations – and the potential for transforming both. In this sense, the public-space character of transport practices (e.g. routes such as streets, transport hubs such as stations, modes such as buses) makes transport practices about more than accessibility. It is also simultaneously about mobility, 'that is, the freedom and right of all citizens to move in public space with safety and security – and without censure and social control' (Levy 2013b, 26).

In reality, globally women experience more violence in the public spaces of transport systems than men. For example, women travelling to work in Delhi, India, experience daily sexual harassment on transport modes and in walking to connect to transport (Anand and Tiwari 2006). Some men, on the basis of social identities such as race or sexuality, may also experience a higher level of violence than other men. Thus, public space and 'the public realm of transport is contested space, imbued with power and meaning in all societies' (Levy 2013b, 26). The centrality of the public–private dichotomy in constructing gender inequality makes gender relations fundamental in articulating this power and meaning, so that in most societies the mobility of women in public space is subject to a range of mechanisms of control, including gender-based violence. This means that, particularly for women, decisions about travel – where, when, and how – are often negotiated in the private sphere of the household and extended family networks, influenced by the perceptions of women themselves and other household members, together with their actual experiences of being in the public sphere.

Therefore, along with accessibility, mobility, and the restrictions on the public space mobility of women and some men, is another reason why travel patterns do not reflect the actual travel needs of women and men. Mobility is also a factor in the differential and unequal potential of women and some men to access work and other urban facilities, with implications for the differentially distributed potential for the accumulation of assets. Moreover, recognition of freedom of movement or mobility in public space – in policy and planning, as well as in the attitudes of household members and the wider community – is a powerful symbol of the potential for social equality on the basis of gender, class, ethnicity, religion, age, and sexuality, depending on the context.

Moreover, mobility in public space reflects more than recognition of freedom of movement by others. It also has the potential for self development, and potentially a challenge to oppression which

> consists in systemic institutional processes which prevent some people from learning and using satisfying and expansive skills in socially recognised settings, or institutionalised social processes which inhibit people's ability to play and communicate with others or to express their feelings and perspectives on social life in contexts where others can listen.
>
> (Young 1990, 38)

In this sense, the differential mobility of diverse women and men in the city is more than just a reflection of their differential urban experience. It has the potential to touch 'existential mobility', that is, 'to move our mind, heart and soul … to make sense of and value the world as we pass through it and it passes through and around us, (Kronlid 2008, 25). In this way, mobility also offers the potential for learning – albeit a spatially and socially distributed process on the basis of social position of transport users and the structure of the city: 'Learning emerges through a relational co-constitution of city and individual, where the individual's experiences, perceptions, memories, agendas and ways of inhabiting the city cannot be read as urban experiences alone' (McFarlane 2011, 3).

Even more relevant to the argument here about self-development, and to the principle of reciprocal recognition, is the fact that 'learning is a name for the specific processes, practices and interactions through which knowledge is created, contested and transformed, and for how perception emerges and changes' (McFarlane 2011, 3). Thus, although this is an unequally distributed process on the basis of the social position of transport users, the potential to learn is also the potential to acquire new knowledge in and about the city, which opens the possibility for self-reflection and potentially a different consciousness about the fairness or otherwise of one's social position. Individually such a change in self-perception is transformative in character. If translated into a collective arena such as a community-based organisation, the potential for raising collective consciousness about inequality, and thus for building the basis for transformation, is enhanced. In terms of asset accumulation, such knowledge is beyond the traditional notion of human capital as an economic asset. As Sen (1997) argues, the notion of human capital needs to be extended to incorporate not just its links to economic development, but also to social change.

Thus 'practice mobility' in the sense of the freedom of diverse women and men both to move and to learn in public space also has a symbolic quality, symbolic of the transformative potential to achieve social justice and in the process to exercise substantive citizenship and the right to appropriate the city.

Gender relations in transport practices: political participation

As implied in the previous sections, there are everyday politics in the struggle for both accessibility and mobility, and the opportunities they open up for transformative change. However, mobilised claim-making for both redistribution and reciprocal recognition in transport practices ultimately requires engagement with the principle of *parity political participation*. As discussed earlier, the two dimensions of parity participation (Fraser 1996) and self-determination, that is, challenging domination or 'institutional conditions which inhibit or prevent people from participating in determining their actions or the conditions of their actions' (Young 1990, 38), open up a fruitful line of enquiry in exploring the transformative potential of transport practices.

Despite the centrality of transport practices in enabling women and men to balance and manage their daily activities in time and space, on the whole, contemporary transport planning in most cities has left debatable assumptions in the discipline unquestioned, and failed to properly address the public space character and potential at the heart of transport practices. Until recently, they have also been an essentially top-down practice in most cities. Even in contexts where there is a statutory duty to include participation in the local transport planning process, for example, in the UK, there is a tendency for at least three constraining trends to emerge, trends which also played out in context-specific ways in planning in cities of the Global South. First, there is a lack of conceptual clarity about the meaning of participation. Transport planners and policy-makers tend to 'discuss participation, interchangeably with involvement and consultation, and in this sense fail to establish a link to real empowerment or a requirement to listen to and act upon the outputs to result' (Bickerstaff *et al.* 2002, 71–2). The consequence is that, often, public engagement tends to be extractive in character, focusing more on supplementing transport surveys than real participatory decision-making.

Second, the definition of the 'public' in these exercises has often been narrowed to 'stakeholders'. Given the wide-ranging privatisation in the transport sector, the notion of stakeholder tends to focus less on transport users and more on service providers within partnership frameworks (Hodgson and Turner 2003). Moreover, these categories are seldom disaggregated on the basis of gender or any other social identity, except in some cases where women are treated as a special-interest group, along with the disabled and other groups with special accessibility needs. Finally, any 'public' engagement often takes place late in the planning process, once plans are already formulated, and in formats or using methods which are difficult for ordinary urban citizens to engage with, for example, public enquiries. Thus, where the process exists, political participation is poorly defined and comprises few elements of either *parity* or self-determination so that, in most cases, '[civic deliberations] … in their current form can be interpreted as part of a system of domination rather than emancipation' (Bickerstaff and Walker 2005, 2140).

This treatment of participation belies the fact that urban transport is an urgent and personally felt issue in most cities around which diverse women and men mobilise collectively. Given the powerful impact of transport on the structure of the city, land markets, and the everyday lives of urban citizens, different groups of citizens have mobilised, lobbied and protested, largely as a form of resistance to the negative impacts of top-down transport decisions. In matters relating to the performance of the transport system associated with fare rises and particularly to safety, transport has proved to be an issue around which it is possible to build solidarity across diverse women and men. For example, the shocking case of rape of a young girl on a bus in Delhi, India, galvanised protest across gender, class, and caste. In the context of the drive to create 'world class cities', investment in infrastructure and roads in Indian cities has led to forced eviction of groups such as pavement dwellers and small businesses, and has resulted in political mobilisations in which women as well as men have played a central role (see, for example, Patel *et al.* 2002). In other situations of urban renewal or flooding which has resulted in the forced evictions and/or relocation of low-income communities, often onto the periphery of cities, groups have mobilised to demand basic infrastructure and transport, for example, in Ahmedabad and Bangkok (Chen 2014). Finally, in the context of those employed in the formal and informal provision of urban transport, many cities have experienced the mobilisation of transport workers in response to policy changes like privatisation, the building of bus rapid transports (BRTs), and the regulation of the informal providers. Primarily an area of male employment, in the context of competition and limited political participation, workers' organisations in the transport sector reflect tough and often violent forms of protest.

What these different mobilisations demonstrate is a shift in the process of reciprocal recognition from individual to collective consciousness and political engagement by vulnerable groups to protect fragile processes of assets accumulation in the face of top-down decisions about transport planning. It also re-emphasises the relationships between the accumulation of financial, physical, productive, human, and social forms of capital, an interrelationship in which transport accessibility and mobility is an important integrating mechanism.

Routes to the just city

What kind of strategies can create, support, and sustain 'routes' to a city in which transport practices contribute to the operation of the principles of redistribution, reciprocal recognition, and parity political participation – in a gender-sensitive manner? As this chapter has shown, such strategies have a range of possible origins – for example, individual perceptions triggered in part by the learning potential that movement in public space might offer; collective mobilisation against top-down transport decisions and protest against gender-based violence in transport-related spaces; and planned intervention in transport and related aspects of the city by local and central governments. The discussion has also shown the relationships among these strategies and the interplay with asset accumulation.

Exploring transport practices through a gender lens shows how women and men are constantly making trade-offs about their use of transport in order to carry out activities essential to the effective functioning and quality of their lives. 'These trade-offs are deeply gendered, and reinforced by other social relations. They are not optimal free "choices", as transport planning assumes' (Levy 2013b). It is, rather, a process in which trips are negotiated in the household and, sometimes, the community; trips that may be made, postponed, suppressed or re-routed. In this sense, freedom of movement is about much more than transport – it has symbolic power relating to the individual and collective struggle for gender equality, the right to appropriate the city, and in the process the right to accumulate and control assets.

Viewing transport practices in this way points to both possible entry points as well as the limitations of transport planning to address gender equality and its role in asset building for more just cities. A critical starting point for transport planning is the development of a transport system that recognises the diverse needs and complex daily experiences of urban citizens, along with the public-space character of transport practices. Research has provided evidence of the need for this change, which can be accelerated by incorporating that experience directly through the active and parity-political participation of women and men, supplemented by data collection and processing that is sensitive to the social position of users, which can then be fed into all components of transport planning methodology.

The discussion above has also demonstrated the potential redistributive multiplier effects of managing transport accessibility on the accumulation of assets at the levels of individuals, households, and workers' organisations. For example, although not normally considered a mechanism of poverty alleviation, adjustments to the costs of transport can impact directly on women's and men's different strategies to balance household budgets and their capacities to build differential stocks of assets. Similarly, careful attention to the design of defensible spaces in the transport system can contribute in part to addressing gender-based violence.

Other planning initiatives at the city level offer other opportunities for change. As examples of planning in cities such as Medellín in Colombia have shown, fostering integration and coordination between transport planning and the planning, design, and maintenance of public space in the city can be a powerful tool in addressing violence and reconstituting a more-inclusive civic engagement (Levy and Dávila forthcoming). Another major potential mechanism of redistribution at city level is to capture and redistribute the surplus in land value generated from investment in transport infrastructure. Whether this surplus is then used to foster more equitable transport development is dependent on the extent to which social relations such as class and gender are recognised in the formulation and implementation of transport and land planning.

In the process of change, both the instrumental and intrinsic value of transport is critical (Moser 2014). It is instrumental in accessing activities that contribute to the accumulation of financial, physical, productive, human, and social capital. Given the increasing separation of home, work, and other essential activities in most cities, the social relations underpinning transport accessibility has a crucial instrumentality with distributional consequences. It is intrinsic in the mobility in public space that transport offers, meaningful to women themselves, their self-development, and their freedoms, as well as being symbolic of their reciprocal recognition and participation in urban life. Under certain conditions, such accessibility and mobility, and the political struggles to improve them, combined with planning that addresses gender equality, may carry individual and collective transformative potential to challenge the intertwined ideologies of patriarchy and other social relations – and so to construct routes to the just city.

References

Allen, Adriana and Apsan Frediani, A. (2013), 'Farmers, not gardeners: The making of environmentally just spaces in Accra', *City: Analysis of Urban Trends, Culture, Theory, Policy, Action*, Vol. 17, pp. 365–81.

Anand, A. and Tiwari, G. (2006), 'A gendered perspective of the shelter–transport–livelihood link: The case of poor women in Delhi', *Transport Reviews*, Vol. 26, No. 1, pp. 63–80.

Bickerstaff, K. and Walker, G. (2005), 'Shared visions, unholy alliances: Power, governance and deliberative processes in local transport planning', *Urban Studies*, Vol. 42, No. 12, pp. 2123–44.

Bickerstaff, K., Tolley, R., and Walker, G. (2002), 'Transport planning and participation: The rhetoric and realities of public involvement', *Journal of Transport Geography*, Vol. 10, pp. 61–73.

Bocarejo J.P.S. and Oviedo, D.R.H. (2012), 'Transport accessibility and social inequities: A tool for identification of mobility needs and evaluation of transport investments', *Journal of Transport Geography*, Vol. 24, pp. 142–54.

Burnham, L. and Theodore, N. (2012), *Home Economics: The Invisible and Unregulated World of Domestic Work*, New York: National Domestic Worker Alliance.

Chen, M.A. (2014), *Informal Economy Monitoring Study Sector Report: Home-Based Workers*, Cambridge, MA: WIEGO.

Cresswell, T. (2010), 'Towards a politics of mobility', *Environment and Planning D: Society and Space*, Vol. 28, No. 1, pp. 17–31.

Cresswell, T. and Uteng, T.P. (2008), 'Gendered mobilities: Towards an holistic understanding', in Tanu Priya Uteng and Tim Cresswell (eds), *Gendered Mobilities*, Aldershot, Ashgate Publishing, pp. 1–12.

Ernste, H., Martens, K., and Schapendonk, J. (2012), 'The design, experience and justice of mobility', *Tijdschrift voor Economische en Sociale Geografie*, Vol. 103, No. 5, pp. 509–15.

Fraser, N. (1996), 'Social justice in the age of identity politics: Redistribution, recognition, and participation', *The Tanner Lectures on Human Values.* Stanford University 30 April to 2 May. http://tannerlectures.utah.edu/lectures/documents/Fraser 98.pdf, accessed 30 May 2013.

Fraser, N. (1998a), 'From redistribution to recognition? Dilemmas of justice in a "post-socialist" age', in C. Willet (ed.), *Theorising Multiculturalism: A Guide to the Current Debate*, Malden, MA and Oxford: Blackwell, pp. 19–49.

Fraser, N. (1998b), 'A rejoinder to Iris Young', in C. Willet (ed.), *Theorising Multiculturalism: A Guide to the Current Debate*, Malden, MA and Oxford: Blackwell, pp. 68–72.

Hodgson, F.C. and Turner, J. (2003), 'Participation not consumption: The need for new participatory practices to address transport and social exclusion', *Transport Policy*, Vol. 10, pp. 265–72.

IEMS (2014), The urban informal workforce: Waste pickers/recyclers. Sector Report, WIEGO and Inclusive Cities.

ILO (2013), *Women and Men in the Informal Economy: A Statistical Picture*, Geneva: ILO and WIEGO.

Kronlid, D. (2008), 'Mobility as capability', in Tanu Priya Uteng and Tim Cresswell (eds), *Gendered Mobilities*, Aldershot: Ashgate Publishing, pp. 15–33.

Law, Robin (1999), 'Beyond "women and transport": Towards new geographies of gender and daily mobility', *Progress in Human Geography*, Vol. 23, No. 4, pp. 567–88.

Levy, C. (1992), 'Transport', in L. Ostergaard (ed.), *Gender and Development*, London: Routledge, pp. 94–109.

Levy, C. (2009), 'Gender justice in a diversity approach to development? The challenges for development planning', *International Development Planning Review*, Vol. 31, No 4, pp. i–xi.

Levy, C. (2013a), 'Travel choice reframed: "Deep distribution" and gender in urban transport', *Environment and Urbanization*, Vol. 25, No. 1, pp. 47–63.

Levy, C. (2013b), 'Transport, diversity and the socially just city: The significance of gender relations', in J.D. Davila (ed.), *Urban Mobility and Poverty: Lessons from Medellín and Soacha, Colombia*, London: UCL & Universidad Nacional de Colombia, pp. 23–9.

Levy, C. (2014), 'Addressing gender equality in transport: Routes to the just city?', Briefing paper for panel on Gender, Asset Building and Just Cities organised by Caroline Moser, funded by the Ford Foundation, World Urban Forum, Medellín, Colombia, 5–11 April.

Levy, C. and Dávila, J. (forthcoming), 'Planning for mobility and socio-environmental justice? The case of Medellín', in A. Allen *et al.* (eds), *Environmental Justice and Resilience in the Urban Global South: An Emerging Agenda*, Palgrave.

Levy, C., Allen, A., Castan Broto, V., and Westman, L. (forthcoming), 'Unlocking urban trajectories: Planning for environmentally just transitions in Asian cities', in F. Caprotti and Yu Li (eds), *Sustainable Cities in Asia*, Routledge.

Little, J., Peake, L., and Richardson, P. (1988), *Women in Cities: Gender and the Urban Environment*, London: MacMillan.

McFarlane, C. (2011), *Learning the City: Knowledge and Translocal Assemblage*, Chichester: Wiley-Blackwell.

Moser, C.O.N. (1989), 'Gender planning in the Third World: Meeting practical and strategic gender needs', *World Development*, Vol. 17, No. 2, pp. 1799–825.

Moser, C.O.N. (2014), Gender, asset building and just cities. A briefing document for WUF7 Networking Event.

Murthy, Kavya (2011), 'Urban transport and the right to the city: Accessibility and mobility', in Marie-Hélène Zérah, Véronique Dupont, Stephanie Tawa Lama-Rewal (eds), *Urban Policies and the Right to the City in India: Rights, Responsibilities and Citizenship*, New Delhi: UNESCO.

Nussbaum, M. (1995), 'Human capabilities. female human beings', in M. Nussbaum and J. Glover (eds), *Women, Culture and Development*, Oxford: Clarendon Press, pp. 61–104.

Patel, S., d'Cruz, C., and Burra, S. (2002), 'Beyond evictions in a global city: People-managed settlement in Mumbai', *Environment and Urbanization*, Vol. 14, No. 1, pp. 159–72.

Robeyns, I. (2003), 'Sen's capability approach and gender inequality: Selecting relevant capabilities', *Feminist Economics*, Vol. 9, No. 2–3, pp. 61–92.

Salon, Deborah and Sumila Gulyani (2010), 'Mobility, poverty, and gender: "Travel choices" of slum residents in Nairobi, Kenya', *Transport Reviews*, Vol. 30, No. 5, pp. 641–57.

Sen, A. (1997), 'Editorial: Human capital and human capability', *World Development*, Vol. 25, No. 12, pp. 1959–61.

Srinivasan, Sumeeta and Rogers, Peter (2005), 'Travel behaviour of low-income residents: Studying two contrasting locations in the city of Chennai, India', *Journal of Transport Geography*, Vol. 13, pp. 265–74.

Tran, Hoai Anh and Schlyter, Ann (2010), 'Gender and class in urban transport: The cases of Xian and Hanoi', *Environment and Urbanization*, Vol. 22, No. 1, pp. 139–55.

Vasconcellos, E (2001), *Urban Transport: Environment and Equity – The Case for Developing Countries*, London and Sterling, VA: Earthscan.

Venter, Christoffel, Vokolkova, Veera, and Michalek, Jaroslav (2007), 'Gender, residential location and household travel: Empirical findings from low-income urban settlements in Durban, South Africa', *Transport Reviews* Vol. 27, No. 6, pp. 653–77.

Young, I.M. (1990), *Justice and the Politics of Difference*, Princeton, NJ and Chichester: Princeton University Press.

Young, I.M. (1998), 'Unruly categories: A critique of Nancy Fraser's dual systems theory', in C. Willet (ed.), *Theorising Multiculturalism: A Guide to the Current Debate*, Malden, MA and Oxford: Blackwell, pp. 50–67.

9   Gender-based violence and assets in just cities

Triggers and transformation

Cathy McIlwaine

Introduction

Gender-based violence (GBV) and specifically violence against women and girls (VAWG) is not only one of the main obstacles to achieving gender equity everywhere in the world, but also is now recognised as being a particular challenge facing women in urban areas. Although the relationship between urbanisation and GBV is contradictory, there is a general consensus that women experience heightened levels of insecurity and conflict in cities (McIlwaine 2013; Moser and McIlwaine 2014; Shaw *et al.* 2013). Such violence and associated fear severely limit women's right and ability to move freely around the city, as well as their capacity to engage in key economic, social, and political activities. Although the root causes of GBV relate to deep-seated patriarchal forces, there is also a host of specifically urban-specific constraints that act as important triggers in the perpetration of VAWG. This chapter explores the relationships between these forces and wider gender transformations from an asset-framework perspective. In exploring the utility of such an approach, the discussion identifies the nature of these urban-based triggers that exacerbate GBV, but also how assets can be mobilised to reduce GBV in cities. It makes the distinction between accumulating first-, second-, and third-generation assets (see Moser, Chapter 1) as ways of addressing GBV and the gender inequalities underlying it in the short and long term. In effect, this means building and accumulating assets that improve women's lives in a practical sense, as well as those which address strategic empowerment through ensuring their equal rights to the city as well as their ability to live economically sustainable lives. As gender transformations evolve, there is some potential for challenging the deep-seated gender inequalities that underpin GBV, as well as the urban-specific catalysts.

Background context: gender-based violence globally and in cities

Gender-based violence refers specifically to the situation whereby the sex of the victim and perpetrator of the violent act is central to constructing the motive for the violence, which revolves around the exercise of social, economic, or political power. In turn, the nature of gender ideologies and inequalities in a given society underlie the prevalence and forms of GBV (McIlwaine 2013). Although men can be victims and women can be perpetrators of violence, especially during armed conflict (Cockburn 2013; Moser and Clark 2001), GBV invariably refers to violence against women and girls. Drawing on the seminal 1993 United Nations Declaration of the Elimination of Violence against Women as the benchmark statement, this usually denotes some form of physical, sexual or psychological harm by an intimate partner or non-partner with the focus on the first two types. Within these broad descriptors, GBV and VAWG can take a wide range of forms that include female genital mutilation, female infanticide, honour killings, trafficking of women, forced marriage, rape as a tool of war, and dowry-related violence (Green and Sweetman 2013). It is now widely acknowledged that VAWG is a human rights violation, a major public health risk, and an insidious form of gender discrimination (UNFPA 2013). Despite increasing recognition of GBV as a 'new dominant global agenda' (Moser and McIlwaine 2014), not least among United Nations (UN) agencies in relation to everyday GBV and that related with armed conflict, there remains a tendency to invisibilise the former, especially GBV within the private sphere of the home in contexts of marked political violence and armed conflict (see Esser 2014).

There is increasing acknowledgement that VAWG is endemic with around 35 per cent of women globally having experienced either physical or sexual intimate-partner or non-partner sexual violence. Much of this is among intimate partners; 30 per cent of all women who have been in a relationship have experienced violence. A high proportion of this violence is fatal, with 38 per cent of all murders of women committed by intimate partners (WHO 2013, 2). Non-partner violence tends to be less prevalent with, for example, 7.2 per cent of women reporting non-partner violence globally (Abrahams *et al.* 2014, 1648). Despite such prevalence, it is also acknowledged that GBV and VAWG are under-reported, with Palermo *et al.* (2014) stating that only 7 per cent of women victims worldwide report to a formal source such as the police and/or some other judicial entity.

Bearing in mind this major caveat, prevalence rates of VAWG vary according to a host of different factors including place, social identity, and economic status, in intersecting ways. For instance, lifetime prevalence rates of partner and non-partner violence are highest in the African region at 36.6 per cent and lowest in the Western Pacific region at 24.5 per cent (WHO 2013, 17). Of particular importance here is the nature of GBV in cities, with one estimate stating that women are twice as likely to experience violence in cities, especially in the Global South (UN-HABITAT 2006). Although men are often more likely to experience urban violence and to die from it, especially those involved in gangs, this is not usually as a result of GBV (Moser and McIlwaine 2004). Instead, women are more likely to be vulnerable to such violence, especially in urban slums (Chant and McIlwaine 2013). However, these patterns are not clear-cut in that some evidence suggests that intimate partner violence is less prevalent in cities than the countryside, while violence by a non-partner is higher in urban areas. For example, 47 per cent of women in rural areas in Thailand experienced intimate partner violence compared with 41 per cent in cities. In contrast, 14 per cent of women in rural areas experienced non-partner violence compared with 20 per cent of women in cities (WHO 2005 cited in McIlwaine 2013, 67). City-dwelling can therefore potentially severely exacerbate GBV through a series of urban-based risk factors.

Urban-specific triggers of gender-based violence: an asset-framework perspective

It is important to note that urbanisation and living in a city is not a cause of GBV in itself. Among the range of different conceptual frameworks that have been developed to explain why GBV occurs, it is generally acknowledged that no single cause at a specific level or scale generates such violence, but that constellations of factors may create situations where gender-based political, economic, and social violence is more likely to be perpetrated. These frameworks range from those situating male violence against women in biological differences or 'impaired masculinities' linked with socialisation to those that locate it firmly within prevailing patriarchal relations, with GBV being the ultimate weapon for men asserting power and control over women (O'Toole and Schiffman 1997). With explanations that emphasise natural and immutable factors being widely critiqued (Green and Sweetman 2013), it is now accepted that the causes of GBV extend beyond individual relations to much wider structural processes within communities, cities, and nations related to armed conflict, socio-economic change, and poverty, all of which are underpinned by unequal power relations between women and men (McIlwaine 2014; Pickup *et al.* 2001). However, many aspects of these wider structural phenomena intersect with a series of risks that are specific to urban living that can precipitate the likelihood of experiencing GBV in cities. These are closely interrelated with the erosion or lack of women's asset portfolios that can be viewed in relation to first-, second-, and third-generation assets; the lack of these can precipitate GBV and their gradual consolidation over time can potentially reduce it (see Moser, Chapter 1).

Erosion of first-generation assets and gender-based violence

First-generation assets are those that focus on the provision of 'basic needs' revolving around provision of land, housing, basic services, and micro-finance, and which are closely linked to the structural causes or driving forces underpinning GBV. In the context of GBV, first-generation asset erosion relates to income poverty, housing, infrastructure, alcohol consumption in public spaces, and education as a human capital asset whose erosion can catalyse GBV.

Income poverty

Income poverty is central to understanding how basic needs are met as well as the incidence of GBV. It is often argued that in certain contexts, poverty may precipitate GBV even if it is important to remember that such violence occurs regardless of a socio-economic position (Morrison *et al.* 2007). In turn, the prevalence of poverty in slum areas of cities of the Global South is arguably related with low levels of asset ownership, which can also make GBV more likely to occur. For example, in Lima, Peru, it was found that poor married women experienced higher levels of psychological, physical, and sexual violence than their counterparts in middle-class areas, although prevalence was still high among the latter (Gonzales de Olarte and Gavilano Llosa 1999). Poverty can therefore act as an 'aggravating factor' in the incidence of GBV that is closely interrelated with asset ownership (Krug *et al.* 2002, 99). Indeed, it is not always income poverty which increases the propensity for GBV to occur, but the fact that the poor, and especially poor women, have limited asset ownership individually and collectively, which can make them more exposed to the phenomenon (see Moser 2009). Economic insecurity is closely linked with personal insecurity, which is undermined by lack of access to a range of different assets related to housing, employment/income, and infrastructure (see below). This resonates with Kabeer's (1999, 149) claim that poor women are often the most vulnerable to harm because: 'they are most exposed to the risk of violence and least able to remove themselves from violent situations'. Being able to remove oneself from a violent situation is closely linked with asset ownership and the ways in which this intersects with prevailing gender ideologies and inequalities.

Housing as a physical asset

Limited access to housing in cities of the Global South can make poor women in particular more likely to experience GBV. Residing in makeshift dwellings which are insecure and in communities where everyday violence is endemic makes women vulnerable to burglary, theft, and rape (Chant 2013). While this can exacerbate non-partner GBV, intimate-partner violence also flourishes in overcrowded conditions where people live in 'stress-inducing' conditions (Hindin and Adair 2002). Therefore, although limited access to assets such as secure housing is partly linked with wider structural forces such as urbanisation and poverty – not to mention patriarchal relations that underlie male bias in inheritance, property, and land rights (Chant and McIlwaine forthcoming; Rakodi, Chapter 5), it acts as an important trigger for the occurrence of GBV. Indeed, in India, Panda and Agarwal (2005) showed that women who did not own a house and land were much more likely to experience GBV in the home than those who did own them.

Urban public space and infrastructure

Another set of related risk factors underpinned by driving forces relates to the configuration of urban spaces and the nature of the activities therein. This links closely to women's access to basic infrastructural assets and, again, how their compromised access can precipitate the likelihood of GBV. Although intimate-partner violence is prevalent in the private spaces of the home, non-partner GBV is concentrated in certain public spaces such as at and around toilets and in secluded areas such as narrow lanes and open fields, especially where they are poorly lit (see Bapat and Agarwal 2003 on India; Moser *et al.* 2005). For example, in Johannesburg, South Africa, one study noted that 31 per cent of rapes were perpetrated in open public spaces (Jewkes and Abrahams 2002). Similarly, women as the primary water collectors can face assault when water standpipes are located far from their homes and/or in isolated areas (see Khosla and Dhar 2013 on Delhi). Potential attacks on public transport also affect women's mobility and generate fear (Levy 2013; see Chapter 8 and also below).

Urban public space and alcohol consumption

Other spaces in cities of the Global South that are often linked with widespread GBV and which undermine women's right to move freely around the city are those where alcohol is bought and consumed. Indeed, there is a strong relationship between the incidence of GBV and, especially, sexual violence in and around bars or taverns. In Guatemala City, women living in one poor community reported being afraid to go near *cantinas* (bars) because they thought they would be raped or assaulted by men (Moser and McIlwaine 2004, 134). Women who do frequent bars often face the risk of experiencing GBV, especially those who participate in 'survival sex' or 'sexual exchange' (informal sex for money as distinct from commercial sex workers) as well as commercial sex workers (see Chant and Evans 2010 on the Gambia; Wojcicki 2002 on South Africa). These associations are partly related to the fact that alcohol is recognised as a primary trigger in the perpetration of GBV affecting non-conjugal and intimate-partner violence (Flake and Forste 2006). For instance, in a study of seven countries, women whose partners got drunk regularly were four-to-seven times more likely to suffer violence (Kishor and Johnson 2004). There is also some evidence that in a small minority of cases, alcohol abuse can also lead to intimate-partner violence perpetrated by women (see Ansara and Hindin 2009 on the Philippines).

Education as a human capital asset

Somewhat contradictorily, attending school can increase girls' risk of GBV in cities of the South and is another way in which GBV can erode women's asset base, in that education is a primary human capital asset. Indeed, estimates suggest that 60 million young women are sexually assaulted either at or going to and from school every year globally (Oxfam 2013). School violence is often linked to male gangs or predatory men targeting girls arriving and leaving school grounds (see Moser and McIlwaine 2004 on Colombia). Within schools themselves, there is evidence of male students and teachers perpetrating GBV and especially sexual violence and exploitation; in the case of teachers, this is a serious breach of trust and abuse of power (Abrahams *et al.* 2014; Chant and Touray 2012; Jewkes *et al.* 2002). While school-related GBV also affects women in rural areas, the concentration of schools in cities and higher population densities means that schools are invariably larger and this may foster more violence. School-related violence can therefore deter young women and girls from attending, which will ultimately lead to lower levels of human capital. This process can be cyclical in that lower levels of education are also widely identified as a risk factor in women's greater likelihood of experiencing GBV (Morrison *et al.* 2007). The perception and reality of schools as violent places in cities also affects young men's attendance and subsequent attainment, which also has implications for GBV; it has been found that men with lower levels of education are more likely to perpetrate VAWG (Morrison *et al.* 2007).

Erosion of second-generation assets and gender-based violence

Second-generation assets in the context of GBV refer primarily to individual, household, and community social capital in cities. GBV can be provoked when these assets are eroded through the fragmentation or absence of social-support functions and the ways in which gender ideologies and tolerance of conflict changes in urban as compared with rural areas. Therefore, their erosion also prevents processes of strategic empowerment in terms of gender relations.

Individual, household, and community social capital as assets

The nature of access to social capital assets can lead to GBV in complex ways. From one perspective it has been argued that positive social capital and social relations have been disrupted in cities of the Global South not least because of neoliberal economic policies, rising inequalities, and a reconfiguration of state–society relations (Watson 2008). A central element of this has been the growth and proliferation of urban violence, of which GBV is an important component (Moser and McIlwaine 2014). Therefore, endemic everyday urban violence can be both the cause and outcome of the erosion of social capital (Moser and McIlwaine 2006), even if communities have emerged as being extremely resilient in the face of such conflict (Muggah 2014). A core aspect of eroding social capital in the first place is gendered intra-family violence which closely interrelates with a panoply of different insecurities (McIlwaine and Moser 2007). Furthermore, for women who might already be at risk of GBV, weakened social relations and/or a compromised social-asset base may act as a further trigger. Indeed, where social-capital assets such as friendship circles are limited, women may be less able to remove themselves from situations of GBV, especially in the home (Heise *et al.* 2002). In turn, women without much social support may be less likely to seek formal help when they do experience GBV (Kabeer 2008).

Beyond networks and social support are values; another pertinent set of social-capital assets are norms and ideologies (Bebbington 1999; Moser 2009) which affect the incidence of GBV in fundamental ways. It is generally thought that gender ideologies are more flexible in cities than rural areas, where social relations tend to be more conservative (Chant 2013; Shaw *et al.* 2013). More specifically, patriarchal strictures tend to be more relaxed in cities, meaning women are able to function more independently and challenge GBV violence (Chant, see Chapter 2; Hindin and Adair 2002; Rao 1997). However, even in contexts where more flexible gender ideologies prevail, at the micro-level of the household, if women dominate decision-making processes this can aggravate and threaten men who sometimes react violently (see Hindin and Adair 2002 on the Philippines). In Colombia, for example, Pallitto and O'Campo (2005) note that increasing 'female autonomy' did not necessarily lead to a reduction in VAWG, because of a violent backlash among some men.

These processes tie in broadly with the 'sanctions and sanctuary' framework advanced by Krug *et al.* (2002, 99), who proposed that the likelihood of GBV is greatest where community sanctions fail to condemn it and/or where shelter or support for women does not exist. Although this varies according to context, tolerance tends to be higher in rural areas where women can be pressurised into accepting gender-based violence as the norm (Heise *et al.* 2002). In urban areas, by contrast, women are more likely to voice concerns and to seek help in situations of GBV, thus mobilising the positive dimensions of changing gender ideologies that are more probable in urban areas (McIlwaine 2013). However, although the erosion of these types of social-capital asset can trigger GBV in cities, they can also be harnessed for prevention purposes (see below).

Erosion of third-generation assets and gender-based violence

Third-generation assets relate to those that ensure financial and institutional stability over time and which maximise the linkages among different assets. In the context of GBV, this mainly relates to access to work, mobilising labour power, and generating financial capital. The inability to mobilise these, or their depletion, can precipitate GBV in cities and prevent gendered empowerment and transformation.

Work and financial capital

Within the context of a 'global feminisation of labour', there has been a ubiquitous increase in female labour force participation over the past three decades, with marked increases in cities of the Global South (Chant 2013). Although not explicitly couched within an asset-accumulation framework, there has been a long-standing debate on the ways in which women's access to paid employment can lead to empowerment and gender transformations in households, the labour market, and wider society (Kabeer 2008). While mobilising their labour as an asset is often positive for women, however, it is also necessary to recognise the type of paid work involved as well as the ways in which women's other responsibilities, especially for caring, are renegotiated as a result of their employment (Kabeer 2008). Similarly, the relationship with GBV is equivocal. In the context of GBV in the home, building financial assets can allow women potentially to leave a violent household. By the same token, it can also be construed as threatening and lead to a backlash against women in the form of GBV (see Bhattacharyya *et al.* 2011 on India). In the case of the Philippines, for example, one study showed that when women earned more than 50 per cent of the household income they reported more domestic violence than those who earned less (Hindin and Adair 2002). In addition, those employed in low-paid and casual jobs are generally more likely to experience GBV in the home than those working in better-paid, higher-quality jobs (see Kabeer 2008, 48 on Bangladesh). Women engaged in certain types of job, such as sex work, are also more likely to be exposed to GBV, especially sexual violence and trafficking (Watts and Zimmerman 2002).

While it is indisputable that access to financial assets such as that generated through paid work facilitates greater decision-making power and a degree of economic independence, this can also aggravate the power balance within households and beyond. Indeed, at the household level, working women who live with male partners who are unemployed or have irregular jobs are more likely to experience GBV (Krug *et al.* 2002). This also has much wider implications, as cases of brutal killings and assaults known as femicides in Mexico and Central America illustrate. Women's disproportionate employment in export-manufacturing electronics and garment factories or *maquilas* vis-à-vis men has been associated with a marked increase in VAWG. The explanations behind this phenomenon are complex but seem to point to a backlash from men who are resentful of women's status as preferred workers and their resulting apparent greater independence, together with the fact that they are effectively transgressing the boundaries of 'acceptable womanhood' (Sweet and Ortiz Escalante 2010; Prieto-Carrón *et al.* 2007; Staudt 2008). Again, while accessing and accumulating financial assets through this type of work can potentially improve women's well-being in relation to GBV, it also brings serious risk of increasing its incidence both in households and in the public sphere.

Outcomes and corollaries of GBV: barriers to asset accumulation in cities

While the erosion of first-, second-, and third-generation assets can lead to urban-specific triggers of GBV, such violence further compromises women's socio-economic well-being and mobility in cities as well as acts as a barrier to subsequent asset accumulation. For example, GBV has many physiological and psychological health effects that include immediate injuries such as fractures and haemorrhaging, miscarriage, stillbirth, anxiety, and post-traumatic stress disorder (PTSD), as well as greater susceptibility to human immunodeficiency virus (HIV) and sexually transmitted infections (STIs) (WHO 2013, 21–2). Also important are harmful alcohol and drug use, depression and suicide, and rape-trauma syndrome (Morrison *et al.* 2007; Oxfam 2013; WHO 2013). While these affect women regardless of their residence, the fact that GBV is disproportionately concentrated in urban areas can influence the wider health and economic sustainability of cities.

The direct and indirect health effects of violence undermine women's ability to function productively, thus severely eroding financial as well as human capital assets. For instance, in Nagpur, India, 13 per cent of women had experience of being unable to participate in paid work because of the health effects of partner violence, resulting in missing an average of seven work days per incidence of abuse (cited in Krug *et al.* 2002, 102–3). This also affects husbands' ability to work, with 42 per cent of women who reported an injury in another Indian study stating that their husband had absented themselves from work following a GBV incident (ICRW 2000 cited in USAID 2014, 10). The actual income lost was the equivalent to nearly 100 per cent of women's average monthly income for a labouring job in urban slum communities (ICRW 2000 cited in USAID 2014, 10). Furthermore, when women are unable to work to their potential due to limited human capital, disability, stress, or distraction, they end up 'making ends meet' in informal and poorly remunerated jobs (Duvvery *et al.* 2013). A damaged psychological state also influences social capital as women survivors often withdraw from friendship and social networks for fear of shame, stigma, or rejection, especially in cases of sexual violence (Heise *et al.* 2002). These social costs also affect families and children when primary female caregivers withdraw from this role. There are also marked inter-generational effects of children who witness GBV and VAWG, who are at increased risk of anxiety and depression often resulting in poor performance at school (Duvvery *et al.* 2013). This clearly reduces the potential for inter-generational asset transfer, especially in terms of their human capital accumulation.

Another outcome of GBV is the loss of power at the intra-household level, whereby GBV within the home can be used as a 'coercive instrument' to erode women's decision-making abilities (Bobonis *et al.* 2009 cited in Duvvury *et al.* 2013, 14). This can mean they are less likely to leave the violent household. This is exacerbated by lack of access to human and financial capital through paid employment, although the relationship is somewhat contradictory (Vyas and Watts 2009; see also above).

GBV generates costs at community, city, and national levels, in that it puts pressure on health-care facilities, which are invariably concentrated in cities. As such, collective as well as community assets are undermined. In Vietnam, for instance, the average health-care spend for a case of domestic violence is US$12.6 (cited in Duvvury *et al.* 2013, 9). This links to wider costs to judicial and social services. In Colombia, for example, the national government spent US$73.7 million in 2003 to prevent, detect, and offer services to survivors of family violence. This was equivalent to around 0.6 per cent of the national budget (Sanchez *et al.* 2004 cited in Morrison *et al.* 2007). There are also costs to the wider economy as well as to individuals: one estimate of the economic effects of intimate-partner violence based on data from nine countries suggested a loss of 1–2 per cent of GDP, which nearly equalled government spending on primary education (Duvvury *et al.* 2013). In the case of Bangladesh, the direct monetary costs of VAWG to victims, perpetrators, and families, as well as costs to the state and to non-state actors, were estimated at 12.5 per cent of the total government expenditure and 2.1 per cent of the GDP. This contrasted to a mere 0.12 per cent spend of expenditure on combating VAWG (USAID 2014, 10).

The final major outcome of GBV in cities is fear and insecurity, which is not only a direct outcome of GBV but which also affects the ability of women to accumulate first-, second-, and third-generation assets. Although fear affects women and men in cities, it is widely acknowledged that women experience higher levels due to a combination of patriarchal relations and the perception that women face more danger from GBV in cities. In Delhi, India, for example, more than 80 per cent of women said they were sexually harassed on public transport, while 62 per cent stated they had been harassed on the streets (Whitzman 2013, 39). Even if perception and incidence of GBV are not always directly linked (McIlwaine and Moser 2007), the psychological power of perception can severely constrain women's freedom to move around the city in terms of using public transport and operating freely in open public spaces (Whitzman 2014). In the case of Guatemala City, spatial freedom was severely restricted among women due to their fear of sexual assaults, itself fuelled by gossip about gang rapes (Winton 2005). Similarly, in Mumbai a study of headcounts of people in public spaces showed that only 28 per cent were women (Phadke 2007 cited in Whitzman 2013, 41).

Forced immobility not only leads to lack of choice and isolation for women, but also affects the accumulation of assets, especially human and social capital assets. For example, the limited social interaction imposed by immobility is a central element of the erosion of social capital. This can be individual and collective; in relation to the latter, participation in political and community events is affected when meetings take place in the evenings, when women are most fearful of travelling, especially between communities (see Cárdia 2002 on Brazil). Such erosion can be experienced by women in relation to a wide range of situations that also undermine the accumulation of other assets. For instance, in Colombia and Guatemala, because of fear young women's ability to attend night school was reduced, thus eroding human capital (Moser and McIlwaine 2004). The range of productive opportunities available to women, and thus their financial assets, are also reduced if they have to travel long distances on insecure public transport. As outlined above, such compromised access to a stable asset base can lead, in somewhat circular fashion, to even greater risk of GBV actually occurring.

Conclusions

This chapter has outlined how an asset-based perspective can potentially provide important insights into understanding GBV and VAWG in cities of the global south. While the roots of GBV lie in unequal gendered power relations and patriarchy and their intersections with processes of urbanisation, poverty, and inequality, lack of access to or the erosion of a series of first-, second-, and third-generation assets act as important urban-specific triggers for the perpetration of GBV. As such, women have partial and compromised experiences of a just city in that they are rarely able to exercise their full rights to the city on an equal basis with men (Whitzman 2013). Generally speaking, women's limited access to a range of physical, human, social, and financial capital assets can put some at greater risk of GBV. However, the accumulation of certain assets can also help them guard against GBV in the longer term as well as feeding into wider processes of gender transformation. Crucial to reducing vulnerability to GBV in the first instance is the building of first-generation assets. But along with this is a move towards a more integrated approach that focuses on building second- and third-generation social capital and financial assets. Such an approach ultimately can result in more sustainable challenges to the gender inequalities that underlie GBV, as well as the potential backlashes that can occur as gender transformations evolve. Therefore, an assets-based approach allows for the deconstruction of the causes, triggers, and effects of GBV in cities in ways that ultimately help in thinking how it might be reduced through gendered empowerment and transformation processes in the longer term.

Acknowledgements

I would like to thank Caroline O.N. Moser and Sylvia Chant for their helpful advice and comments in revising this chapter.

References

Abrahams, N., Devries, K., Watts, C., Pallitto, C., Petzold, M., Shamu, S., and García-Moreno, C. (2014). Worldwide prevalence of non-partner sexual violence: a systematic review. *Lancet.* 383, 1648–54.

Ansara, D.L. and Hindin, M.J. (2009). Perpetration of intimate partner aggression by men and women in the Philippines: prevalence and associated factors. *Journal of Interpersonal Violence.* 24: 9, 1579–90.

Bapat, M. and Agarwal, I. (2003). Our needs, our priorities: women and men from the slums of Mumbai and Pune talk about their need for water and sanitation. *Environment and Urbanization.* 15: 2, 71–86.

Bebbington, A. (1999). Capitals and capabilities: a framework for analysing peasant viability, rural livelihoods and poverty. *World Development.* 27: 12, 2021–44.

Bhattacharyya, M., Bedi, A.S., and Chhachhi, A. (2011). Marital violence and women's employment and property status: evidence from north Indian villages. *World Development.* 39: 9, 1676–89.

Cárdia, N. (2002). The impact of exposure to violence in Sao Paulo: accepting violence or continuing horror, in S. Rotker (ed.) *Citizens of fear: urban violence in Latin America*, New Brunswick, NJ and London: Rutgers University Press, 152–83.

Chant, S. (2013). Cities through a 'gender lens': a golden 'urban age' for women in the global south? *Environment and Urbanization.* 25: 1, 9–29.

Chant, S. and Evans, A. (2010). Looking for the one(s): young love and urban poverty in the Gambia, *Environment and Urbanisation.* 22: 2, 353–69.

Chant, S. and McIlwaine, C. (2013). Gender, urban development and the politics of space, *E-IR.* www.e-ir.info/2013/06/04/gender-urban-development-and-the-politics-of-space (accessed 21 February 2015).

Chant, S. and McIlwaine, C. (forthcoming). *Cities, slums and gender in the global south: towards a feminised urban future*, London: Routledge.

Chant, S. and Touray, I. (2012). *Gender in the Gambia in retrospect and prospect*, Kanifing, the Gambia: GAMCOTRAP. www.gamcotrap.gm/content/images/stories/documents/Chant_Touray.pdf (accessed 25 February 2015).

Cockburn, C. (2013). War and security, women and gender: an overview of the issues. *Gender & Development*. 21: 3, 433–52.

Duvvury, N., Callan, A., Carney, P., and Raghavendra, S. (2013). *Intimate partner violence: economic costs and implications for growth and development*. Washington, DC: World Bank.

Esser, D. (2014). Security scales: spectacular and endemic violence in post-invasion Kabul, Afghanistan. *Environment and Urbanization*. 26, 373–88.

Flake, D.F. and Forste, R. (2006). Fighting families: family characteristics associated with domestic violence in five Latin American countries. *Journal of Family Violence*. 21: 1, 19–29.

Gonzales de Olarte, E. and Gavilano Llosa, P. (1999). Does poverty cause domestic violence? Some answers from Lima, in Morrison, A.R. and Biehl, M.L. (eds) *Too close to home: domestic violence in the Americas*. Washington, DC: Inter-American Development Bank, 35–49.

Green, C. and Sweetman, C. (2013). Introduction to conflict and violence. *Gender and Development*. 21: 3, 423–31.

Heise, L., Ellsberg, M., and Gottmoeller, M. (2002). A global overview of gender-based violence. *International Journal of Gynaecology and Obstetrics*. 78, Suppl 1, S5–S14.

Hindin, M.J. and Adair, L.S. (2002). Who's at risk? Factors associated with intimate partner violence in the Philippines. *Social Science and Medicine*. 55, 1385–99.

Jewkes, R. and Abrahams, N. (2002). The epidemiology of rape and sexual coercion in South Africa: an overview. *Social Science and Medicine*. 55: 7, 1231–44.

Jewkes, R., Levin, J., Bradshaw, D., and Mbananga, N. (2002). Rape of girls in South Africa. *Lancet*. 359, 1423–9.

Kabeer, N. (1999). *Reversed realities: gender hierarchies in development thought*. London: Verso.

Kabeer, N. (2008). Paid work, women's empowerment and gender justice: critical pathways of social change. Pathways Working Paper 3, IDS, University of Sussex.

Khosla, P. and Dhar, S. (2013). Safe access to basic infrastructure: more than pipes and taps, in Whitzman, C., Legacy, C., Andrew, C., Klodawsky, F., Shaw, M., and Viswanath, K. (eds) *Building inclusive cities: women's safety and the right to the city*. Abingdon: Routledge, 117–41.

Kishor, S. and Johnson, K. (2004). *Profiling domestic violence: A multi-country study*. Calverton, MD: ORC Macro.

Krug, E.G., Dahlberg, L.L., Mercy, J.A., Zwi, A.B., and Lozano, R. (eds) (2002). *World report on violence and health*. Geneva: WHO.

Levy, C. (2013). Travel choice reframed: 'deep distribution' and gender in urban transport. *Environment and Urbanization*. 25: 1, 47–63.

McIlwaine, C. (2013). Urbanisation and gender-based violence: exploring the paradoxes in the Global South. *Environment and Urbanization*. 25: 1, 65–79.

McIlwaine, C. (2014). Gender- and age-based violence, in Desai, V. and Potter, R. (eds), *The companion to development studies*, 3rd edn. London: Arnold, 493–9.

McIlwaine, C. and Moser, C. (2007). Living in fear: how the urban poor perceive violence, fear and insecurity, in Koonings, K. and Kruijt, D. (eds), *Fractured cities: social exclusion, urban violence and contested spaces in Latin America.* London: Zed Books, 117–37.

Morrison, A., Ellsberg, M., and Bott, S. (2007). Addressing gender-based violence: a critical review of interventions. *The World Bank Observer*, 22: 1, 25–51.

Moser, C. (2009). *Ordinary families, extraordinary lives: assets and poverty reduction in Guayaquil, 1978–2004.* Washington, DC: Brookings Press.

Moser, C.O.N. and Clark, F. (2001). Gender, conflict and building sustainable peace: recent lessons from Latin America. *Gender and Development.* 9: 3, 29–39.

Moser, C.O.N. and McIlwaine, C. (2004). *Encounters with violence in Latin America,* London: Routledge.

Moser, C.O.N. and McIlwaine, C. (2006). Latin American urban violence as a development concern: towards a framework for violence reduction. *World Development.* 34: 1, 89–112.

Moser, C.O.N. and McIlwaine, C. (2014). New frontiers in twenty-first century urban conflict and violence. *Environment and Urbanization.* 26: 2, 331–44.

Moser, C., Winton, A., and Moser, A. (2005). Violence, fear and insecurity among the urban poor in Latin America, in Fay, M. (ed.), *The urban poor in Latin America.* Washington, DC: World Bank, 125–78.

Muggah, R. (2014). Deconstructing the fragile city: exploring insecurity, violence and resilience. *Environment and Urbanization.* 26: 2, 345–58.

O'Toole, L.L. and Schiffman J.R. (eds) (1997). *Gender violence: interdisciplinary perspectives.* New York and London: New York University Press.

Oxfam (2013). *Ending violence against women: The case for a comprehensive international action plan.* London: Oxfam.

Palermo, T., Bleck, J., and Peterman, A. (2014). Tip of the iceberg: reporting and gender-based violence in developing countries. *American Journal of Epidemiology.* 179: 5, 602–12.

Pallitto, C.C. and O'Campo, P. (2005). Community level effects of gender inequality on intimate partner violence and unintended pregnancy in Colombia: testing the feminist perspective. *Social Science and Medicine.* 60: 10, 2205–16.

Panda, P. and Agarwal, B. (2005). Marital violence, human development and women's property status in India. *World Development.* 33: 5, 823–50.

Pickup, F., with Williams, S. and Sweetman, C. (2001). *Ending violence against women: a challenge for development and humanitarian work.* Oxford: Oxfam.

Prieto-Carrón, M., Thomson, M., and Macdonald, M. (2007). No more killings! Women respond to femicides in Central America. *Gender and Development.* 15: 1, 25–40.

Rao, V. (1997). Wife-beating in rural southern India: a qualitative and econometric analysis. *Social Science and Medicine.* 44, 1169–80.

Shaw, M., Andrew, C., Whitzman, C., Klodawsky, F., Viswanath, K., and Legacy, C. (2013). Introduction: challenges, opportunities and tools, in Whitzman, C., Legacy, C., Andrew, C., Klodawsky, F., Shaw, M., and Viswanath, K. (eds) *Building inclusive cities: women's safety and the right to the city.* Abingdon: Routledge, 1–16.

Staudt, K. (2008). *Violence and activism at the border: gender, fear and everyday life in Ciudad Juárez.* Austin, TX: University of Texas Press.

Sweet, E. and Ortiz Escalante, S. (2010). Planning responds to gender violence: evidence from Spain, Mexico and the United States. *Urban Studies,* 47: 10, 2129–47.

UNFPA (2013). *The role of data in addressing violence against women and girls.* New York: UNFPA. www.unfpa.org/sites/default/files/resourcepdf/finalUNFPA_CSW_Book_20130221_Data.pdf (accessed 23 January 2015).

UN-HABITAT (2006). *State of the world's cities 2006/2007*. Nairobi: UN-HABITAT. www.unwomen.org/en/what-we-do/ending-violence-against-women/facts-and-figures#notes (accessed 23 January 2015).

USAID (2014). *Toolkit for integrating GBV prevention and response into economic growth projects*. Arlington, VA: USAID.

Vyas, S. and Watts, C. (2009). How does economic empowerment affect women's risk of intimate partner violence in low and middle income countries? A systematic review of published evidence. *Journal of International Development*. 21: 577–602.

Watson, V. (2008). Seeing from the south: refocusing urban planning on the globe's central urban issues, *Urban Studies*. 46: 11: 2259–75.

Watts, C. and Zimmerman, C. (2002). Violence against women: global scope and magnitude. *Lancet*. 359, 1232–7.

Whitzman, C. (2013). Women's safety and everyday mobility, in Whitzman, C., Legacy, C., Andrew, C., Klodawsky, F., Shaw, M., and Viswanath, K. (eds), *Building inclusive cities: women's safety and the right to the city*. Abingdon: Routledge, 35–52.

Whitzman, C., Andrew, C., and Viswanath, K. (2014). Partnerships for women's safety in the city: 'four legs for a good table'. *Environment and Urbanization*. 26: 2, 443–56.

WHO (2013). *Global and regional estimates of violence against women: prevalence and health effects of intimate partner violence and non-partner sexual violence*. Geneva: WHO.

Winton, A. (2005). Youth, gangs and violence: Analysing the social and spatial mobility of young people in Guatemala City. *Children's Geographies*, 3: 2, 167–84.

Wojcicki, J.M. (2002). 'She drank his money': survival sex and the problem of violence in taverns of Gauteng Province, South Africa. *Medical Anthropology Quarterly*. 16: 3: 267–93.

10 The gendered destruction and reconstruction of assets and the transformative potential of 'disasters'

Sarah Bradshaw and Brian Linneker

Introduction

This chapter explores the transformative potential of 'disasters' through examination of the differential gendered destruction and reconstruction of assets through individual, collective and external strategies. Who provides assets and the use, access and control over them is gendered. The services assets provide may influence individual and community well-being and the development of more gender-transformative and just societies. The chapter examines the extent to which extreme weather events can lead to the reconstruction of more gender-equitable societies and just cities. It addresses a number of questions: is there a gendered impact to disaster asset destruction including loss of life? Is the erosion and destruction of assets gendered? How do women and men rebuild their asset base? What is the role of institutions and outside agencies and the gendered impact of asset accumulation and reconstruction? How does the destruction and reconstruction of assets impact on gender perceptions of improved well-being? What does this mean for gender transformative relations? The chapter draws on two evidence bases from post Hurricane Mitch, Nicaragua: (1) an in-depth local community study that separately interviewed both women and men in the same household; and (2) a large-scale national-level household survey – the Social Audit.

Natural hazards and disasters

Disasters are seen as extraordinary events that break the 'normal' routine of everyday life, notwithstanding the frequency with which they occur. Disaster academics have long pointed out that the natural hazards that may potentially produce a disaster are often not unusual or surprise events. They have also pointed out there is no such thing as a 'natural disaster', since a natural hazard becomes a disaster only when it results in significant loss of life and/or property, and this is as much determined by the ability of people to respond to an event as the event itself. Disasters should be understood as the outcome of historical development processes that create vulnerability and are as much political as natural events (Bankoff 2001). While originally the focus of disaster professionals was on the hazard and technical fixes to limit hazards, more recently the focus has shifted towards vulnerability, addressing 'underlying risk factors' at the local project and international policy levels (Bradshaw and Linneker 2014).

Vulnerability in the disaster literature is generally defined as the diminished capacity of an individual or group to 'anticipate, cope with, resist, and recover from the impact of a natural or human-made hazard' (Blaikie *et al.* 1994). The causes of vulnerability lie with the lack of access to the resources and assets that allow people to cope with hazardous events, such as income, education, health, social networks, institutions, regulation, and governance – and this access is gendered. Evidence on the gendered impact of disasters, how different women experience disasters diversely, has grown in recent years (Bradshaw and Fordham 2013; Bradshaw and Linneker 2014). However, this evidence has not necessarily informed the policy discourse around disasters, which still mainly result from assumptions relating to links between poverty and vulnerability, and gender and poverty (Bradshaw 2010). In terms of the poverty–vulnerability debate, DFID, in their call to 'disaster proof development,' note that poorer people tend to be more susceptible to hazards and that disaster can 'wipe out any gains that may have been made through poverty reduction programmes or pro-poor economic growth' (DFID 2004, 3). It has also been suggested that 'women always tend to suffer most from the impact of disasters' (UN-ADPC 2010, 8), and recent events have seen women targeted within reconstruction initiatives designed to rebuild lives and livelihoods post-disaster. DFID further suggest that as female-headed households are the 'more asset poor' they may be more impacted by natural hazards. However, there is little empirical evidence to support this assertion, since gender disaggregated data are scant, and the assumption rests on the contested notion that female heads are the 'poorest of the poor' (see Chant in Chapter 2).

The disaster discourse of DFID suggests that, on the one hand, asset ownership is a good predictor of vulnerability, and that, on the other, disasters can destroy assets. The discourse also refers to the potentially transformative nature of 'disasters'. The idea that opportunities for transformation exist after a disaster is largely based on the profound changes that such an event may produce in the lives of the people involved (Bradshaw 2013). Just as the destruction of old buildings provides a unique opportunity to rebuild anew, so too disasters are seen at least temporarily to affect, damage, or destroy existing social structures and relations, presenting a window of opportunity for new social articulations to develop in their place. There is an opportunity to reconstruct and potentially transform the physical and social asset base of communities and households. As disasters reveal the 'normal' order of subordination and inequality (Hewitt 1983), including within intimate relations (Enarson and Morrow 1998), it is also suggested that an opportunity exists for the transformation of gender roles and relations (IRP 2009). At the very least, the change in day-to-day gender roles means alternatives might be more easily introduced.

Assets are not only resources which support practical livelihood needs, but they can also create agency leading to changes in gender relations which may be socially transformative. From the perspective of disaster, a dynamic asset frame-work includes a number of different assets and their services, both public and private, in the natural and built environments. Tangible assets include physical assets such as land, buildings, housing, and productive assets such as resources, transport infrastructure, tools, capital equipment, economic, financial, and liveli-hood assets. Environmental assets are also productive and include urban blue and green space and their ecosystem services, which are important in disaster risk reduction. Environmental services often depend on land use and urban and regional development planning and include *regulatory* services such as climate temperature, water purification, and flood protection, *provisioning* services such as food, water, and fuel, and *cultural*, recreational and social services (Wade and Lundy 2011). Intangible assets include social and human capital such as neigh-bour reciprocity networks, education, physical and mental health, violence, security, community organisation, institutions, local and central government ser-vices, governance, legal inequalities, and regulation and enforcement in asset provision, access, and use. Human and physical assets are dynamic and interact in both positive and negative ways in sustainable development processes and influence people's well-being. Human behaviour may influence physical and environmental assets and the regulatory services provided, through urban sprawl, pollution, and non-sustainable use eroding or destroying services, leading to climate change and extreme weather events. Physical assets also influence intan-gible social assets through presenting and developing hazards, often leading to cultural and community organisation to reduce people's vulnerability and dis-aster risk.

In this chapter, evidence from post-Mitch Nicaragua[1] explores the gendered nature of asset destruction and reconstruction in the disaster context, and the extent to which it may potentially bring transformative gender change. It draws on an in-depth study of four communities impacted by the hurricane (Bradshaw 2001a; 2001b; 2002) along with evidence from a three-stage national-level 'Social Audit' survey of impacted communities undertaken by the Civil Coordi-nator for Emergency and Reconstruction (CIET-CCER 1999a; 1999b; 2001).[2] The differential impact of the event on eroding the asset base of women and men, and the impact of reconstruction strategies and programmes on their ability to rebuild assets, is explored using an 'asset lens'. It examines how differing individual and collective asset portfolios, and how they were obtained, influence the well-being of women, men, and different household types post-disaster. Finally, the chapter examines the extent to which the changing gender roles associated with asset reconstruction can be important in transforming gender relations and producing more just and gender-equitable societies.

Gendered disaster asset destruction

In the short and the long term a range of assets may be impacted by an event. In the short term, physical productive assets (roads, land, vehicles, tools) and physical assets (housing and goods within the home) may be lost or destroyed.

The event may also destroy social infrastructure such as schools and hospitals, reducing the ability to invest in building human capital. The question then is: are more of the assets of women than men eroded or destroyed, including loss of life?

Gendered inequalities in fatalities and the erosion of assets

While reliable fatalities data disaggregated by gender and generation are still largely missing (Mazurana *et al.* 2011), it has been suggested that women, boys, and girls are 14 times more likely than men to die during a disaster (Peterson 2007). The Indian Ocean tsunamis were important in establishing the general belief that women and girls are more likely to die in such an event (Rofi *et al.* 2006). This gendered vulnerability has been linked to social constructions of gender as much as biological differences – that more women drowned was not because they were 'weaker' but because women were not taught to swim, for example. However, if it is the social construction of gender identities that is important, then predicting impact is not straightforward. For example, in Australian bushfires men are most often killed outside while attempting to protect the home and other assets, while most female and child fatalities occur while sheltering in the house or when fleeing (Haynes *et al.* 2010; Whittaker *et al.* 2012). More generally, gendered ideology and gendered practice give rise to systematic gender differences in the perception of risk (Gustafson 1998), with men displaying more risk-taking behaviour (Waldron *et al.* 2005). Social constructions of maleness and the need to prove themselves as protectors may have led to riskier behaviour by Nicaraguan men during Mitch and may help explain why an estimated 54 per cent of those that died were male. Thus in societies such as in Latin America, where masculinities are pronounced, there may be a masculinised loss of life (Bradshaw 2004).

The most often cited study to suggest disaster deaths are 'feminised' is that of Neumayer and Plümper (2007). The study constructed indicators of disaster magnitude and women's socio-economic status and explored how these related to the size of the gender gap in life expectancy. They did not (and could not) explore existing gender-disaggregated data on disaster deaths as these do not exist. The study concluded that in countries where a disaster has occurred, where the socio-economic status of women is low, more women than men die or die at a younger age. What the study highlights is not that more women die, but that where gender inequalities are high, women are more likely than men to be vulnerable to the negative effects of hazards (Neumayer and Plümper 2007). This suggests that access to and control over assets are important in determining gender inequality in fatalities.

The importance of loss of life to those that remain might seemingly be clear. Over and above the emotional affect on well-being (see below), the loss of a wife will result in the erosion of 'assets' related to work within the home and carer responsibilities – tasks that could be undertaken by a daughter or new wife. For women, the loss of a husband might have greater implications for access to assets since, if women have the right to own land, land rights may be disputed by male relatives, and the ability to claim ownership of housing may also be problematic without legal documents to prove marriage or land title (Bradshaw 2007). However, while the physical asset base widows can claim against may decline, it should not be assumed asset destruction is always negative. Feelings after an event may be ambiguous: a woman in the post-Mitch community study noted that she felt peaceful, a feeling associated with the loss of her (abusive) husband during the hurricane. It is important to realise that the experience of a disaster, and indeed the extent to which an event is perceived to be, or bring, 'disaster', differs among individuals.

Destruction and damage of physical assets including housing

Evidence from Honduras suggests equal numbers of men and women made homeless by Mitch were present in public refuges (Bradshaw 2004). However, of the women, over half were women heads of household, a figure significantly higher than the national average (26 per cent). This might seem to support the 'female heads as most vulnerable' thesis, but there is no evidence to show that of the estimated 85,000 houses destroyed or damaged by Mitch in Honduras more were those of female heads. It is also not clear if these women heads were existing heads of household or those widowed by the hurricane.

Being in a refuge may actually demonstrate capacity, not vulnerability. High numbers of women and children immediately after an event may demonstrate that they, rather than men, leave for and reach a 'safe haven'. Women heads who are able to make the decision to evacuate themselves may be more inclined to do so than male heads, and more able to do so than female partners, thus explaining the high numbers in refuges post-Mitch. Even if the numbers of women in refuges points to their greater vulnerability, it is important to note that it is not being a woman per se that creates vulnerability, but characteristics associated with being a woman. The evidence suggests that a high proportion of women in refuges did not attend school or did not complete primary education (37 per cent), few had completed secondary education (7 per cent), and fewer had access to tertiary study (1 per cent). Research post-tsunami similarly found the heads of households in public refuge camps had lower education levels than those who took refuge with friends and family, suggesting it may be that more educated people are more likely to have better social networks, or social capital (Rofi *et al.* 2006). Thus human capital may help keep certain groups of people out of a refuge or public camp, and through drawing on social networks they are made 'invisible' within the homes of others. Female heads may have both lower levels of human capital and social capital, and if women living alone are stigmatised it may also explain their greater presence in public refuges.

In terms of physical and financial asset destruction, comparisons between men and women are often difficult. Post-disaster assessments do not conventionally include estimates of the direct erosion of financial capital to households or the private sector, but tend to focus on damage to infrastructure, public sector service provision, utilities, and housing stock (Lal *et al.* 2009). What is measured and how it is measured raise difficult issues for understanding gender disparities in asset destruction. Losses recorded tend to be land and large 'productive' resources such as mechanised farming equipment, large livestock like cattle, and housing, all of which are generally owned by men. In urban settings the destruction of assets critical to women's livelihoods, such as sewing machines, micro-enterprises or small livestock and chickens, are less often recorded, and items used for reproductive activities, such as ovens and cooking utensils, tend not to be recorded. However, women's asset destruction can be substantial in terms of their opportunity cost. Post-Mitch estimates suggested the financial value of losses in subsistence egg production alone was between US$90,000 and US$120,000 per month immediately after the event (Bradshaw 2004). Gender comparisons of who suffers the greatest physical asset erosion and/or destruction are not always possible as women's losses are generally not even recorded.

Impact on human capital: education and health

Losses in 'non-productive' assets such as school clothes and books will generally not be recorded, despite impacting on the lives of young people in the short and longer term, preventing the return to education post-disaster. Existing evidence points to a gendered erosion of education as a human capital asset, at least in the medium term, since girls more than boys may be kept out of school if they do not have the 'right' clothes, and will be restricted in returning to school if the trip is deemed to be too 'dangerous'. Schooling is more closely linked to economic costs for girls than for boys, and if there is a feminised fatality girls may be taken out of school to take over their mother's role in the home, or be married young to older male widowers (Plan International 2013). The extent of gender disparities in the erosion of educational assets will be seen only over the longer term.

In terms of health, the gendered nature of life-changing injuries and levels of ill health post-disaster are often not recorded over time. However, the impact on mental health is increasingly being recorded globally. In Nicaragua the first two phases of the Social Audit asked respondents if Hurricane Mitch had severely emotionally affected someone in their family. Immediately following the disaster more than one in five people reported that someone in their household was very emotionally affected by the event, and more female heads reported a person in the household being affected compared with male-headed households. As the data also suggest that men and younger people are less likely to report emotional impacts, the latter finding may be explained by the age and sex of the head of household rather than any inherent characteristics of female-headed households. However, three-quarters of those reported as emotionally affected were women or girls. More generally research does support the fact that women may suffer more or more severely from an event than men. However, care needs to be taken with this finding since during 'normal' times the double standard of mental health sees more women in therapy, on medication, or in institutions, and this finding post-disaster may be less to do with them being women than to do with their position and situation in society as women (Bradshaw 2013). As women tend to occupy a lower socio-economic position than men, they may be more susceptible to psychological problems. Emotional health is also related to physical health, and due to reproductive health risks and the social and economic limitations around dealing with these, women tend to be less physically healthy than men.

The Nicaraguan study highlighted significant and positive relationships between reporting emotional affects and other variables, including suffering material damages and spending time in a shelter. Spending time in a refuge led to higher numbers of people reporting emotional affects independently of other losses (CIET-CCER 1999a; 1999b). This suggests the disaster response efforts have an independent impact, and their effects need to be considered as part of the event itself. The most important predictor of reporting emotional affect was the loss of human life within the family. In 50 per cent of those households that had suffered loss of life, it was reported that someone had been impacted emotionally (compared to 22 per cent in households with no loss of life). The impact of poor mental health on other assets, including income-generating activities and human capital associated with educational attainment, may be great, and may be gendered in the long term – but again, we do not have the research evidence to state this with any certainty.

The gendered impact on the asset base of women and men is not easy to discern as the erosion and destruction of women's assets are often unrecorded, evolve over the longer term, or are more intangible in terms of health and well-being. What is clear is that women and men experience asset erosion and destruction differently, however, and even loss of life and its impact cannot be known with any certainty. The literature suggests it is now accepted as a 'known' that more women than men die. If this is the case then women should be the targets of pre-event disaster risk reduction projects and male survivors should be the target of post-disaster relief and asset reconstruction initiatives. However, the reverse is often the case, with evidence from Nicaragua showing that women, particularly female heads, were more involved in non-governmental organisation (NGO) and state-sponsored reconstruction initiatives post-disaster. Thus both men and international agencies saw women as responsible for asset reconstruction.

Gender differences in disaster response

Coping strategies tend to focus on income-generating initiatives and changing or diversifying in terms of who is working and in what activity; at the same time, external interventions put pressure on people to engage in reconstruction activities either collectively or individually, and this creates an asset accumulation trade-off with implications for women's and men's access to and control over assets.

Trade-offs between productive work and asset reconstruction

The post-Mitch community study suggests the proportion of women involved in productive income-generating work declined markedly after the disaster, in particular among women with a male partner. This might be linked to the fact that these women might not have been 'allowed' to take on the work that existed after the disaster if it meant travelling outside the community. Associated with this was a rise in the number of households that depended on a single source of male income, making the households more vulnerable in the face of future shocks. In contrast, women heads continued with their productive work and also were involved in reconstruction activities.

Post-Mitch women were targeted as 'beneficiaries' for a range of 'reconstruction assets' by different agencies. House titles were often put in women's names, and non-traditional potentially financially remunerative assets such as cows gifted to them (often as a collective asset shared among a number of women). Women were also targeted to 'participate' in group activities including rebuilding housing and roads. Many agencies focused on women's practical material needs in asset reconstruction, rather than addressing women's strategic and more transformative gender interests (Molyneux 1985; Moser 1989). While some organisations attempted strategic initiatives, including consciousness-raising activities within the projects, often these were not well received by the women themselves, who were focused on acquiring practical material assets.

The Social Audit indicated that a greater proportion of female-headed households that suffered damages received aid for housing, as compared with male-headed households with similar damages. However, while benefiting in material terms, fewer women heads felt their opinions were taken into account as to 'where' (55 per cent) and 'how' (35 per cent) to construct the houses than male heads and their partners (66 per cent and 49 per cent, respectively). This raises two issues. First, that the targeting of assets such as housing and animals was not necessarily based on event impact and need, but rather assumptions around the needs of female heads prior to the event. Second, there was a need to distinguish between being a beneficiary of, and participating in, asset reconstruction.

The community study highlights that being beneficiaries did not mean women benefited. While half the women interviewed identified themselves as having participated most in the projects for reconstruction, only one-quarter felt that women benefited from reconstruction projects. The majority stated that it was the family that benefited from their participation. This lends weight to the 'feminisation' of post-disaster reconstruction initiatives, with women being targeted as 'virtuous-victims' rather than as women per se (Bradshaw 2010; Bradshaw and Linneker 2014). The women were also clear why they were participating – for 'practical' not 'strategic' reasons – and in many ways they did not expect reconstruction to be transformative in terms of gender relations, only in terms of material gain.

It is clear that women were involved in reconstruction and through this involvement gained important physical and productive assets for the household.

What is less clear, however, is whether the large number of women involved in reconstruction was due to the increase in time available to them on account of the lack of productive work, or whether the reverse was the case; namely, the proportional reduction in productive work recorded was due to a lack of time, arising from their involvement in reconstruction. In either case, by comparison, women heads continued to work in both productive and reconstruction activities, meaning they could replenish eroded material assets equally (or more so) than male heads. For women heads the trade-off was not productive work for reconstruction, but work for well-being, with the greater time burden possibly further eroding intangible assets such as health and making them even more time-poor.

There were other intangible outcomes to the trade-off between productive work and reconstruction work, relating to gender differences in how each was perceived. Women placed greater value after the disaster than before on their reproductive and asset reconstruction activities. In contrast, men valued women's productive work more after the disaster than before, with their recognition of women's reproductive work consequently decreasing post-Mitch. The outcome was that while women without productive work had a greater recognition of their own contribution after the disaster, their partners did not share this opinion. While women were bringing material resources into the home, these were less valued by men than resources 'earned' through 'work'; while important, such material resources did not carry equal value with those earned. The self-perception of female heads of their contribution to the household actually fell post-Mitch – more often naming an adult son as the main contributor to the household – despite the fact they continued with income-generating activities and added reconstruction activities to their workload.

Post-disaster migration and changing household structures

Worldwide, migration is a common disaster response. While long-term external migration may change gender identities in progressive ways, remittances from short-term migrant workers may not necessarily do so. In Nicaragua, short-term migration was mainly to Costa Rica, and after Mitch some 17 per cent of households reported migration by one or more persons, 48 per cent of whom were women. One in four migrants returned after a short time, usually due to an inability to find work. In contrast, in Honduras one major outcome of Mitch was suggested to be the migration of male household heads. Linked to this, it was also suggested that the proportion of households with a female head doubled (Delany and Shrader 2000). Diverse scenarios were presented to explain the 'massive' increase in female-headed households, including the fact that some households stated that they had become a female head in order to obtain assistance. Anecdotal information from Nicaragua and El Salvador suggests this could well have been the case (Bradshaw 2004). Since the Social Audit in Nicaragua also showed that a greater proportion of women heads received assistance than did male-headed households, this self-declaration as female head may have had a strong rationale. In this case, female headship was not just a choice made by woman (to leave a male partner), but a benefit-driven strategic decision taken jointly to separate, at least until a house or other physical assets had been acquired, thereby increasing the household asset base and improving the well-being of the entire household.

As with gendered asset destruction, understanding how women and men rebuild assets during reconstruction processes is complex. While physical assets can be gained via reconstruction, the gender values placed on tangible and intangible assets may differ, depending on how and through whom they were acquired. This relates to women's and men's perceived contribution to the household, linked to their decision-making roles (see below). Female heads may rebuild stocks of material assets to the detriment of their health and well-being. Yet the post-disaster focus on women heads by international agencies may also drive the formation of female-headed households. Thus, reliance on assumptions around the perceived needs of female heads may have longer-term implications not only for their well-being, but also that for women, men, and children more generally.

Asset destruction and reconstruction and the gendered impacts on well-being

The impact of capital asset destruction and reconstruction on gendered improvements in well-being were explored using the Social Audit survey of 7,799 poor households in 102 communities in all departments of Nicaragua between 1999 and 2001 (Linneker and Bradshaw 2004; Bradshaw *et al.* 2002). The influence of different environmental, economic, social, and institutional assets on reported improvements and declines in well-being were explored for women, men, and different household types. The well-being indicator reflected a respondent's perceptions of whether the household situation had got 'better' or 'worse' between two post-disaster survey periods and related to individual and collective household-asset portfolios, and the institutions that provided asset reconstruction assistance.

The survey showed that household receipt of remittances, and having a fixed income improved well-being relating to individual financial assets, particularly for men.[3] Unexpected expenses, livelihood 'shocks' and the inability to cope with such shocks led to a decline in men's well-being, perhaps due to challenges to their social role as household 'provider'. Having a resilience strategy to go forward in times of crisis was important, and those with no strategy, especially women heads, were more likely to report a decline in well-being. Community preparedness for a future disaster improved perceptions of well-being, again particularly for woman heads. Factors influencing perceptions that 'things had got worse' over the period included financial asset destruction, associated with running up debts and reducing other household assets to cover illness costs. Households with a child in school were more likely to report declines in well-being, particularly women heads, which may have been income-related, reflecting the higher opportunity cost of schooling. Social assets were also important for well-being, including the right to live free from violence. Those who reported that this right had not been fulfilled were more likely to report declines in well-being, particularly women heads. The perception that conflict and arguments in households had increased was associated with declines in well-being in all households (Linneker 2002).

For women as a whole, the key individual and community assets portfolios improving well-being (in order of significance) were: identifying local government as the main organisation working to improve the community, community disaster preparedness, having a fixed income, the presence of national civil society community organisation, and receiving remittances. For women with a resident male partner, improvements in well-being were related to key assets such as community disaster preparedness, identifying local government as the main organisation working to improve the community, and having a fixed income. Interestingly, social capital assets, such as identifying someone to go to in times of crisis, improved well-being, but having been the recipient of assistance from family in times of need reduced the likelihood of well-being improvement being reported.

Men's views on sources of asset assistance in times of need differed from those of women. Male well-being improved when receiving resources from organisations, family, and neighbours in times of need. The presence of a community group working in the community, for instance, improved well-being for male heads who had not necessarily participated in the group; this was in contrast to the negative influence on women with a male partner. The importance for men of being seen to be unable to provide for their families is also reflected in the fact that running up debts or selling assets to cover health costs negatively impacts their well-being.

For women heads of household the main factors increasing well-being (to over 90 per cent) were identified as the presence of an NGO or civil society organisation working for the community, community disaster preparedness, local government working to improve the community and having been able to ask for help in times of crisis. One notable difference between women heads and women partners was that a fixed source of income was not as important in improving well-being for women heads as for women partners. This may highlight the fact that women reliant on a male partner place a higher value on the regularity of available income than do women heads who control their own income; similarly, resources sent directly to women by family members living outside the household may have more significance for women who live with a male partner than for women heads. The presence of a civil society organisation working in the community may also be important in explaining the absence of 'economic' variables in women heads reporting improvements. As noted above, post-Mitch reconstruction targeted women and privileged female heads of household in particular. This may have led to an over reliance of female heads on alternative sources of income. While getting help improved well-being for different groups of women, if the source of help was family or friends this was viewed more negatively by female heads than by women with a male partner. This finding suggests women heads preferred help from civil and local government organisations, rather than using stocks of social capital. However, it may also indicate that women heads had already eroded their social capital, the goodwill of family and neighbours.

What does asset destruction and reconstruction mean for gender relations?

One important measure of change in gender relations relates to women having greater decision-making ability in the home. Household decision-making models suggest perceptions of relative contribution to the household to be important in determining voice, and this in turn is linked to assets brought to the household, including income and physical assets associated with house titles, as well as more intangible assets such as social capital associated with familial networks (Agarwal 1997; Sen 1990).

The community study suggests that women's opinion as to who makes the more important contribution to the household had changed after the disaster, with a greater number of women post-Mitch suggesting that they contributed most to the household, despite the fact that there was a decline in the number of women in income-generating activities. However, there were differences between women. On the one hand, some women who pre-event had named the man as contributing most to the household, post-event had greater recognition of their own contribution, representing a progressive change. However, of those women who had stated pre-event that the couple made an equal contribution, post-event more had suggested it was the man alone. This may relate to women withdrawing from productive activities and becoming dependent on a male income, representing a regressive change in gender relations. Moreover, men and women often disagreed regarding household contribution. Of the women who reported that both of them equally made the most important contribution to the household, over half of their male partners reported that it was they, the man, who made the most important contribution, suggesting a potential point of conflict.

One consequence of disaster events is said to be an increase in violence against women and girls (VAWG). In addition to this, a rise in other harmful practices such as early and forced marriage, transactional sex, and trafficking, often represent a 'secondary disaster' for women (Bradshaw and Fordham 2014). While an increase in VAWG post-disaster has become received wisdom, there is still little robust evidence to support this assertion. The Social Audit in Nicaragua provides one of the few national-level surveys on the perceptions of post-disaster changes in VAWG. The evidence suggests that the situation is not as clear-cut as is often presented. Of all the men and women interviewed, 21 per cent reported an increase in violence against women post-Mitch; 32 per cent reported no change, and 34 per cent reported a decrease. However, in considering gender differences in violence reporting, some 33 per cent of women and only 17 per cent of men reported an increase in VAWG. There were no significant links between increased violence and the key variables of asset destruction or of asset reconstruction. Rather than violence increasing post-disaster, the nature of violence may change or its visibility may be increased – especially when living in a refuge. Violent behaviour persists in such environments and may increase, owing to frustration (on account of living conditions), jealousy (women are in 'public' spaces with other men), or opportunity. There were anecdotal reports in Honduras that women's former spouses would arrive at the refuges for the sole purpose of beating them up (Bradshaw 2004).

Refuges do not always offer safe spaces for women, and broader reconstruction projects may also have had unintentional negative outcomes. In the community study, for instance, perceptions that violence and arguments had increased in households related to the belief that there had been problems with reconstruction projects (Bradshaw 2001a; 2002). This was associated with a generalised disquiet about the priorities of reconstruction projects, such that women, whether or not they were participating in projects, identified similar problems. This suggests that problems with reconstruction projects tended to stem from inclusion and issues associated with the provision of assets, rather than from exclusion and disappointment associated with non-receipt of assets.

The implications for building just societies

This chapter has applied an 'assets lens' to explore asset destruction and the opportunity for asset reconstruction post-disaster, and what this might mean for gender roles and relations. It highlights the complexity of the situation, and the fact that men and women not only experience disasters differently, but that different women have different experiences of the same event. In particular, women heads of household and women who live with a male partner may experience the event and its aftermath very differently, with the experience not always being negative. While gendered asset destruction often reveals the extent of inequality in gender roles and relations, it also presents an opportunity for the transformation of gender relations; while disasters bring great destruction, they can also bring the possibility for transformation. In the same way that the destruction of the physical infrastructure may provide the opportunity for urban planners to 'build back better' housing, education and health facilities, public buildings and transport networks, so too the temporary destruction of social infrastructure may allow changes to established social norms, including gender norms. Just as disasters may force women and men to take on new roles, they may also result in related changes in gender relations.

Many reconstruction initiatives are based on assumptions that while pre-disaster women heads have fewest assets, post-disaster women are best at distributing and reconstructing assets. This results in the targeting of women with potentially transformative physical assets, including title to newly built homes, productive assets such as livestock ownership, human capital assets such as new skills in non-traditional areas (such as house construction), and intangible social assets gained through participating in rebuilding communities. Such reconstruction and reconfiguration of women's assets may help to promote transformative change in gender relations and build more just societies. However, the evidence presented here suggests there are barriers to such transformative change being achieved that need to be addressed.

The very basis of targeting, seemingly grounded on perceived need and assumed roles, may help explain the lack of the hoped-for transformative change. If any new roles taken on by women are seen as based on, or extensions of, existing roles, then rather than changing gender relations they will only add to women's responsibilities. The assets gained and the ways in which they are acquired may limit the transformative potential of reconfiguring women's asset base. There may be a trade-off, particularly for female heads of household, in increasing stocks of physical assets and reductions in other, more intangible, assets such as health, time, and perceptions of self-worth, leaving them feeling worse-off overall. For women with a male partner the trade-off may be between productive work and unpaid work in reconstruction projects. While women may value the contribution to the household asset base that their reconstruction work brings, male partners who more highly value financial capital earned through productive work may not share this valuation. Gender differences in external sources of post-disaster asset reconstruction demonstrate that who provides such assets is also important in determining if they do more than just improve the practical physical asset base of the individual or household.

Access to assets while bringing short-term practical improvements in well-being could also incrementally drive longer-term strategic gender transformations. The research shows how the gendered effect of asset reconstruction varied from being regressive to being progressive, depending on who, how, and what asset reconstruction was undertaken. Identification of the necessary conditions for post-disaster transformative change, and the role that NGOs and social movements can play in transforming gender relations, are both important issues for further attention. The research suggests that greater consideration is needed as to how and why different women are targeted, to ensure the new roles do not become just new responsibilities, reinforcing rather than transforming gender relations. The trade-off between tangible and in-tangible assets means that women's time poverty can become a negative outcome of reconstructing the household asset base. If women's contribution is to be valued by them and others, a better understanding of how assets are differentially regarded by men and women is required. Overall, post-disaster interventions, rather than reconstructing the household asset base, should aim to facilitate the reconfiguring of gendered asset bases as a strategic policy outcome, not a means to meet a practical policy need.

Notes

1 While the evidence base was first used in 2000, successive events such as the Indian Ocean tsunamis and Hurricane Katrina have proved to have similar outcomes for women (Bradshaw and Fordham 2013).
2 The community study was undertaken while working with the feminist NGO *Puntos de Encuentro* and the valuable input of all those involved in the research needs to be

recognised with thanks. Both authors worked closely with the CCER in the design of the Social Audit and the analysis of the data. The opinions expressed here are of the authors alone, as are any errors and omissions.

3 Households in northern and western areas of the country significantly under-reported improvements in well-being during the reconstruction period. This may have related to environmental vulnerability from seismic volcanic activity and flash flooding in these areas.

References

Agarwal, B. (1997) Bargaining and gender relations: within and beyond the household, *Feminist Economics*, 3, 1, 1–51.

Bankoff, G. (2001) Rendering the world unsafe: 'vulnerability' as Western discourse, *Disasters*, 25, 1, 19–35.

Blaikie, P., Cannon, T., Davis, I., and Wisner, B. (1994) *At Risk: Natural Hazards, People's Vulnerability, and Disasters*, London and New York: Routledge.

Bradshaw, S. (2001a) Reconstructing roles and relations: women's participation in reconstruction in post-Mitch Nicaragua, *Gender and Development*, 9, 3, 79–87.

Bradshaw, S. (2001b) *Dangerous Liaisons: Women, Men and Hurricane Mitch/Relaciones Peligrosas: Mujeres, Hombres y el Mitch*, Managau, Nicaragua: Puntos de Encuentro.

Bradshaw, S. (2002) Exploring the gender dimensions of reconstruction processes post-hurricane Mitch, *Journal of International Development* 14, 871–9.

Bradshaw, S. (2004) *Socio-economic Impacts of Natural Disasters: A Gender Analysis*. United Nations Economic Commission for Latin America and the Caribbean. www.cepal.org/mujer/reuniones/conferencia_regional/manual.pdf, accessed 10 March 2015.

Bradshaw, S. (2007) Gender dimensions of land rights and conflict resolution in disaster management situations. Draft revised manual for the Food and Agriculture Organisation of the United Nations.

Bradshaw, S. (2010) Feminisation or de-feminisation? Gendered experiences of poverty post-disaster, in Chant, S. (ed.), *International Handbook on Gender and Poverty*, Cheltenham: Edward Elgar, 627–32.

Bradshaw, S. (2013) *Gender, Development and Disasters*, Northampton: Edward Elgar.

Bradshaw, S. and Fordham, M. (2013) *Women, Girls and Disasters: A Review for DFID*. Department for International Development. www.gov.uk/government/uploads/system/uploads/attachment_data/file/236656/women-girls-disasters.pdf, accessed 10 March 2015.

Bradshaw, S. and Fordham, M. (2014) Double disaster: disaster through a gender lens, in Collins, A. (ed.), *Hazards, Risks and Disasters in Society*, Oxford: Elsevier, 233–55.

Bradshaw, S. and Linneker, B. (2014) *Gender and Environmental Change in the Developing World*. International Institute for Environment and Development Working Paper. http://pubs.iied.org/pdfs/10716IIED.pdf, accessed 10 March 2015.

Bradshaw, S., Linneker, B., and Zúniga, R.E. (2002) Social roles and spatial relations of NGOs and civil society: participation and effectiveness post Hurricane 'Mitch', in McIlwaine, C. and Willis, K. (2002) (eds), *Challenges and Change in Middle America: Perspectives on Development in Mexico, Central America and the Caribbean*, Harlow: Pearson Education.

CIET-CCER (1999a) *Social Audit for the Emergency and Reconstruction: Phase 1*, Managua, Nicaragua: Carqui Press.

CIET-CCER (1999b) *Auditoría Social para la Emergencia y la Reconstrucción – Fase 2*, Managua, Nicaragua: CCER.

CIET-CCER (2001) *Principales Resultados de la Auditoría Social Sobre la Condición de la Pobreza – Fase 3*, Nicaragua: CCER.

Delaney, P. and Shrader, E. (2000) Gender and Post-disaster reconstruction: the case of Hurricane Mitch in Honduras and Nicaragua. Decision review draft presented to the World Bank, January.

DFID (2004) *Adaptation to climate change: making development disaster-proof*, DFID Key Sheet 06.

Enarson, E. and Morrow, B. (eds) (1998) *The Gendered Terrain of Disasters*, Westport, CT and London: Praeger.

Gustafson, E. (1998) Gender differences in risk perception: theoretical and methodological perspectives, *Risk Analysis*, 18, 6, 805–11.

Haynes, K., Handmer, J., McAneney, J., Tibbits, A., and Coates, L. (2010) Australian bushfire fatalities 1900–2008: exploring trends in relation to the 'Prepare, stay and defend or leave early' policy, *Environmental Science and Policy*, 13, 3, 185–94.

Hewitt, K. (1983) *Interpretations of Calamity from the Viewpoint of Human Ecology*, London: Allen & Unwin.

IRP (2009) Gender issues in recovery. Executive briefs for recovery: Extracts from key documents series. Compiled by International Recovery Platform.

Lal, P., Singh, R., and Holland, P. (2009) Relationship between natural disasters and poverty: a Fiji case study. SOPAC Miscellaneous Report 678, April.

Linneker, B. (2002) Gender comparisons of capital influences on women and households experiencing poverty in Nicaragua. Working Paper, Coordinadora Civil, August. www.linneker.pwp.blueyonder.co.uk/docs/logit_wmb.pdf, accessed 10 March 2015.

Linneker, B. and Bradshaw, S. (2004) Gender comparisons of capital asset influences on the well-being of women and households in poverty in Nicaragua. Working Paper, Centro de Información y Servicios de Asesoría en Salud, February. www.linneker.pwp.blueyonder.co.uk/docs/logit_finaledit_feb.pdf, accessed 10 March 2015.

Mazurana, D., Benelli, P., Gupta, H., and Walker, P. (2011) Sex and age matter: improving humanitarian response in emergencies. Feinstein International Center, Tufts University, August.

Molyneux, M. (1985) Mobilization without emancipation? Women's interests, the state, and revolution in Nicaragua, *Feminist Studies*, 11, 2, 227–54.

Moser, C. (1989) Gender planning in the third world: meeting practical and strategic gender needs, *World Development*, 17, 11, 1799–825.

Neumayer, E. and Plümper, T. (2007) The gendered nature of natural disasters: the impact of catastrophic events on the gender gap in life expectancy 1981–2002, *Annals of the Association of American Geographers*, 97, 3, 551–66.

Peterson, K. (2007) Reaching out to women when disaster strikes. Soroptimist, White Paper. www.soroptimist.org/whitepapers/WhitePaperDocs/WPReachingWomenDisaster.pdf, accessed 1 March 2015.

Plan International (2013) The state of the world's girls 2013: in double jeopardy – adolescent girls and disasters. Plan International. http://plan-international.org/files/global/publications/campaigns/biag-2013-report-english.pdf, accessed 1 March 2015.

Rofi, A., Doocy, S., and Robinson, C. (2006) Tsunami mortality and displacement in Aceh province, Indonesia, *Disasters*, 30, 3, 340–50.

Sen, A. (1990) Gender and co-operative conflicts, in Tinker, I. (ed.), *Persistent Inequalities: Women and World Development*, Oxford: Oxford University Press, pp. 129–49.

UN-ADPC (2010) Disaster proofing the Millennium Development Goals (MDGs).

UN Millennium Campaign and the Asian Disaster Preparedness Center. www. preventionweb.net/files/16098_16098brochuredisasterproofingmdg1.pdf, accessed 29 May 2015.

Wade, R. and Lundy, L. (2011) Integrating sciences to sustain urban ecosystem services, *Progress in Physical Geography*. Special issue: Creating a new prosperity: Fresh approaches to ecosystem services and human well-being, 35, 5, 657–74.

Waldron, I., McCloskey, C., and Earle, I. (2005) Trends in gender differences in accidents mortality: relationships to changing gender roles and other societal trends, *Demographic Research*, 13, 415–54.

Whittaker, J., Handmer, J., and Mercer, D. (2012) Vulnerability to bushfires in rural Australia: a case study from East Gippsland, Victoria 2012, *Journal of Rural Studies*, 28, 2, 161–73.

11 Challenging stereotypes about gendered vulnerability to climate change

Asset adaptation in Mombasa and Cartagena

Caroline O.N. Moser and Alfredo Stein

Introduction

Climate change and natural disasters are often closely interrelated, such that they comprise an overlapping continuum. Consequently, they are frequently conflated, both analytically in terms of the conceptualisation of local populations as vulnerable, but also operationally in terms of associated policies and programmes designed to prevent and overcome their negative impacts. These range from disaster risk reduction, through disaster risk management, to climate change adaptation. The tragic outcomes for local populations of climate change-related disasters, as well as other types of natural disaster such as the Asian Tsunami, and the Central American Mitch and New Orleans Katrina hurricanes, have resulted in a tendency to focus on dramatic big disasters. In such events the profound gender-related vulnerability of elderly, women, and children has been well documented. This has included women drowning because of their inability to swim, a deficit in human capital; women unable to flee because of their domestic 'reproductive' responsibilities to care for children and the elderly, linked to household social capital; and the prevalence of gender-based violence associated with displacement, resulting in the erosion of their human and social capital. All of these affect the capabilities of women, and therefore make them more vulnerable and less resilient to these types of climate-related disaster. At the same time, the essential, invaluable role that women play in post-disaster reconstruction, based on their community social capital, also has been broadly recognised (see Bradshaw 2013; Liu 2007).

Therefore, at the outset it is necessary to clarify the difference between two, often conflated, weather patterns: first, the dramatic 'extreme' weather associated with disasters; and, second, the 'severe' weather linked to climate change. This confusion or lack of conceptual clarity has led to the assumption that women are equally vulnerable in both weather-related contexts. Yet increases in the severity and intensity of adverse weather associated with climate change are not necessarily dramatic, immediate, time-bound 'shocks'. These are far more likely to comprise temporally slow, incremental impacts of long-term trends in the increasing severity of weather, which because it is not dramatic 'is likely to be ignored, which is much more invidious' (Moser *et al.* 2010, 16). Indeed, the fact that climate is seen only through the lens of disaster means this presents a very partial picture (Bradshaw and Linneker 2014). This chapter, therefore, is intended to start to fill this gap.

Following on from Sarah Bradshaw's chapter on disasters, this chapter focuses specifically on the gradual changing 'severe' weather patterns more likely to be associated with climate change. It uses an asset adaptation framework to address stereotype assumptions about gendered vulnerability as well as adaptive capacity. It seeks to explore whether local knowledge of weather is gendered, whether women in urban contexts are more vulnerable to climate change than men, and the extent to which adaptive responses differ. This allows for consideration of whether adaptation changes gender roles, and the contexts in which this can lead to transformative changes in gender relations. Using the evidence base from two participatory appraisals of local community adaptation to climate change in Mombasa, Kenya, and Cartagena, Colombia, the chapter is intended to contribute to debates about gendered asset adaption to climate change, the extent to which this has the potential to empower women, and whether subsequent gendered transformations contribute to a more just city.

Background: conceptual framework and participatory methodology

Chapter 1 of this book introduced the concept of assets, the asset accumulation framework, and the nexus linking gender, assets, and just cities. To address climate change, however, requires a shift in emphasis from asset accumulation to asset adaptation, and an associated two-fold operational and conceptual framework that focuses both on vulnerability to severe weather as well as on adaptation strategies to build and strengthen resilience to its impacts. An asset vulnerability analytical framework identifies the links between different vulnerabilities and the poor's capital assets. These relate both to external shocks and stresses, as well as to internal capacities to resist or withstand them. Vulnerability has long been recognised as an important constraint for asset accumulation. The more and diverse assets people have, the less vulnerable they are; and the greater the erosion of their assets, the greater their insecurity (see Moser 1998). Climate-change vulnerability obviously is closely linked to assets, but also introduces the uncertainty of future as against present risk. Vulnerabilities can be economic, political, social, and psychological in nature, and can affect different groups, especially women and children (Moser and Satterthwaite 2010). The assets of low-income populations are particularly vulnerable to climate change and this applies not only to individual assets such as human and social capital, but also to household, small business, and community assets such as financial and productive assets.

An asset adaptation operational framework, in turn, explores and classifies the asset adaptation strategies of different local social actors as they exploit opportunities to develop resilience, cope and resist, or recover from, the negative effects of severe climate-related weather. Three closely interrelated phases can be identified: asset adaptation to build long-term resilience; asset damage limitation and protection during severe weather events, and asset rebuilding after such weather. The framework also includes a mapping of institutions associated with climate change and their associated policies at both national and local level. Together, both sources of information provide the basis for policy-makers and other stakeholders to propose concrete climate-change adaptation policies and programmatic interventions, implemented by local institutions, and with positive impacts on poor households and communities (Moser and Stein 2011).

Turning to research methodology, in the past decade, with some exceptions, vulnerability assessments have tended to be 'top down' and not engaged directly with the 'bottom up' realities of local urban communities living in the most hazardous areas of cities, who, because of a lack of basic services and adequate infrastructure, are most vulnerable to adverse weather (Bicknell *et al.* 2009; Moser *et al.* 2010). Recognition of the importance of understanding local people's perceptions of severe weather, their vulnerabilities, and adaptation measures, has resulted in the development of a climate-change-specific participatory methodology. This was adapted from participatory urban appraisal (PUA), developed by modifying Robert Chamber's participatory rural appraisal (PRA) (Chambers 1994). PUA was first used in studies on local urban community perceptions of violence and insecurity and the erosion of assets undertaken in urban areas in Jamaica, Colombia, and Guatemala (Moser and Holland 1997; Moser and McIlwaine 1999). It was then expanded into a participatory consensus-building methodology for strengthening the capacity of women's organisations in Colombia to participate in the peace process. Finally, in recent climate change studies it was broadened beyond an appraisal tool to also incorporate a participatory planning methodology (Stein and Moser 2014).

Using this participatory methodology, the two-fold climate change asset adaptation framework has been empirically tested in two consecutive studies undertaken in four secondary cities across the Global South. The first study, termed a participatory climate change adaptation appraisal (PCCAA), was undertaken in four low-income settlements in each of the cities of Mombasa, Kenya, and Estelí, Nicaragua, with support from the World Bank's Social Development Department. Its objective was to document local people's perceptions as to how poor households, small businesses, and communities coped with the impacts of severe weather, as well as to identify how policy and institutional systems could best build on local realities to develop pro-poor urban climate change adaptation actions to strengthen resilience (Moser *et al.* 2010; Moser and Stein 2011). The second study changed the methodology's name to reflect its additional planning focus along with the original objectives, and was called asset planning for climate change adaptation (APCA). With support from the Ford Foundation New York, the study was undertaken in one community each in Cartagena, Colombia, and Pondicherry, India, with the focus in the latter case specifically on severe weather impacts on health and environmental hazards. While the second study reduced the number of communities, it extended the methodology by a further stage to include an operational framework to mainstream asset planning for climate change adaptation into city planning.

Rather than individual or household questionnaires, participatory methodology is based on purposive sampling from a range of focus groups that are representative of community members in terms of age, gender, ethnicity, economic activities, and other culturally specific variables. This evidence base for this chapter is drawn from one city in each study, namely Mombasa and Cartagena. The choice of these two cities allows for comparisons between the two methodologies described above. In addition, the fact that I participated in all the stages of study implementation – from training the local teams and undertaking fieldwork in both cities, through to analysing the results and facilitating the community planning process in Cartagena – has enabled me to draw on first-hand knowledge of the data. While all these climate-focused studies 'mainstreamed' gender into their data collection and analysis, gender was not a specific focus, and with hindsight was somewhat invisibilised because the unit of analysis was primarily the household. Writing this chapter, therefore, has been salutary; it has required me to return to the raw data in the original focus group reports and re-review them with a 'gender lens'. This has generated comparative quantitative and qualitative data from men and women's focus groups (see Table 11.1 for breakdown details). The next section locates the chapter within the context of current gender and climate change debates, while the final section then focuses on the insights these studies contribute to these debates.

Contextual issues: gendered and climate change debates

How is climate change gendered? It is useful to start by clarifying the ways in which gender or women have been integrated or incorporated into climate change debates. The fact that this is a relatively new issue means that robust frameworks are still being developed. One important constraint relates to the fact that climate change is often identified as a highly masculinised concept, emerging from the scientific establishment, structured within techno-scientific framing (Israel and Sachs 2013). Consequently, while in some institutional contexts 'climate change processes have largely assumed gender neutrality' (Bradshaw and Linneker 2014, 19), in others, as it has happened in past developmental debates, it is still more a matter of 'add women and stir' than any fundamental structural change (Moser 1993). This has been particularly prevalent in formal documentation, such as those of institutions in the UN system, where critical lobbying to 'bring women in' has resulted in the inclusion of the word 'women, or gender' without necessarily including analytical or operational reference as to its relevance (Alber 2011).

Another important constraint relates to the paucity, until very recently, of an urban focus. Even though this has changed in the most recent Intergovernmental Panel on Climate Change (IPCC) documents (especially since 2012), policy responses in the majority of cases are still embedded in ministries of environment and natural resources, and when urban issues are introduced they are treated exclusively in terms of disaster risk reduction/management (Moser *et al.* 2010). Most gendered research continues to focus on women's positioning within a largely rural phenomenon (Demetriades and Esplen 2008), with growing concern for insecurity and climate-related conflict resulting in a focus on heightened competition and growing scarcities in natural resources such as water and arable land (Röhr 2006).

To date, the main focus on women and climate change in urban areas as much as rural has been on their assumed 'vulnerability', and its relation to gender roles. Its origins are closely linked to the poverty and inequality literature that identifies women as the most disadvantaged, and subsequently the 'poorest of the poor', with disaster and climate change-related shocks and inequality exacerbating their risks. In a much-cited urban-related quote, Satterthwaite *et al.* (2007, 45) argue that: 'Within low-income populations women often have particular vulnerabilities as a result of gender-related inequalities.' The associated policy implications have been impressive; for instance, the UN-HABITAT resolution on Cities and Climate Change of the 22nd session of the UN-HABITAT Governing Council mentions women among the most vulnerable groups, while the UN-HABITAT's Climate Change Strategy 2010–2013 refers to the 'special vulnerability of women to climate impacts' (UN-HABITAT 2009, 22; Abler 2011, 14). However, as Bradshaw and Linneker argue, policy knowledge where women have been constructed as a vulnerable group 'is as much due to their supposed characteristics as actual studies to demonstrate this' (Bradshaw and Linneker 2014). This is one of the substantive issues this chapter addresses.

A number of frameworks have been developed to identify the range of inequalities and injustices that lead to differential impacts of climate change on men and women. Abler, for instance, argues that at the global meta-level cities are facing enormous justice issues in terms of polluters and impacted people, and use of scarce resources such as urban space, water, and air (Abler 2011, 49). Her framework focuses on the ways in which differences in roles and gender power relations result in gendered differences in needs and associated opportunities. This framework treats cities and climate change separately, considering first generic issues of power relations and gender participation in urban policy and practices.[1] This is followed by an examination of sectors of activities that most require gender-sensitive policy formulation and implementation, such as energy, transport, and consumption, which should lead to greater gender justice. While this is not climate change-specific, it provides a checklist against which factors contributing to gender inequality in climate change contexts can be identified (Jabeen 2014).

Another framework builds on Chambers' *Web of Poverty Disadvantages* (2005, 46) and 'identifies connections between poverty, gender inequality and vulnerability/resilience to environmental stress and shocks' (Demetriades and Esplen 2008, 25). These include physical and mental health, ascribed and legal inferiority, discrimination in the labour market, and poverty of time. Of particular significance to this chapter is the identification of 'lack of political clout'. With 'women and girls conspicuously absent from decision-making processes at all levels' (p. 27), participation in decision-making is said to contribute to addressing gender inequalities by raising the profile and status of women and girls in the community and challenging traditional assumptions about their capabilities. Although the Cartagena asset adaptation planning process is focused at the local rather than city level, it nevertheless provides an opportunity to empirically contribute to this debate.

An additional important urban-specific element to climate change concerns broadening the focus on inequalities or vulnerabilities within local populations to include space and the built environment, referring here not only to buildings, streets, and infrastructure, but also to the ways in which people interact with them. As Alber comments, historically the urban built environment has been gender blind:

> with male dominated and fossil-fuel intensive urban structures and infra-structures including the segregation of housing from the workplace, and public transport geared towards the needs of computers, rather than the complex and manifold trips of women who combine care work and employed work.
>
> (Alber 2011, 11)

Urban space is representational in the sense that gender power relations often define separate spheres for men and women's use; most widely known is the determination of the public realm or the city for men, and the private domestic spaces of the home for women. The 'social production' of space means cultural social norms influence the spaces women and men inhabit, to live and work in, as well as the types of activity they carry out in their houses and neighbourhoods. Of importance here is the fact that the social dynamics of gender, traced in these representational spaces and reflected in spatial practices, has implications for differences not only in men's and women's vulnerabilities to climate change, but also their adaptive capacities to cope with it (Jabeen 2014, 5–11).

A final contextual issue relates to the widespread tendency to define debates in principle in terms of the gendered nature of climate change, but in practice to exclude men and focus only on women. This has been justified on the grounds that 'androcentrism' in power relations has meant a male perspective tends to dominate most policy domains (Alber 2011, 15), while the entrenched structural disadvantages and inequalities faced by women in cities across the Global South makes it important to better understand separately their experiences of severe weather. Yet there are limitations in focusing on women in isolation, since in reality they live in communities, in families, and, above all, with men. As Demetriades and Esplen (2008, 25) comment:

> abstracting women from their social realities eclipses the relational nature of gendered power and the interdependency of women and men, and paints a distorted picture of women's vulnerabilities, choices and possibilities.

This chapter therefore seeks to bring together the focus on both women and men within an asset framework, identifying their relative vulnerabilities, as well as recognising their differing roles in gender empowerment processes.

The evidence: gendered asset adaptation to climate change in Mombasa and Cartagena

It is widely recognised that the severity of climate change is context-specific, with global generalisations being of limited relevance. In describing the results from the two studies, at the outset it is necessary to acknowledge limits in terms of comparative results, while at the same time providing the shared characteristics used as the basis for city selection. In summary, Mombasa in Kenya and Cartagena in Colombia are both medium-sized, fast-growing secondary cities in coastal towns, chosen because the cities did not fall into existing 'high-profile' categories for climate change impacts, but both of which are in flood- and drought-prone regions, and affected by recurring flooding and sea level rises. Despite the limitations of climate projections downscaled to city level, available data from both cities suggest that ongoing climate change-related severe weather trends will continue and intensify in the future[2] (Moser *et al.* 2010; Stein and Moser 2014).

Is local knowledge of severe weather gendered?

The first research question concerns local, so-called indigenous, knowledge of weather, and the extent to which it is gendered – in the sense that men and women understand weather differently. While some maintain that 'women tend to be more concerned about climate change than men' (Alber 2011, 11), others recognise slight differences between men and women when weather-related changes occur. However, to date the predominant focus has been rural, where 'men focus on implications for farming production issues while women describe the wider impacts on the health for the family' (Lambrou and Nelson 2010, cited in Bradshaw and Linneker 2014, 22).

Women and men in local communities in both Mombasa and Cartagena,[3] despite their urban location and the fact that they did not conceptualise or articulate the term 'climate change', nevertheless had a great awareness of weather and its impact on their lives.[4] Listings and rankings from participatory focus groups in both cities showed similar perceptions of severe weather, but also some more nuanced gendered differences. As Table 11.1 shows, rain and associated flooding was perceived as the most serious weather problem in both Mombasa and Cartagena. This perception was identified from both the universe of all focus groups (72 in four communities in Mombasa; 22 in one community in Cartagena) (Moser *et al.* 2010), as well as when disaggregated by gender-specific focus groups undertaken separately with men and women.

However, underlying reasons differed, illustrating the importance of local context. While in Mombasa the local population's greatest preoccupation was

Table 11.1 Women- and men-only focus group perceptions of severe weather in Mombasa and Cartagena (by percentage and focus group rankings)

Cities disaggregated by gender	Categories of severe weather					
	Rain/flooding		Wind		Heat/sun	
	%	Ranking totals	%	Ranking totals	%	Ranking totals
Mombasa						
Women	59	30	18	9	23	12
Men	55	48	17	30	28	24
Cartagena						
Women	48	20	19	8	33	14
Men	56	18	25	8	19	6

Notes
Mombasa: women's focus group 12 ($n=78$); men's focus group 21 ($n=87$).
Cartagena: women's focus group 8 ($n=55$); men's focus group 6 ($n=36$).

the impact of flooding on housing, in Cartagena the flooding of canals that affected roads, mobility, small businesses as well as housing was specifically identified. As a local middle-aged woman in Policarpa explained: 'Truly the rain is the problem because it fills the canals, the canals overflow and flood the streets, and from the streets the inundation enters the house. Then the water company cuts its service – it's crazy.'

At the same time there were a few who disagreed that severe rain was their biggest problem, often because of impacts on their productive assets associated with income-generating activities. Thus fishermen living on the edge of Tudor (one of the four Mombasa communities), reflecting their traditional role as providers, had a different perception of rain, commenting: 'Floods are a blessing. They bring nutrients to the ocean and this increases our catch.'

In both cities, rain and flooding were not the only climate-related problems. The universe of focus groups in Mombasa and Cartagena identified heat and sun as of second importance, followed by wind and associated pollution. However, within specific cities there were interesting gendered variations in second and third priorities; in Mombasa some men were more concerned with heat, and women with wind; in Cartagena the reverse was true. While men were more concerned with wind, women ranked heat as more important. At the same time, in their individual comments both men and women linked heat and illness. One older woman said: 'When there is heat I suffer which is worse that when there is flooding – then I do not sleep.' In a slightly different vein, an older man commented: 'Heat generates emotional and psychological problems; the people feel bad, they despair from not being able to sleep.' In both cases they illustrated the ways in which severe heat affected their well-being, eroding health-related human capital.

What are the gendered prioritisations of asset vulnerability to climate change?

A well-known concern in the emerging urban literature focuses on the extent to which women in such contexts are more vulnerable to climate change than are men (Bradshaw and Linneker 2014). Following the climate change-related definition of vulnerability as the relationship between the impacts, exposure, and sensitivity of severe weather, and the capacity to adapt and respond to it (Romero Lankao and Qin 2011), the contribution of an asset framework is that it moves beyond individual gendered 'social' vulnerability, to focus on assets, identifying how these are gendered and their associated level of exposure, sensitivity, and capacity to adapt to the impacts of severe weather. In principle the question then becomes one of the gendered disaggregation of assets and the assessment of whether women's assets are more vulnerable to climate change than those of men. However, reality is more complex; while some individual assets may be gender-specific, others are part of collective household asset portfolios, while further assets may pertain specifically to small businesses. In this case a more relevant question concerns the gendered perceptions of prioritisation of asset vulnerability to climate change, as well as the strategies used to adapt them to the impact of severe weather.

This complexity was reflected in both the Mombasa and Cartagena case studies when data on prioritisation of asset vulnerability to climate change were disaggregated by gender (even though the data from the two studies are not directly comparable because of methodological differences). In Mombasa, the first of the studies, where tools were tested in an exploratory manner, lengthy listings and ranking of assets vulnerable to climate change were undertaken. Table 11.2 identifies the extensive range of assets perceived as being vulnerable to severe weather, as well as differences in perceptions by gender. While men overwhelmingly prioritised their business-related financial and physical assets associated with the generation of income, and to a lesser extent housing, women's perceptions related to a more complex asset portfolio that included physical capital such as housing, but also both human capital associated with

Table 11.2 Women's and men's perceptions of prioritisation of asset vulnerability to climate change in Mombasa (by percentage and ranking)

City	Vulnerable assets					
	House	Electrical goods	Human health	Children's health	Septic tank	Business stock/tools
Women (%)	23	14	21	18	9	15
Ranking	10	6	9	8	3	7
Men (%)	28	4	8			60
Ranking	7	1	2			15

Notes
Mombasa: women's focus group 12 (*n*=78); men's focus group 21 (*n*=87); mixed focus group (*n*=39); total focus group (*n*=72).

health generally, and more specifically child health. Indeed, if these two categories are added together, human capital health becomes the overriding priority
for women. In a context where not all the women had small-scale enterprises,
business stock and tools were less important, though still figured.

In Cartagena, in a much more rapid study, focus groups verbally discussed
and prioritised their most vulnerable asset rather than undertaking listings and
rankings. They then undertook causal flow diagrams of the causes and consequences of severe weather on the specific asset identified. While descriptive
and qualitative, the results from Cartagena still point to the same gendered
differentiation of roles and identities. Again, men's perceptions of climate-
related vulnerability prioritised business-related assets that related to their
narrow income-earning productive responsibilities, while for women housing
was their priority. But as in Mombasa, women were also preoccupied with
climate impacts on a more extensive asset portfolio associated with their triple
role of reproductive, productive, and community-managing responsibilities
(Moser 1993). This is illustrated by Figure 11.1, a causal flow diagram drawn by

Figure 11.1 Women's causal flow diagram of asset vulnerability resulting from rain,
Cartagena (source: focus group of eight women from Las Flores and Central
sector, Policarpa, Cartagena).

a focus group of eight women from the Central and Las Flores sectors of Barrio Policarpa that shows the effects of rain on different assets, including septic tanks, electricity, and health, as well as on streets and houses.[5]

Do women and men's asset adaptation strategies to climate change differ?

While the gender and environment literature widely acknowledges that 'men and women have distinct and valuable knowledge about how to adapt to the adverse impacts of environmental degradation' (Demetriades and Espen 2008, 29), such information is entirely rural in focus and not necessarily specific to climate-change associated severe weather.[6] In both Mombasa and Cartagena data from a range of participatory tools, that did not lend themselves to quantification, descriptively identified adaptation strategies implemented by households, small businesses, and the community to build long-term resilience before severe weather, protect and limit damage during such events, and rebuild after severe weather events.

As with asset vulnerability, gender disaggregation of asset adaptation strategies is complex. In Mombasa and Cartagena data from gender-specific focus groups showed that women and men, regardless of title rights, saw housing as a joint asset with a common adaptation strategy before, during, and after severe weather. A diversity of adaption matrices showed women and men taking collaborative responsibility for the adaptation of this collective household asset without differentiating gendered responsibilities between internal space, mainly inhabited by women, and external space, mainly used by men. Indeed, in Mombasa, differentiation between homeowners and tenants was identified as more important in terms of responsive strategies than those of gender (Moser and Stein 2011, 478; Jabeen 2014). As a middle-aged woman from Bofu commented, 'floods are not such a problem for me as I am a tenant'.

Linked to their reproductive and community-managing role, mentioned above, in both cities women took primary responsibility for collective community assets even though located in public spaces. For instance, a women's focus group in Bofu, Mombasa, identified the local well as their most important asset. They provided a 'technical' drawing to illustrate how floods from severe weather causes water to seep in from the sides as well as entering from the top, resulting in contaminated water. They identified maintenance as their responsibility; this included putting a slab on as a cover before the rains came, and then repairing and cleaning the well after the floods had subsided.

In Mombasa far fewer women were involved in income-generating activities outside the home than was the case in Cartagena. In the latter context, linked to their productive role, a women's focus group prioritised community nurseries (*hogares comunitarios*) that provide childcare for working mothers. As shown in Table 11.3, they revealed a detailed knowledge of building problems in listing and ranking solutions to build resilience and protect the buildings from rain, as well as using the opportunity to identify solutions to generally improve them.

Table 11.3 Listing and ranking of solutions for the impact of rain and floods on community nurseries (*hogares comunitarios*), Policarpa, Cartagena

Solutions	Votes by focus group participants
(1) Improvement of bathrooms, floors, and walls	19
(2) Elevating the base of community houses	12
(3) Improve high voltage cables	5
(4) Expanding house space	1
(5) Building multiple-activity spaces	1
(6) Study of land conditions	0

Source: focus group of eight mothers aged 30–48, from different sectors.

Gender divisions of labour in small-scale enterprises were reflected in the impact of severe weather on work space. Figure 11.2, for instance, shows a causal flow diagram undertaken by men tailors in Mombasa renting workspace. Their particular concern was dust caused by strong winds, which not only resulted in ill health, preventing them from working, but also the malfunction of their sewing machines when sand got inside them. The renter–landlord power relations were illustrated by the tailors' distinction between their own modest adaptation strategies as renters to clean their sewing machines and the more permanent solutions that landlords could provide, such as introducing glass doors. Motorcycles, entirely operated by men, were the primary transport mode in both cities, with men's focus groups identifying damage to their motorcycles as their priority asset vulnerability in hazardous weather, and elaborating detailed strategies of adaptation. In Cartagena, for instance, a group of four men identified lubricating the chain, waxing, and the use of silicone before severe weather, working away from the neighbourhood when flooding occurred, and borrowing

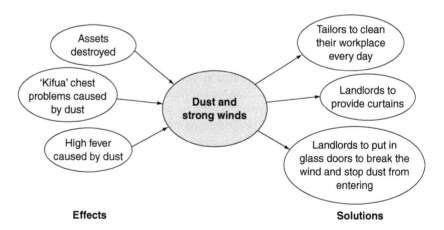

Figure 11.2 Men tailors' identification of the effects of and solutions to dust and strong winds in Ziwa la Ngombe, Mombasa (source: focus group of 15 tailors aged 20–35 years old).

money to get help with repairs afterwards to 'rebuild' their asset. In this case, regardless of whether men owned or rented their motorcycles, they took responsibility for the maintenance of their asset.

A comparable trend in both cities for women's focus groups was a primary concern with the impact of severe weather on their small sales businesses – located either in their homes or in small shops. Detailed stock adaptation strategies depended on the type of weather. Focus groups in Cartagena, for instance, identified that severe sun and heat led fresh-food sellers to set up stalls under trees and cover with coconut palms, while in the case of rain to cover with plastic and put sand in the selling area so mud did not affect customers. During severe weather a common strategy was to sell fast by lowering prices. In the case of Mombasa, a women's focus group in Tudor distinguished between preserving stock in a good place before severe weather, reducing stock as there would be few customers during weather events, and looking for new stock and starting up the business again after the event was over. As self-employed informal sector workers, women recognised such actions as essential for economic survival, though they were nevertheless empowered by their ability to successfully adapt their small businesses to such weather conditions.

Does climate change adaptation change gender roles, and if so, does it lead to changes in gender relations?

To the extent that women assume new responsibilities beyond those traditionally ascribed to them in their gendered roles, in principle severe weather linked to climate change can empower them individually and collectively as they adapt their assets, particular those located in public spaces. However, in practice although women may take on such responsibilities as they improve and repair their housing or deal with flooded wells and septic tanks – tasks customarily undertaken by men – it does not necessarily change gender roles or relations. Such tasks are done either in collaboration with men, or if men are focusing on productive assets and generating income, women take on the responsibility for such 'non-productive' assets as housing and water, required for reproductive tasks.

As urban planning associated with climate change adaptation shifts from 'top down' to more 'bottom up' participatory processes, this may provide more opportunities for women to be empowered. However, this will not occur simply with the inclusion of women's 'voices', but requires women's negotiation and bargaining power to be reflected in decision-making around asset adaptation strategies. One early example in support of this thesis comes from Cartagena which, as mentioned in above, incorporated a participatory planning process (Stein and Moser 2014). This process did not a priori seek to empower women, yet as briefly described below, their participation as equal social actors resulted in the prioritisation of their demands. The participatory planning process started with consultations with public and private institutions identified as important in supporting climate change, environmental, or poverty initiatives in Barrio Policarpa, gaining their agreement, and identifying representatives to participate in an asset adaptation planning workshop (APW). Simultaneously, focus group facilitators together with community leaders identified barrio representatives using selection criteria that included a balance between women and men, different age groups, from different sectors of the barrio, and representative of the different community local groups. The one-day APW, held in July 2011, comprised 51 participants (excluding facilitators), of which 10 of 23 barrio representatives were women, with 10 of the 28 representatives from different public and private organisations also being women.

Key to the participatory process was the division of participants into groups with different stakeholders equally represented, with each addressing one of five themes identified as critical during the focus group analysis. This meant that the priorities identified within gender-specific focus groups, namely housing improvements, small businesses, health, infrastructure, and community facilities, were transferred into the planning exercise. After facilitators had introduced the specific theme, participants listed and ranked solutions, and in a highly participatory process those prioritised were then analysed and weighted in terms of the criteria of urgency, technical feasibility, and legal and administrative feasibility. Prioritised solutions were then shared in plenary, with participants subsequently returning to their groups to elaborate detailed asset adaptation plans. The first two priorities from each group were then merged into a barrio asset plan that became the starting point for negotiations with the local municipality, private institutions, and NGOs. As the study did not have resources for project implementation, it has not been possible to follow which of these priorities have actually been undertaken by different local institutions.

Conclusion: towards gender asset adaption pathways to empowerment and transformation

To date there is limited concrete evidence on the gendered nature of vulnerability and adaptation to climate change in cities. Therefore, this chapter, first and foremost, is intended to extend our knowledge base of this increasingly important issue, while contributing both theoretically and operationally through the introduction of an asset adaptation framework. Debates on gender power relations tend to assume that increases in women's power reduce those of men. Yet the cumulative focus group evidence from both Mombasa and Cartagena on collaborative adaptation of housing by both men and women together provides a contrary example. Women were quite clear in the focus group discussions that it was the immediacy of severe weather events that often results in them individually empowering themselves by taking on tasks previously done by men.

The asset adaptation planning workshop in Cartagena, while only an anecdotal example, nevertheless points to the importance of women's role in collective decision-making in mixed-gender groups. While women participated across all groups, they took on leadership roles with more 'political clout' in those groups that addressed housing improvements and health, both prioritised by women's focus groups in terms of asset adaptation solutions. A 25-minute documentary video filmed during the workshop provided visual evidence of the contrast between the strength of women's 'voice' and participation in debating solutions in the two groups, as against their passivity in male-dominated groups focusing on technical issues such as economic infrastructure and community services (such as illegal electricity and sports facilities). In the housing group the presence of a charismatic woman leader, at that time heading Corvivienda, a housing programme run by the Housing Department of the District of Cartagena, provided crucial leadership in identifying improvements to community nursery houses as one of four priority solutions. Other priorities such as a topographic and pluviometric survey, dredging and widening of the canals, and the implementation of the Healthy Housing Minimum Improvement Programme, while highly technical, were suggested and endorsed by women as much as men in the group (see Stein and Moser 2014, 179). Women's engagement in planning processes around climate change asset adaptation is crucial in moving towards a just city, in which the transformative potential of gendered collective action can be realised by both identifying as well as implementing such agendas at the local level. However, this requires moving beyond academic studies to providing committed support and resources to actually implement initiatives such as the climate change asset adaptation planning process initiated in Cartagena.

Notes

1 This includes divisions of labour (men working primarily in paid labour/women doing unpaid work); differentials in income/economic resources (more women are poorer than men; levels of wealth held by women are much lower than those for men); and gendered aspects of responsibility for/access to resources (e.g. energy production and consumption) (Alber 2011, 16).
2 For documentation of gradual but sustained changes in weather patterns during the last decades in Mombasa, see Moser *et al.* (2010); for the case of Cartagena, see Stein and Moser (2014).
3 In Mombasa the study was undertaken in the four communities of Tudor, Ziuwa La Ngome, Timbwane, and Bofu, while in Cartagena in the barrio (neighbourhood) of Policarpa. For the sake of simplification in the text the generic terms Mombasa and Cartagena are used throughout the text, except when evidence from specific focus groups is provided.
4 Local residents, particularly in Mombasa, were not familiar with the term 'climate change', while the term 'disaster' was avoided in order to understand the slow incremental effects of changing weather variability. In Mombasa agreement was reached as to the specific meaning of weather in Kiswahili, while in Cartagena Spanish terms such as *tiempo* (weather) and *clima* (climate) were commonly used.
5 Although the direction of some of the arrows in Figure 11.1 may not seem logical, these represent the perceptions of the focus group members who drew the causal flow diagrams.
6 See, for instance, references in Demetriades and Esplen (2008).

References

Alber, G. (2011) Gender, cities and climate change. http://unhabitat.org/wp-content/uploads/2012/06/GRHS2011ThematicStudyGender.pdf
Bicknell, J., Dodman, D., and Satterthwaite, D. (eds) (2009) *Adapting Cities to Climate*

Change: Understanding and Addressing the Development Challenges, Earthscan, London and Sterling, VA.

Bradshaw, S. (2013) *Gender, Development and Disaster*, Edward Elgar, Northampton.

Bradshaw, S. and Linneker, B. (2014) *Gender, Environment and Disasters in the Development Context: Parallel Pathways and Common Concerns*, IIED, London.

Chambers, R. (1994) 'The origins and practice of participatory rural appraisal'. *World Development*, 22, pp. 953–69.

Chambers, R. (2005) 'Participation, pluralism and perceptions of poverty', paper for the Many Dimensions of Poverty Conference, Brazil, August.

Demetriades, J. and Esplen, E. (2008) 'The gender dimensions of poverty and climate change adaptation', *IDS Bulletin*, 39, 4, pp. 24–31.

Israel, A.L. and Sachs, C. (2013) 'A climate for feminist intervention: feminist science studies and climate change', in Alston, M. and Whittenbury, M. (eds), *Research, Action and Policy: Addressing the Gendered Impacts of Climate Change*, Springer, the Netherlands.

Jabeen, H. (2014) 'Adapting the built environment: the role of gender in shaping vulnerability and resilience to climate extremes in Dhaka', *Environment and Urbanisation*, 26, 1, pp. 147–65.

Liu, A. (2007) 'Hurricane Katrina: impact on assets and asset building approaches to poverty reduction', in Moser, C. (ed.), *Reducing Global Poverty: The Case for Asset Accumulation*, Brookings Institution Press, Washington, DC.

Moser, C. (1993) *Gender Planning and Development: Theory, Practice and Training*, Routledge, New York and London.

Moser, C. (1998) 'The asset vulnerability framework: reassessing urban poverty reduction strategies', *World Development*, 26, 1, pp. 1–19.

Moser, C. and Holland, J. (1997) 'Urban poverty and violence in Jamaica', in *Viewpoints*, World Bank, Washington, DC.

Moser, C. and McIlwaine, C. (1999) 'Participatory urban appraisal and its application for research on violence', *Environment and Urbanisation*, 11, 2, pp. 203–26.

Moser, C. and Satterthwaite, D. (2010) 'Towards pro-poor adaptation to climate change in the urban centers of low- and middle-income countries', in Mearns, R. and Norton, A. (eds), *Social Dimensions of Climate Change*. World Bank, Washington, DC.

Moser, C. and Stein, A. (2011) 'Implementing urban participatory climate change adaptation appraisals: a methodological guideline', *Environment and Urbanisation*, 22, 2, pp. 463–86.

Moser, C., Norton, A., Stein, A., and Georgieva, S. (2010) *Pro-Poor Adaptation to Climate Change in Urban Centers*, World Bank, Washington, DC.

Röhr, U. (2008) 'Gender aspects of climate-induced conflicts', *Environment and Conflict Special Edition Newsletter on 'Gender, Environment, Conflict'*, Adelphi Research.

Romero Lankao, P. and Qin, H. (2011) 'Conceptualising urban vulnerability to global climate and environmental change', *Current Opinion in Environmental Sustainability* 3, pp. 142–9.

Satterthwaite, D., Huq, S., Pelling, M., Reid, H., Romero Lankao, P., and IIED (International Institute for Environment and Development) (2007) *Adapting to Climate Change in Urban Areas: The Possibilities and Constraints in Low- and Middle-Income Nations*, IIED, London.

Stein, A. and Moser, C. (2014) 'Asset planning for climate change adaptation: lessons from Cartagena, Colombia', *Environment and Urbanization*, 26, 1, pp. 166–83.

UN-HABITAT (2009) *Climate Change Strategy 2010–13*, UN-HABITAT, Nairobi.

Index

Page numbers in *italics* denote tables, those in **bold** denote figures.

For Product Safety Concerns and Information please contact our EU
representative GPSR@taylorandfrancis.com
Taylor & Francis Verlag GmbH, Kaufingerstraße 24, 80331 München, Germany

www.ingramcontent.com/pod-product-compliance
Ingram Content Group UK Ltd.
Pitfield, Milton Keynes, MK11 3LW, UK
UKHW021828240425
457818UK00006B/120